THE STORY OF YORKSHIRE POP MUSIC

YFPPUBLISHING PROUDLY PRESENT

A CRAIG FERGUSON BOOK

I'LL GO TO T'FOOT OF OUR STAGE
THE STORY OF YORKSHIRE POP MUSIC

ISBN 978-0-9545333-8-0
Cover by Duane Hobden

A copy of this book is available at the British Library. If it isn't on the shelf at the time, there's probably a mad rocker reading it on his lunch break.

Printed and bound in the UK by CPI Mackays, Chatham ME5 8TD

Typeset Myriad Pro Regular & Bold Condensed

Every effort had been made to clear and obtain copyright for images used in this book.

yfppublishing.com

I'LL GO TO T'FOOT OF OUR STAGE:

The story of Yorkshire Pop Music

About the Author

Born in Normanton, Craig Ferguson lived his first 18 years in deepest, darkest West Yorkshire, before defecting over the Pennines to Manchester. Whilst making gallant but unsuccessful attempts to be a pop star, with The Dannys Boys then Raintree County, he wrote articles for music publications including *Record Mirror* and the *NME*, before embarking on a career in television, scripting anything from sketches for *Spitting Image* and Russ Abbot, to full episodes for Basil Brush and *Shaun the Sheep*. His first book, 'The DVD Book of Leeds United', was published in 2008. He has two daughters, a son, and a lingering, but slim hope of writing a chart-topping pop song.

For Madge and Red,
"Turn that bloody noise down!"

Acknowledgements.

Thanks to Les and Andrew at YFP Publishing for their belief and support - they knew where I was coming from right from the beginning. Thanks to all my willing interviewees (their management and PR) for their valued time and enthusiasm – Chrissie, Brad, Trevor, Dave, Jeff, Bill, Jon, Andy, Glenn, Gary M, David, Jez, Rick, Richard and Gary J. And thanks even to those Yorkshire pop and rock stars who decided against talking to me. Without them, there wouldn't be a book anyway.

Thanks to the Yorkshire Post Newspapers for providing the pictures.

Also, thanks to Dave Simpson, Luke Bainbridge and Neil Jeffries for their help and advice. A hearty thank you to all my friends for their encouragement, and special thanks to my brothers Pete and Ian, my sister Kathryn, and their families, for their loving support. And last but not least, thanks and love to my beautiful children, Ruby, Evie and Billy.

Chapters page

Introduction

Earth To Yorkshire, Come In Yorkshire...

"David Bowie is not from earth. He is from outer space, and with his Spiders from Mars, he is invading us, flooding the planet with irresistible, cosmic rock 'n' roll."

Chuck Swanson, New Orleans *Figaro*, December 1972.

You can see where Chuck was coming from. Even at the tender age of eleven, I would have perhaps taken his words only too literally, had I actually read them back then. The funny looking bloke with the body-hugging jump suit, dark nail-polish and electric-shock mullet certainly looked like he came from a different planet to this raw young pop-picker sat transfixed to the black-and-white telly in deepest West Yorkshire.

In fact – and my Mam and Dad would have undoubtedly backed me up on this - the funny looking bloke looked 'funny peculiar'; both Bowie and his backing band scared me as much as excited me. It wasn't quite on par with hiding from the Daleks behind the sofa – did anyone really do that? - but they did look like a set of bad buggers from *Doctor Who*. Still, the fact is, I liked the music they were playing/miming to, and I'd never seen anything like them before. Surely that was exactly how pop stars should be?

Until that point, my main interest in life had been exclusively football – playing it, watching it and trying to replicate the excitement of the game on a scaled-down level with Subbuteo Table Football – despite what it said on the ads, Subbuteo technique was about so much more than 'just flick to kick'.

Football was enough for me; so-called 'pop stars' had thus far been boring, long-haired hippy types in my eyes, and of no great interest until Bowie invaded us with his cosmic rock 'n' roll (thanks Chuck).

That element of, shall we say, disconcertion, instilled as I watched a *Top of the Pops* performance of 'Starman', stayed with me for thirty years, obviously fading to a very distant memory of pre-pubescent unease as I entered my painfully grown-up forties. But any remnant of the exciting mystique that worked its strange magic that night was blown away for good when, in 2002, I tuned in to David Bowie chatting to Michael Parkinson, as he recalled the very early days of that, his most famous pop incarnation, Ziggy Stardust.

Ziggy's band, the wonderfully named Spiders from Mars, comprised Mick Ronson on guitar, Trevor Bolder on bass, and Woody Woodmansey on drums. Though all were very talented musicians, and what's more they looked the part (Bolder sported a massive pair of silver bushy sideburns later borrowed by Woolpack landlord Amos Brearly on *Emmerdale Farm*), it transpired the trio were more accurately Tetley Bittermen from Hull than Spiders from Mars.

In his TV interview, Bowie recalled the three Yorkshiremen's less-than-unpredictable reaction when, backstage, prior to the Ziggy Stardust tour's

9

opening gig, they were told that they were expected to dress in a similar manner to their leader, and that included a liberal application of make-up. "No bloody way", they probably said. Or words to that effect. Two nights later, after 'the Spiders' had been on the receiving end of some serious female attention during the shows, it seems that Ziggy had a job on to even get his hands on the make-up bag.

At the punch line of the anecdote, Bowie performed arguably his finest piece of acting ever, adopting a perfectly acceptable Yorkshire accent to represent the new attitude of Ronson, Bolder and Woodmansey that night, in one telling line – "eh Trevor – has tha' finished with t'mascara?"

And as if that wasn't enough to dispel the remaining wonderment first cast on yours truly three decades before, your man also revealed, in that very same interview with one of Yorkshire's favourite sons, he didn't come from Outer Space at all, far from it. Bowie's dad was born in Tadcaster. Bloody Tadcaster… an old Roman Town between Leeds and York! Ziggy Stardust came not from the furthest reaches of the Cosmos but from the loins of a Yorkshireman. Maybe that's why he could do such a good Yorkshire accent. A cameo in the 40th series of *Last of the Summer Wine* surely beckons.

In less than three minutes, Bowie had both re-activated, and partly answered a question that had puzzled this pop loving Yorkshireman for many a year – why had my county, the biggest in the whole of the province we still call Great Britain, never been a celebrated hotbed of pop talent?

It's true. In the fifty-odd years since Elvis and his brethren invaded these shores with their revolutionary new music, I estimate the White Rose county has produced few more than the same number of acts to trouble the pop historian, acts deemed successful by the criteria of either having a Top Ten single, best-selling album, gracing the cover of a celebrated music magazine or paper, making a prime-time appearance on national television, in fact having a career at least equal to the Warholian fifteen minutes of fame in the public consciousness. Fifty-odd, or if you bend the rules and show maximum generosity of judgement, perhaps sixty, sixty-five tops. Count them yourself – well don't, that's what I'm here for.

Whilst the likes of Manchester, Glasgow, Liverpool of course, and even more of-course, of course London, have seemingly produced successful pop stars at a rate of fifty a decade, the Land of Tykes has, on average, produced just one act worthy of note a year. Or, more accurately, one and a bit.

A couple of years ago, a survey carried out by a musicians magazine put Manchester at the top of their list in terms of successful acts produced from within its boundaries, with, wait for it, 500-plus acts. Excessive doesn't quite do this calculation justice; we can only assume that every turn that produced more than one recording in the last fifty years has been included in the count, and – ahem (rubs nails against lapel) - that would mean my own mighty combo of years ago figures amongst this number since we ourselves hatched our musical master plan in the Rainy City. That is, we lived there.

But it's not just about the acts themselves. The UK's pop history is dotted with numerous 'scenes' or 'movements', these usually being born in some vital nightclub or similar venue. But, to my eternal disappointment, none of these were ever Yorkshire-based – 'the scene' always happened in other counties, in other cities. I've often looked on in envy as these exciting high points in British music were given the official seal of cool approval by first the press, then by the music-listening youth at large.

When the angry white-headed spot that was punk broke out in late 1976, the arse that it broke out on was London – so where were our gobbing cretins when we needed them? When Two Tone revived Ska, skinhead fashions and the political consciousness of the nation's youth whilst filling the dance floors towards the end of that same decade, the highly unfashionable city at its epicentre was Coventry – why not the alienated young boot boys of Doncaster or Huddersfield? When the refreshing 'Sound of Young Scotland' was the bees-knees in the early 1980s with its jingle-jangle pop that was more often than not wilfully amateurish yet determinedly funky, we could have done that, even if it was unintentionally amateurish yet accidentally funky.

Long-coated miserabalism was surely second nature to the gloomy youth of Yorkshire, yet it was bands from Liverpool and Manchester who made it hip in the first half of the 1980s. The list goes on – the Mad-For-It baggy scene of the late eighties… the drug-fuelled dance scene that took the 80s through to the 90s… etc. Where were we?! Each scene, with the rapturous endorsement of the media, had me praying it was Yorkshire's turn next, and dreaming of the moment when that Yorkshire-inspired, or better still, Yorkshire-based scene was the envy of the rest of the nation, and I could regularly deliver the 'ay-up… I come from Yorkshire' line, knowing the recipient would be suitably impressed.

And what of the legendary venues that become synonymous with a hip and happening scene, mystical, almost mythical? Where was our Cavern, 100 Club, or Hacienda when we needed it? There have even been shops that have taken on a semi-legendary status in pop folklore, places where bands met and decided to make music together. Malcolm McLaren's Sex boutique in London, or even Probe Records in Liverpool has become pop landmarks, worthy of column inches if not blue plaques. And it didn't have to be a shop… Morrissey had Southern Cemetery in Manchester. Yorkshire could have at least had a famous fish and chip shop, park or public toilet. Okay, best stick with a fish and chip shop.

As far as I'm aware, it never happened.

How can that be? Though, admittedly, we Yorkshire folk are not always the most refined of British citizens, aesthetically speaking, we are, by-and-large, a relatively creative tribe. For crying out loud, we've produced acclaimed writers aplenty from the Brontes (not one but three of 'em) to J.B. Priestly, Keith Waterhouse to David Peace; poets like Hughes, Auden and Armitage;

playwrights such as Bennett and Ayckbourn; artists and sculptors of the calibre of Hockney, Moore and Hepworth; fine actors in Judi Dench and Charles Laughton; even a classical composer in bloody Delius. Then there's the Chuckle Brothers.

But until recently, we were struggling in the pop music department – a list that has to include Black Lace to make up the numbers hardly seems worth quoting (though the Black Lace story is perhaps darker and more rock 'n' roll than you would imagine).

But yes, recently… well recently, Yorkshire has become the hip capital of pop music. Yes, the Ridings – as they were known until the early 1970s - are officially cool, at least in terms of the high calibre pop stars the territory is now turning out at a healthy rate. The *NME*, *Q*, and all those other bibles of modern music say Yorkshire is now officially cool, and they must know. Amazing - 'Yorkshire' and 'cool' are two words I had come to accept I'd never see together in a sentence unless the word 'not' was in there as well.

The Arctic Monkeys and The Kaiser Chiefs have led the way, with the likes of The Cribs and Richard Hawley, amongst other respected, lauded, prize-winning acts emanating from the White Rose County. Sheffield's Arctic Monkeys have hardly stopped winning awards since their first album became the fastest selling debut album in the history of British pop industry in 2005. The same year, The Kaiser Chiefs of Leeds impacted in a blaze of Brit-winning glory themselves, becoming kings of the catchy chorus. Hailing from the sexy city of Wakefield, The Cribs - now new and improved with 24-carat guitar-legend Johnny Marr in their ranks - were called the biggest cult act in the UK by *Q* Magazine in 2008. And also hailing from Sheffield, Richard Hawley has carved out a uniquely nouveau-retro niche for himself, picking up a dizzy number of awards and nominations in an admirably quiet fashion along the way. And in flying the flag, all, to the greater extent, have managed to reach their respective heights and stay there without pretending to be something that they are not.

Quite right. The acts at the forefront of the White Rose revolution have continued being themselves, not wishing to hide their Yorkshireness, indeed writing and singing songs about their roots, complete with local landmark name checks, and sometimes delivered in a singing voice not dissimilar to the one they speak in. And when they've been put in front of a camera and microphone, none have pretended to be from anywhere else but their home-cities of Sheffield, Leeds or Wakefield.

We might be turning out acclaimed pop stars on a regular basis now but it's been a long time coming and the fact remains that, in the accepted sporting parlance, Yorkshire has severely underachieved in the world of popular music. With a population of between 5.5 and 6 million – Greater Manchester has less than half that number, and Liverpool and its surrounding area, not even a quarter - Yorkshire has more folk within its boundaries than Ireland, Denmark, Finland or New Zealand. Its populace is on par with Israel! We surely should have gathered up more pop winners medals, if only through the laws of probability.

Don't get me wrong. The two biggest cities in the county, Sheffield and Leeds have had their moments in pop's past, but certainly until the 1980s, they were hardly what you could call place-names to drop. Wannabe pop stars from these parts were more likely to have been ridiculed than respected. Really the last thing you were going to do if you wanted to be a pop star, was wear your Yorkshire heart on your sleeve. And back in 1972, pop fans never wanted their pop heroes to look and sound like they came from around the corner. At least I didn't. Outer Space was much more…. Sorry, covered that.

Yes, Yorkshire cities have indeed had their moments in pop history, Sheffield perhaps more than most, and many of the finer moments at that. In the early 1980s, the Steel City regularly topped both the singles and album charts thanks to the Human League, ABC and Heaven 17. Very good though these top turns were, here were people who were dressing up with wacky haircuts, nail varnish and eyeliner, and in suits of the zoot and lame variety.

14

Not a million miles from David Bowie, Ziggy and his reluctant Spiders from Mars, just ten years earlier.

Let's be straight – you would expect no less - Yorkshire popsters have never been good at dressing up and pretending to be something they're not. It's not in their, erm, make-up. And these days they don't have to pretend. In the 21st Century, the bullshit of old has been blown away. No need to dress up, no cheese please, Louise. Modern pop musicians can be themselves, in fact it's demanded, and if there's one thing that we Tykes are pretty good at doing, it's being ourselves. Bowie had no problems making himself up like a tart in the name of his art. His band, like bricklayers turned glam rockers, had to see tangible proof of its benefit before they'd lay a finger on a mascara brush.

But is it really just a reluctance to get dressed up and painted that has held back generations of young Tyke rockers and popsters? Surely not.

Is it just a reluctance to perform? It's amazing how even the gobbiest Yorkshireman can become the quietest when he's given a microphone in front of an audience. Yes, we're all larger-than-life characters after a few drinks down the pub but when it comes to the crunch... The fear of looking stupid holds most performers back until they think *fuck it*, what's the worst that can happen?

Is it a lack of talent? The debate could admittedly be dealt with in half-a-dozen words over a pint…

Q: Why have so relatively few Yorkshire pop acts been successful?
A: Because most of them are crap.

There is a certain amount of truth in this, obviously, but every other British region has produced its fair share of stinkers and that hasn't hurt their success quota.

Which leads us to a conspiracy theory – there had to be one didn't there? Nobody likes us. The rest have the country have long had an aversion to

Yorkshire folk, their ways and traditions (the fact that a lot of Yorkshire folk feel the same way doesn't come into it), and that perhaps includes the powers that be. Given this, we've had to try that little bit harder than everyone else.

Chip on my shoulder? I like to think I'm a well-balanced Yorkshireman – I've got a chip on both shoulders. And don't get us started on the subject of having an inferiority complex. They come bigger and better in Yorkshire.

If pop music is the cultural art form of the last fifty years, have we had little or nothing to say on the human condition, the state of the world, or the price of fish?

But this really is just scratching the surface. Many of these factors must surely come into play – some artists will have encountered obstacles to success that we couldn't even dream about.

And, you have to look at the audience, the great Yorkshire public. It has to be said that there has always been an inbuilt reluctance to embrace anything new. The same can be said of old and young Yorkshire folk alike, though that's maybe less so these days. But the old Yorkshire maxim of 'we know what we like and we like what we bloody well know' still prevails in many quarters. Whether the current generation of young Tykes have banished such a barrier from their sensibilities is arguable; for every 16-year-old from Castleford who is brave enough to dye his hair and dress like a dandy, I'll wager there are five more who would rather take the stairs than be stuck in a lift with him. Either that or they'd beat him up. Maybe there's a traditional conservatism (with a small c) at work here, I don't know.

But consequently, Yorkshire audiences – in the past at least - have hardly been quick to accept and adopt musical revolutions – on average these have arrived and took effect in Yorkshire at least eighteen months after the rest of the country. Legend has it that punk hit Rotherham in 1981.

We could go on. And given the chance, we will. For fourteen more chapters to be precise. But why is all this really so important? It's important because to this raw young Tyke, a child of the sixties, born in Normanton, hidden away in the gruff and grimy pit district of Yorkshire, pop stars were an entity at the top of the 'wannabe' list, above astronauts and on par with footballers. I presumed that every young lad in the country felt the same. Pop stars were amazingly unreachable, mysterious figures both exotic and exciting. Yes, you wanted your pop stars to be from somewhere far, far away from your normal day-to-day life. But imagine if one of them had actually lived in the next street…

At the risk of getting all socio-analytical - God forbid - Yorkshire, Britain, and the world is, of course, a much different place in 2009 to what it was in 1972. That's another book completely but if modern culture holds a mirror up to the world that produced it, we have to at least pay some attention to a young society that would rather stay in and watch the *X Factor* final than go out and find a good time.

Yorkshire's time never arrived while I was still young and stupid enough to enjoy it, swigging and a-ligging at the bar down some sweaty venue, crammed in a dark, dank tent at some waterlogged festival, queuing up outside the secret gig that everyone knew about. And that's perhaps the frustration that makes this quest a personal necessity. If only the Arctic Monkeys and Kaiser Chiefs had happened in the mid-1980s, or even in the mid-1990s.

Maybe this is just a personal concern, the need to exorcise pop demons from my pop-picking psyche. Because once music appeared on my radar, I consumed it, loved it, even made it myself – or at least tried. And the big frustration is that it was only when the love of music became a less integral part of my life that the land of my fathers (just the one actually) went to the top of the class, top of the charts and, yes, *Top of the Pops* before those pillocks ditched it. Buggeration. You wait ages for a happening Yorkshire band to come along, then two, even three of them turn up at once. The thing is, I'd stopped waiting for it to happen, not really caring if it ever did.

Middle-aged rant over. Volumes have been written on the masses of pop 'legends' that have emerged from other parts of the UK. Five hundred from Manchester, my proverbial arse. To my knowledge, this is the first document to look at those born, bred or both in Yorkshire. This is a quest, a personal one perhaps but nonetheless a quest, in search of the Yorkshire Pop Star. It's like an expedition to find the polar bear. We know they're out there in the frozen wilds of pop history but you have to look in a few dark caves as well as on top of the icecaps, if you want to do a proper headcount. And if there are as few of them as we're led to believe, why is that? Yorkshire pop stars that is, not polar bears.

After a sustained four-years-plus of thumbs-up from critics and punters alike – both here and overseas – The Arctic Monkeys, The Kaiser Chiefs, The Cribs et al, are still winning the plaudits, awards and new fans. They're looking good for another few years at least. Fifteen good minutes in the limelight would have been good but this is something better by far. And there are plenty of other popsters in support, bubbling under, on the rise, waiting in the wings.

I've been waiting 30 or even 40 years to be able to view the pop echelon and say, they're ours, so is he, her too, and them. I can't be alone in that - there must be other young Yorkshire men and women who have asked, at some time or other, where are all our bloody pop stars? Well now they're here and hopefully here to stay. But question is… what took us so bloody long?

Chapter One

You Don't Know You're Bloody Born.

There you are, you've just put some of your hard earned in the incongruously flash jukebox of an old, run down backstreet pub, in lower Wakefield, Doncaster or Halifax, and now you're stood at the bar trying not to meet the eye of the old bugger lurched at the end of it, sporting the remnants of a teddy-boy quiff. Pissed up, he smiles as he finally catches your eye. Crap. You want to escape but you're still waiting for your drink. He staggers closer – he's got you now. Does he... A. Tell you how lucky your generation is? ...B. Tell you how crap music is today? ... C. Tell you about the band he was in once and how they should have been massive? The smart money is on A or B, or both. If it's C, then he really is pissed and perhaps dangerous – forget the drink and make a run for it before he puts his arm around you and starts telling you that

Rock 'n' Roll was born in Yorkshire.

It wasn't. But contrary to popular opinion, the county isn't concealed in a parochial bubble, and certainly wasn't in the 1950s. It wasn't all brass bands. Some of those old codgers actually were there when life got a whole lot more exciting for the youngsters of the region, and some even embraced the dawn of a new cultural era, inspired enough to pick up an instrument and raise a racket of their own. God knows there hadn't been a lot of fun going on since the war.

It was even grimmer than usual up North after the cessation of hostilities in 1945. The incoming Labour government had the unenviable task of overseeing the transition from wartime economy to peacetime economy, a mission that involved the continuing burden of rationing whilst the cost of war was established, precious resources redirected, and ex-servicemen integrated back into normal society. With this in mind, there were significant developments that would change lives forever, not least those working class lives in Yorkshire.

Apart from the founding of the Welfare State, complete with a National Health Service, Clement Attlee's Government set out on a programme of Nationalisation, taking the UK's traditional heavy industries out of private ownership and putting their management in the hands of government controlled bodies. (Bear with me – this is still a book about pop music). Coal was one of the first industries to be nationalised, followed by the railways and the steel industry in the next few years. Coal, textiles, steel and railways accounted for most of the manufacturing output from Yorkshire's work places – farming in the North of the county and fishing in Humberside covered the rest. But these had shown signs of decline even before the war, and clearly the priority in its wake was to establish a period of stability in these industries as a platform for economic regeneration. Happily, the years of austerity and hardship suffered in the immediate post-war period (and moaned about for subsequent decades) would be succeeded by one of affluence and relative economic security. A sustained period of national economic growth, due to the upturn in world trade resulted in an unprecedented consumer boom. Even in Yorkshire.

The succeeding Tory government of 1951 reaped the benefits, though they'd done little or none of the hard work of getting the economy back on track. It heralded the 'you've never had it so good' era as the USA flooded the European market with new, exciting and affordable products including cars, a whole mansion full of revolutionary domestic appliances, and most significant to our story, music.

The music market was opened up with the availability of transistor radios, record players, jukeboxes, musical instruments and a new style of music, hey, just for 'the kids', Daddio. Whether we like it or not – and it's a fair bet that most Yorkshire folk probably didn't then and certainly don't now - the Americans were the pioneers of the modern age. They lit the fuse on the space age, sending a monkey into orbit in 1951, and the same year, Alan Freed, a 'Disc Jockey' in Cleveland, coined the phrase 'Rock 'n' Roll'. Well actually, no, he didn't – it was already an old black phrase for 'rumpy-pumpy' (an old Yorkshire phrase for sex). Freed merely started using the term as a euphemism for black music that was deemed acceptable to a white audience. Claims that the first Rock and Roll record surfaced in the same year – 'Rocket 88', credited to Jackie Brentson and his Delta Cats – remain debatable.

That meant sod all to us anyway. Yorkshire, by-and-large, was still hoarding coal in the bath and listening to *Family Favourites* on a radio the size of a small fridge. And why? Because no one invented 'the teenager' till 1955, that's why. And again it was the Americans who are credited with giving teenagers to the world. Many Yank servicemen had already given the British population a boost in their stay over here during the war. But this was a true cultural revolution… introducing the adolescent with an identity and attitude.
Bill Haley and the Comets' 'Shake, Rattle and Roll' may have hit the airwaves in 1954, but things really got interesting the following year when 'Blackboard

Jungle' hit the cinema screens, and Haley's most famous tune therein, 'Rock Around The Clock', had the nation's youngsters dancing in the theatre aisles, in a 'most unseemly manner'.

But we need to stop right there and rewind a year or three to gauge the musical climate in the United Kingdom before your parents, or even more likely, your grandparents got hip to the beat.

From 1945 up to the early 1950s, the dominant sounds on the airwaves and the dance floors had been decidedly 'nice and easy'. The big star of the 1940s had been Frank Sinatra, whose fan worship by young teenage girls, the 'bobby soxers', was the nearest that any artist had come to frenzied adulation before Elvis surfaced. But even Frankie's recording career hit a dip as he tried to emulate his singing success as a movie actor. His replacements in the affections of music-loving audience stuck with the nice and easy style, but it often strayed into 'safe and bland'.

If that didn't light the fire of the young radicals of Yorkshire – and why would it? – there really was only one other port of call, Jazz. And even that music was going through a revolution of its own, with the more aggressive, abstract sounds of the 'Bebop' players giving rise to the Cool Jazz, Modal Jazz, Free Jazz, all conveniently rounded up under the banner of Modern Jazz. Whatever you wanted to call it, the new form stepped on the toes of the traditional style and divided its listeners. Even today, in terms of the mass audience, it's fair to say that the jury's still out on jazz, full-stop. Alexei Sayle voiced one opinion when he said 'there are two types of jazz... and they're both crap'. Yorkshire was predictably traditional on the whole when it came to its jazz – the prime exponents of the art from the area being the highly respected but less-than-imaginatively named, Yorkshire Jazz Band. You'll have to delve deeper than I'm prepared to if you want to find the White Rose equivalent of John Coltrane or Charlie Parker, taking jazz into wild new territories whilst under the influence of hard drugs. Good luck with that.

Oh, and there was folk music.

But for the mass listeners of the UK, the first half of the 1950s was all about dreamy crooners and smoochy balladeers – Perry Como, Nat King Cole and a young Tony Bennett, all coming over from the States, of course. When the first UK chart – or 'Hit Parade' as it came to be known – was published by the *New Musical Express* in 1952 (it's been around a while), another smooth voiced Yank, Al Martino claimed the nation's first Number One with 'Here in My Heart'.

And this is where the story of the British pop star actually starts. Not to mention Yorkshire's first pop star.

Cue controversy. Some may claim that one David Whitfield surely deserves the latter accolade. Born in Hull, Whitfield's recording career details seem too good to be true – two big Number Ones, another ten Top 10 hits, the first UK male vocalist to earn a hallowed Gold Disc, one of only six artists to have a record at the top of the charts for ten weeks or more, the first UK artist to have a hit in the top ten of the American Billboard charts, and the first artist from Britain to sell over a million copies of one record in the States.

Not too shabby, I grant you. But Whitfield, as talented as he obviously was, is the pop music equivalent of the dinosaur. With a voice and style that was firmly, undeniably operatic, he belonged to a previous musical world, the world of perfect pitch, vocal phrasing of an elocution teacher, and Mantovani and his plush orchestral soundscapes. Whitfield's biggest hit, 'Cara Mia' even co-credits Mantovani on the lavish production. Whitfield's path to success had been undoubtedly paved by that of the great Mario Lanza, an American Italian with a supremely velvety tenor voice. Though not quite in the same league, David Whitfield too had a marvellous voice. But, even the Rodgers and Hammerstein film musicals of the time are more rock 'n' roll than Whitfield.

His star rose in 1953, hit an impressive high a year later and started falling in 1955 just as the UK's musical landscape was being re-developed in a fashion far too wild and radical for some tastes. Harsh it may seem, but David Whitfield was not, by any stretch of the imagination, a 'pop star', never mind Yorkshire's first pop star (I suspect, was the man still around to hear this, he'd be relieved that his talents hadn't been dumbed down to that of something so vulgar). There may be outrage over this decision, I realise. Expect to see riot police surrounding old people's homes in the Humber region.

But Whitfield was a formidable chart rival to all the home grown artists looking to make their mark in those days before Bill Haley opened a rocking new can of worms. Of course, in what became a hit-and-miss formula, all the British crooners took a love song that had been successful in the US, did their own version and hoped for the best – there were sometimes three versions of the same song vying for radio airtime.

A year or too later, another local boy was thrown into the music machine with no greater chance than that of any other young contender. But by virtue of stepping into the spotlight smack-bang-in-the-middle of a cultural revolution, when (adopts old-school BBC broadcaster voice) 'the popular music of the day' became the much cooler, much snappier 'pop music', and not just surviving but thriving, Ronnie Hilton was one of the first British pop stars and certainly gets this vote as the first Yorkshire pop star.

Also hailing from Hull, but growing up in Leeds, the story of Ronnie's rise to stardom is more like the script of an old black and white film, seemingly a million miles from the reality show route to fame and fortune that's forced down our throats these days. But there was a Simon Cowell figure involved; there were indeed dozens of Simon Cowells pulling the strings in the music industry way before Cowell himself was pulling his first short trousers up to meet his armpits.

Born Adrian Hill, Ronnie was an ordinary football-loving Yorkshire lad who could sing more than a bit, his talent having been noticed during his stint in the army, where he was pushed forward to front the regiment band. Back in civvies and working as an engineer in a Leeds sewing plant, Ronnie was entered for a singing contest by his first wife, Joan. Less than pleased about it, he reluctantly turned up for the contest and duly won it, first prize being a month's contract as the singer with Johnnie Adleston's Big Band in the city's Starlight Ballroom. The month turned into three years.

Still Adrian Hill in those days, he was approached to record a demo of a song written by a local songwriter. The demo arrived on the desk of Wally Ridley, top A&R man for EMI's HMV record label; in true Hollywood fashion, Ridley hated the song but wanted to hear more of the singer. You can guess the rest. A name change and a little plastic surgery on an unsightly top lip, and bingo, Ronnie was ready to… croon. No rocking, not yet, and certainly not for Ronnie. After a year of healthy exposure on the radio, Hilton got his first hit in 1954 with 'I Still Believe', a song that had been written for Dorothy Squires by her long-suffering hubby, Billy Reid, but after one of their regular barnies, she told him where to shove it. That was Ronnie Hilton's third big break of many.

But ironically it was 1956 when Ronnie Hilton struck Hit Parade gold, just as rock 'n' roll was taking over the nation's youth hearts, minds and swinging hips. His recording of 'No Other Heart', successfully covered by Perry Como in the States, reached Number One and stayed there for six weeks, keeping no less a record than Elvis's 'Heartbreak Hotel' off the top slot in the process. Ronnie had made it – he was a bona fide pop star. With a career that coincided with a true musical revolution, our man still managed to clock up nine Top 20 hits in three years. It all sounds amazingly straightforward in a local-lad-makes-good style, but Ronnie's widow, Chrissie – his second wife – puts the dream story into a more reality-tinged perspective.

"Ron was a really down-to-earth fella but I think he loved the pop star tag really. What used to really piss him off was his missus (first wife, Joan) always used to call him 'Adrian', in public as well. He thought she was dragging him back and she wasn't recognising his success. When they had arguments, she would always be cursing Ronnie Hilton, and Ron would say 'look around you sweetheart, if it wasn't for Ronnie Hilton you wouldn't have this'. It was almost a double life with two different personas. His wife and three children wanted him to be very ordinary yet they loved the trappings of Ronnie being a star."

It was his original wife, remember, who had first entered 'Adrian' for the singing contest, a man who loved singing but was obviously more reluctant to perform and be judged. Once the industry got its hands on someone who was, from all accounts, an uncomplicated, humble Yorkshire bloke, and gave him a new identity, the marriage became a troubled union.

With his 1950s success as a crooning heart-throb behind him – and yes, apparently, he did enjoy the fringe benefits associated with being a pin-up star - Hilton carved out a career as all-round entertainer, performing at three Royal Variety Performances, becoming a popular radio presenter of a regular oldies show for the BBC, and of course becoming a popular fixture on the Panto and summer-show circuit. But there was still a recording career. The children's favourite 'Windmill in Old Amsterdam' took him back into the charts in the mid-60s, and he recorded nearly a full LP's worth of songs as tribute to his beloved Leeds United, who under the inspired management of Don Revie became Britain's top football team in the late 1960s and early 70s. And it wasn't just his football team that fuelled his local pride. Chrissie confirms that he was passionately proud of his Yorkshire roots.

"People tried for years and years to get him to move down to London because they said that he was missing out on contacts and opportunities by staying up North. He said, 'if I can't sell records from Leeds, where the hell can I sell them from? It doesn't really matter where I am'. He wouldn't move down."

And not even when Haley, Elvis et al took a stranglehold on British teenage sensibilities? "Initially, in true Yorkshire fashion, he saw it as a 'bloody load of rubbish'. Fortunately for Ron and singers of his kind, there were still a lot of people who had struggled through the war, and music like his that moved

26

them emotionally and lyrics that meant something remained important to them. They really just wanted the peace and quiet of a ballad, rather than the agitation of the rock 'n' roll that was coming out at the time."

Ronnie carried on singing in his same comfortable style, and he certainly didn't put on heirs and graces when it came to dealing with music's international community. He recorded a song called 'A Blossom Fell' in the mid-50s; when the song's American writer met Ronnie he said, "My God, how do you sing the way you do, and talk like that?"

His career was a long and yes, mostly glittering one. But not without the odd glitch and extra dollop of troubles. Ronnie had become a big name on the country's thriving variety circuit when he and young dancing girl Chrissie Westoll started an affair in 1963. Chrissie fell pregnant with Ronnie's child in 1966… scandal! Rock and bloody roll! Not really. But it could have been had Chrissie reacted differently to the pressures exerted on her.

"When it leaked out, I was living with my parents in Oxford at the time. The paparazzi, as it were, camped outside for ten days. The papers offered me enough money to buy a house, to put Simon, our son through school, etcetera, if I gave them the story… but I refused to kiss and tell because I knew it would ruin Ronnie."

Of course, had this happened ten years previously, the outcry would have perhaps made the name of Ronnie Hilton synonymous with a Category A scandal, having done a dirty far more rock 'n' roll than anything that any of the so-called rebellious stars from the States were doing at the time.

With his career heading for something of a wasteland and his private life wrapped in complication, Ronnie suffered bouts of depression, and sadly, a rather desperate low when he was convicted for shoplifting. But, in keeping with the dream start to the story, there was an eventual happy ending for Ronnie and Chrissie. After years of staying apart for the sake of the other people involved, they were finally reunited and married, enjoying twelve happy years together before Ronnie, the perhaps reluctant pop star, passed away in 2001.

Ronnie wasn't the only local talent to enjoy a taste of pop success in the mid to late 1950s. Marion Ryan, once dubbed 'the Marilyn Monroe of popular music', was born in Middlesbrough when the vast old gas yard was still as part of the North Riding of Yorkshire, but like Ronnie H, she was brought up and educated in Leeds. Another singer who built up a career singing with big bands in the city's dance halls, Marion's looks got her noticed as much as her voice, and Ray Ellington snapped her up to sing with his band – they'd got the plum gig of the time, adding musical fills for the *Goons Show* on radio, probably the most listened-to show on the airwaves.

Though Marion did register in the charts with 'Love Me Forever' (number five in 1958), she struggled to be a consistently successful recording artist, finding her cover versions of successful American tunes being in direct competition with versions by other artists, as was often the way. But the growing TV industry in the UK was crazy for talent like Marion so it was no surprise that her future lay with the new visual medium as she became the resident singer on Granada TV's *Spot the Tune* – a forerunner of *Name That Tune*. Other regular TV appearances and even a sortie into films - most notably *It's All Happening* with Tommy Steele – kept Marion in the British public eye, but with her chance to crack the big time seemingly behind her, Marion stepped back from the limelight in the mid-sixties, by which time her teenage twin sons were ready to cement the family name in pop chart history. Perhaps Marion's biggest claim to fame was that she sang on the first British record made in glorious stereo ('The World Goes Round and Round') in 1958, a nugget of knowledge that you'll no doubt ever have any use for.

Balladeers like Ronnie and Marion should, and probably would have seen the change coming when they were eventually overrun, at least in the affections of younger Britons, by the invasion of the American Rockers . And if it didn't exactly pave the way for rock 'n' roll, 'Skiffle' laid out a little red carpet.

Home grown skiffle was undoubtedly a warm-up act for Elvis and Co, being the first DIY music that young people could listen to, and then try themselves, regardless of their lack of natural musical talent. At interludes in performances by the big bands of the day (particularly of the jazz variety), a faction of the band would play a short quirky improvised set with a skeleton rhythm section and simple guitar or banjo accompaniment. When this took off as an entity in itself, everybody was doing it with tea chest bass guitar, cheap acoustic guitars, washboards, in fact anything than would give a rhythm or make a sound. Glasgow's Lonnie Donegan was the undisputed Skiffle King, and many skiffle bands were started in Yorkshire, but as always it took a while longer for us to catch on. The legendary '2i's' coffee bar in London may have been the venue for live skiffle in the capital, but up in Yorkshire, the region's exponents wowed eager young punters in pubs and working men's clubs; coffee bars up here were strictly for listening to the new sounds on that new fangled whatsit, the jukebox.

It was almost like busking indoors. Once the youth's imagination had been captured by what was the punk rock of its day, even the more traditional Jazzateers, not to mention, folk musicians, got with the beat.

But unfortunately I have to mention folk musicians. I've got nothing against folk music, believe me, and there are some modern examples of what could be referred to as folk music that I do like. Skiffle was classified as a form of folk music in that anyone and everyone could do it, but by that principle, every form of music is folk music. It's the traditional nature of what we recognise as folk music that doesn't really lend itself to the story of pop music evolution, at least in the early days. It may have been the white man's blues in the States with the likes of Woody Guthrie, and romantic images of living the hobo life, hitching rides in railway boxcars and drinking moonshine. But in Britain, the image was, and to some extent still is more one of fisherman's jumpers, a finger in the ear when you sing, and a pint of real ale in an old pewter tankard. Not cool, not sexy. It wasn't until Dylan in the 1960s that anyone recognised folk music as cool, no matter what anyone says. But it was there in the roots of UK skiffle, mainly because the folk singers saw the opportunity to perform music that didn't send their audience to sleep. It was the elements of jazz, blues and country that made skiffle a vibrant new music, with roots, naturally, embedded in America.

Apart from Lonnie Donegan, skiffle music really didn't make stars of anyone, Yorkshire based or otherwise. Quickly usurped by the bigger, bolder and louder rock 'n' roll, skiffle was a stepping stone for the UK's first wave of Rockin' acts, who in a desperate attempt to emulate the American imports, were of the more manufactured variety. Cliff Richard, Tommy Steele, Marty Wilde and later Billy Fury were all examples of the identikit rock 'n' roller put together by the starmakers of Soho, legendary impresarios like Larry Parnes. Consequently, the provinces really didn't get a look-in when it came to providing talent in these early days – the opportunity to actually make a recording if you were in the North was virtually non-existent. No, their role was to provide the audience for the revolution. And it wasn't just starstruck girls.

The Teddy Boy movement had actually started in the UK before Bill Haley fired the first shots of the rebellion but it was rock 'n' roll that galvanised the Teds, not least when it came to tearing cinema seats up as *Blackboard Jungle* inspired nationwide riots, or what passed for riots in those days. Once they attached themselves to the music, the Teds also became known as 'Rockers', though the movement was as much to do with attitude as it was music. Marlon Brando in *The Wild One* became as much of an idol to them as Elvis. Before long, most teds or rockers were too busy making trouble to spend time making music. And of course, it kicked off every weekend in every town and city in Yorkshire. Whole gangs of them, each of them looking like a rock 'n' roll star anyway – they could leave the music to someone else.

At the time, you really couldn't have predicted where the first, and perhaps only Yorkshire rock 'n' roll star was going to come from. But in retrospect, it was obvious – television.

It hardly took a genius to come up with the catchphrase, 'It's all happening'. Because it was; not only was there a musical revolution under way, there was a media revolution in front of the great British public's eyes. Television was broadening its horizons to meet the needs of young people – with some predictable reservations in high places; it was willing to embrace the revolution. Even the BBC recognised the changing times and the opportunity they offered. Jack Good was the man who sought to put rock 'n' roll on TV in this country. Though ITV, the new commercial channel on the block, had dipped a toe, it was the BBC who dived in with the *Six-Five Special*, the first music-based television show especially made for the nation's teenagers.

And in our quest to uncover Yorkshire starring roles in the evolution of British pop music, we hit pay dirt with *Six-Five Special*. The show made a very unlikely star, but a rock 'n' roll star all the same, out of one Don Lang, better known in his hometown of Halifax as Gordon Langhorn.

It was Don, with his band, The Frantic Five who brought the wild new sounds into British homes for nearly two years, from February 1957 to December 1958, opening the show with the show's catchy, iconic theme tune. He'd been a confirmed jazzman, playing trombone with a variety of bands, both live and recording, before having a crack on his own in the mid-fifties, with some medium-sized success. But it wasn't until maverick producer, Good, married the new musical craze with the rapidly increasingly popular medium of television, that Lang enjoyed the kind of exposure most musicians can only dream about. Lang's son, Brad takes up the story…

"It was Jack Good who took a bit of a shine to me Dad really, because, in all honesty, he was a bit too old to be on that kind of show when you think about it. He was in his early thirties by that time, I think. Jack Good used me old man because he wanted him to put a band together that could read music and back the artists who came on the show - the problem with a lot of the skiffle musicians who'd come through was that very few of them could

31

actually read music. A lot of the big new stars of the time came over from the States and they obviously needed a good band of musicians to accompany them on the show. The idea was that they'd have guys who could play rock 'n' roll and still make sense of their musical part when required."

Find the man via the miracle of the Internet, and as his son says, you will see someone who hardly fits into the sexy young rebel mould a la Elvis and even Cliff in his early days. Not to be unkind, but a less-than-slim happy looking chappy heading for middle-age is nearer the mark. But then again, take a look at Bill Haley whilst you're at it; the man who supposedly paved the way for Elvis, already looks like a middle-aged baker, who's been eating half the profits as he invites you to shake, rattle, and indeed, roll.

Lang and his band quickly became synonymous with what was perhaps the most recognisable TV theme tune of the time. The show had used the original recording of *Six-Five Special* for the first few shows – the song came first before the show - then later on, Don sang the theme in front of his band.

Naturally Don and the Frantic Five used their new high profile to launch a successful recording career of their own, their biggest hit coming in 1958 with the annoyingly catchy 'Witch Doctor'; complete with its nonsensical singalong chorus, the song had been a big hit in the States for the 'genius' who gave the world *Alvin and the Chipmunks*. Getting a hit record was undoubtedly a bonus to someone like Don Lang who, according to son Brad, had a very un-starry take on what he did for a living. "If rock 'n' roll hadn't come along I'd guess that me Dad would still have been playing trombone and leading the band. That's what he did after *Six-Five Special* and all that, touring American air bases and the like with a bigger band. I remember him going off on working trips to the bases in Germany when I was a kid. It was a matter of getting work wherever you could. He would have described himself as a jobbing musician."

As Brad emphasises, Lang Senior had a musical career before the rock 'n' roll monster came along and had one after, despite it not because of it. The icing on a varied and rewarding career came in 1968 when Don played trombone on the Beatles' 'White Album', being one off many session musicians brought in by producer George Martin. "Yeah, the great thing is that the Beatles actually knew who me Dad was when he walked in on that recording – it was like Lennon or McCartney looking up and saying 'bloody hell, it's Don Lang from *Six-Five Special!* which was a really great moment for my Dad. The Beatles recognised him!"

Don passed away in 1992 but Lang Junior is a respected professional musician himself these days, having been an in-demand bass player for hire for twenty-five years. Don Lang brought his son Brad up with a distinctly Yorkshire attitude – to view music as first and foremost, a job of work. Brad's played with ABC, Wham, Robbie Williams, Shirley Bassey, Wishbone Ash and Barbara Dickson, among many, many others. His Dad made sure that the first thing his son did when he picked up his instrument, was learn to read music.

Though he appears to have been very much the pragmatic Yorkshireman, Don Lang enjoyed his five minutes of fame whenever he could. There's a story you can look up about him driving a big pink Vauxhall Cresta (the nearest he could get to Elvis's pink Cadillac) 200-yards to the local shop back in the day when any car was an outrageous luxury item. As Brad Lang happily remembers, "My Dad wasn't averse to being recognised".

As the 60s approached, it was hardly surprising that music shows became an accepted TV staple, with the spectacle of their idols usually performing their hits live being the draw for the young viewer, even if some of the performers looked more like your uncle dressed in your cousin's clothing.

In the slipstream of the highly successful *Six-Five Special* came *Oh Boy!*, *Dig This*, and probably most memorably *Juke Box Jury*. And every hip and happening music show needed a hip and happening theme tune – *Juke*

Box Jury had a cracker. The man responsible was a musician who went on to become one of the finest and most celebrated composers and arrangers in Twentieth Century cinema. And what's more he came from York.

John Barry (real name John Prendergast) may have served an apprenticeship in the early days of UK rock 'n' roll but he was destined to find his proper place in the world of the movies; his father ran a number of cinemas in the area and the young Barry unsurprisingly spent an inadvisable amount of time devouring the films of the day.

Barry, the young musician, played trumpet but soon found his true niche as leader and arranger of his own swinging little jazz combo, The John Barry Seven. Spotted playing a gig in their local York, the Seven were invited to back Tommy Steele on a summer season in Blackpool. Their next break was an invite to appear on the *Six-Five Special*, followed by one from *Oh Boy!* ITV's teen music show, where they became something of a regular fixture. But it was as co-writer and arranger for one of the UK's first rock 'n' roll's stars, Adam Faith (imagine a young Cliff Richard being cast as a market stallholder on *Eastenders*), that Barry first made strides in composing for television, providing the music for *Drumbeat*, yet another teen-targeted show that featured Faith, and then for film, when he scored, arranged and conducted the music for Faith's big-screen debut, *Beat Girl*. There was no looking back for Barry after that; the last fifty years of movie history has his mark indelibly printed on it, with film scores for everything from *Midnight Cowboy* to *Born Free*, *Dances with Wolves* to his most famous work for the James Bond films, winning more Oscars, Grammys and awards than the man could possibly shake his conductor's baton at.

Back in the day, John Barry was hardly what you could call a pop star since you wouldn't have known him had you been sharing a bus seat with him, but this fantastically talented Yorkshireman scored impressively in the charts with no less than a dozen hits, starting with that theme tune for *Juke Box*

Jury, 'Hit Or Miss'. Those early hits created a trademark sound that would see Barry's band rival The Shadows as the country's most popular instrumental combo into the early 1960s, before the movies became the man's bread and butter, not to mention jam and caviar.

So, yes – so far so good, Yorkshire did in fact play a part in the early days of youth-oriented popular music, even if the personnel involved did only appear to be bit players in the wider scheme of things, sometimes grabbing a shaft of limelight more by accident than design, and perhaps in spite of the rock and the roll rather than because of it. Better than nowt, if you like.

But if the fifties was an exciting time for the nation's youth, and the newly liberated teenager, they held nothing on the following decade. How would Yorkshire and its stars-in-waiting fare with the swinging sixties?

Chapter Two

North Of Watford… East Of Liverpool

The Swinging 60s lasted for over 17 years in Yorkshire, with petty crime giving way to serious misdemeanour and all set in a quaint country village to a rocking good soundtrack. Sorry, my mistake – that's *Heartbeat*, ITV's long-running Sunday night drama, that frankly makes you glad you weren't living in the sixties.

Except, yours truly was. The UK Number One on the day of my birth in July 1961 was 'Runaway' by Del Shannon. Try as I might, I can't find any lasting significance in that poptastic fact. But my parents were kind of influenced by pop music when it came to naming me – Craig Douglas was a popular if unremarkable young singer at the time. It could have been worse; they quite liked The Shadows too, featuring Hank Marvin.

At the turn of the decade, the refreshing prosperity of the 1950s still prevailed and our green and pleasant land was gilded with relative contentment and even optimism – even the bits of it that were murky grey and far from pleasant. And it seems that everybody else liked The Shadows too. When they weren't the backing band for Cliff Richard in the most rocking era of his never ending career, the Shads were a Hit Parade fixture with their trademark instrumentals. Starting in 1960 with the iconic 'Apache', Hank and chums enjoyed a dozen straight Top Ten singles, five of which were Number Ones. And if Skiffle had inspired the region's youth to have a go themselves in the late 50s, then it was The Shadows who topped-up the inspiration at the start of the 60s, spawning hundreds of fresh young combos, all eager to reproduce that twanging new electric guitar sound - drowned in an ocean of reverb obviously. Surely every schoolboy practised the 'Shadows Walk' in front of a mirror with a tennis racket or cricket bat in place of Hank Marvin's fiesta red Fender Stratocaster.

And in Yorkshire, the fact that many were actually picking up the real thing (maybe not a 'Strat' but an electric guitar nonetheless) represented a highly significant shift in the aspirations of young male Tykes. Until rock 'n' roll came along, most teenage boys dreamt of making the grade as a professional sportsman, especially so in the sports mad county of Yorkshire.

In the early 1960s, we were the kings of the cricket pitch with heroes like Fred Trueman, Brian Close and a young Geoffrey Boycott helping us to four County championships in five years. In football, the two Sheffield clubs both enjoyed respectable positions in the old Division One before Leeds United became the dominant Yorkshire team from the mid-decade onwards. But at the dawn of the sixties, the game played with the oval ball still dominated Saturday afternoons for legions of the region's young men, with Rugby League giants sprinkled throughout the county. Leeds, Halifax and Huddersfield all had trophy-winning teams and Wakefield Trinity had the most successful period in their history, winning three Challenge Cups in four seasons. The 1963 film *This Sporting Life*, filmed in Wakefield, famously celebrated Rugby League as the sport of gruff, tough, don't-call-me-a-puff Yorkshiremen.

And let's get this straight, playing that there rock and roll, in its infancy at least, was mostly a man thing across the nation, and, it seems, an exclusively man thing in Yorkshire. Being the member of a band wasn't quite as macho as knocking seven shades out of an opponent in the name of sport, but it was much better for picking women up – they were more likely to watch a band in action than a rugby team.

The 1960s represent a complex period of cultural change, not least in popular music. There are at least two decades worth of developments packed into ten small years, so it's more accurate to talk in terms of 'sub-periods', plural, the first of which could be described as 'B.B.' – before Beatles. Those first two-to-three years of the celebrated decade saw changes in the attitude and outlook of young people across the country and yes, even in dye-in-the-wool Yorkshire too. As well as, and sometimes instead of picking up the bat or the ball, young men were picking up guitars and drumsticks.

Finally there were signs of local youngsters getting with the beat, from the Leeds area in particular. Trevor Midgley brandished guitar in one of the city's combos typical of the day, The Raiders, who by Trevor's own admission, were straight copyists of The Shads. But taking the opportunity to play any part in the exciting new musical era was the important thing. "Until rock and roll came along, Leeds was no different to anywhere else in that the kids were just little copies of their mums and dads, and they were listening to the same music too. Then Haley happened. Personally, it was Elvis's 'Jailhouse Rock' in 1957 that really made me want to get involved."

And like every other city in the country, Leeds had coffee bars where you could hang out and listen to the new sounds. But what about live venues in the city where you could see your new heroes and dream of being up on stage in their place? "The theatres - the Empire, the Grand and even the old City Varieties - put the big names on. Then there were the established dance halls, the most famous of which in Leeds was the Mecca Locarno in the County Arcade."

Part of a chain of ballrooms scattered across the county, and indeed the country, the Mecca is most famously the place where one James Savile started making his name in the entertainment business, as manager in the late 1950s. It's Sir Jim, it is claimed – by himself, first and foremost - who 'invented' the Disc Jockey/Disco set-up as we know it today, i.e. some fab and groovy geezer, you see, playing them there records, one after another on a pair of turntables, for the guys and gals to dance to. How's about that then? Huh-uh-uh-uh-huhh! Sorry, couldn't resist.

Come the 1960s, it wasn't just the dance halls and theatres that took the opportunity to get the teenage population through their doors and relieve them of their pounds, shillings and pennies. City Hall in Sheffield, Queens Hall in Leeds, St. George's Hall in Bradford were examples of the grander establishments lowering themselves to accommodate this vulgar new craze, which undoubtedly was still being given the three-word critique by the over-25s - 'it'll never last'. But even the cinemas were getting in on the act all across Yorkshire. The Odeons, ABCs, Gaumont's and Rialto's all hosted shows featuring teen beat sensations, 'as seen on TV'.

But back at grass roots level, the mark of progression for bands like The Raiders was getting a booking anywhere bigger than a pub or working man's club. "We played places like Normanton Baths, and village halls as well as recognised dance halls where big dance bands had played before. They became teen venues because the new beat bands started getting employed to play for the complete night or as back-up for the bigger bands.

"But you didn't even need to have a stage – we set up anywhere. If you had rich parents, you could have a marquee in your garden where a band could play or even in a big house. We played a gig once in such a big house, we set up the full band including the drum kit under the stairs and played."

But as Trevor readily accepts, there was only so much a raw young band could do – we are talking about nearly fifty years ago after all. "Transport was a big problem then as not many people had a car; not many young people could even drive, so groups like the Raiders tended to stay on their home patch. Ambition

39

was limited by resources. As for access to recording facilities, there was nothing. It was even a rarity for anyone to actually own a tape recorder. When you could get hold of one, there was hardly any fidelity on these machines, and to record a band, apart from sticking a microphone right in the middle of the dance floor, forget it.

"To get noticed then, you had to be seen in London of course. There were two or three venues talent-spotters would turn up at, one of which was the '2i's' coffee bar in Soho, because it had the reputation from the Cliff days. We played there but never got anything out of it. And talent contests, of course, were a way to get noticed. *Opportunity Knocks* even, though it was still only on radio back then. Even if you just got an audition, A&R men would turn up there. There was no chance or room for recording a demo and sending it off – just didn't happen."

In those fresh, young, heady days of the UK pop industry, 'flavour of the month' wasn't just a flippant phrase; there was always a new musical revolution just around the corner. When British R 'n' B – that's Rhythm and Blues to you – stepped forward into the spotlight, the days of the Shadows copyists such as Trevor's band were numbered, as the Shadows themselves retreated back into the, er, shadows.

But there were plenty of other bands on the West Yorkshire circuit – "Leeds bands were more competitive than co-operative, though having said that, if someone from a band couldn't make a gig for whatever reason, another player from another band would stand in." For the record, there were The Mustangs from Wakefield, and also from Leeds, The Cresters and The Cherokees, the latter group eventually achieving a top 40 hit with 'Seven Golden Daffodils' in 1963. Under the guidance of famous producer/Svengali Mickie Most, The Cherokees were indeed contenders for a short period. Following their big brush with success, but even they got left behind in the Beatles-led beat revolution, and went missing, re-appearing years later renamed as, wait for it, New York Public Library. Mmm, catchy. Surprisingly they never troubled the chart compiler

40

again.

Another of Trevor's contemporaries was Jeff Christie, starting out himself with The Tremmers, very much 'Shadows derivatives' too. They metamorphosed into The Outer Limits, who for a while looked the Leeds band most likely. But Christie had to wait a while longer for his big moment.

Trevor Midgley himself left The Raiders in 1965, when, inspired by Dylan and fellow American folkie, Phil Ochs, he started developing own 12-string guitar style. He went on to record for John Peel's infamous Dandelion label under the stage names of 'Beau' and 'John Trevor'. Unlike many of those early Leeds pop musicians, he has at least continued a long-term music career, though by his own admission, it has been a part-time pursuit in some periods.

Good to report that Trevor looks back without bitter 'if-only's' though; it was obviously a very good time to be a young music fan. "Once rhythm and blues got a foothold, loads and loads of different, diverse venues opened up. Clubs featuring live music like the Three Coins in Leeds and The Coffin Club in Bradford grew up on back on beat boom. Not surprisingly, they were modelled on the Cavern. It was a winning formula."

Oh yes, the Cavern – everything changed with the success of the Beatles. "The Beatles opened everything up – A&R men started looking for talent outside London. Anyone who could play a note from Liverpool was signed up. And similarly in Manchester. But they didn't tend to look over the Yorkshire side of the Pennines, just on the west."

Perhaps the exception that proves the rule is Dave Berry. Sheffield born and bred Berry – real name, Dave Grundy – was one of the lucky artists who got his chance after the Beatles convinced the London suits in 1962 that there was talent north of Watford. Originally billed with his band, The Cruisers, Berry enjoyed a purple pop patch in the mid-sixties that in practical terms set him up for a long and contented career in the music industry.

"We were very fortunate because there was a flourishing scene in Sheffield when we got going, so we never really had to resort to the Working Men's Clubs.

A lot of the gigs we had were ones we set up ourselves in village halls, upstairs rooms in pubs, etc. We ended up getting so much work that we decided to turn professional before we got a recording contract. We were able to build up an incredible following, mostly around South Yorkshire and also in Manchester because we were being managed by an agency based there – Kennedy Street Enterprises – and they brought us to the attention of labels looking up North for talent. They picked up on us because of our big grass roots following."

The Mecca Locarno Ballroom, Sheffield 'branch', played a significant part in Dave Berry's success story. "That's where I first performed in 1958 with a mate of mine doing an Everly Brothers song in the talent spot there. We won, and that was the start of it for me.

"The cinemas were starting to put on music for young people. The Gaumont in Sheffield put on a show every Saturday, ten–till-midday - it sounds cheesy now but they called it 'the Teenage Show'. There were sometimes eight or nine hundred kids in there to watch you. That's what we all aimed for – moving up from small pub back-rooms to these big stages, us, Joe Cocker, and others."

Yes, that Joe Cocker. The one with the voice that sounds like either the sweet release of a tortured soul, or a drain in pain, depending on your standpoint. Back in the day before the day – if you see what I mean – Dave Berry and Joe Cocker were the young leading lights on the Sheffield R 'n' B circuit, battling it out, in a friendly way, to see who made it big first.

Sheffield's music scene according to Berry, owed much to tradition – "a lot of us had dads and uncles who played music in the area. It was very much a working class pursuit". Both views are evidential in the kind of very Yorkshire career advice that Berry got from his dad, himself a semi-pro jazz drummer. "He used to tell me things like, 'don't own the van with the rest of the band, buy it yourself and pay for running costs between you'. Basic stuff like that. So I took charge of the band, which meant that I was hiring and firing as well.

"I didn't have a plan. Nobody did in those days. We all thought if we could get a few decent years out of playing music, we would have done well – I'm sure

Keith Richard and Mick Jagger thought the same. We were all from working class backgrounds so you didn't really have any plans for your life anyway. I was going to technical college, learning how to be a welder – but when I started getting some success with the music, I stopped going. But I always knew that I could fall back on it. You didn't worry about it - if it didn't work out with the music you could go and get another job.

"The plan came later when I was having the hits, and I realised that those chart songs could be the bedrock of my career. As long as I could keep the same attitude, adding new material, trying new stuff as I went on, I thought I'd be okay. I didn't just want to keep rehashing those songs from the 60s and nothing else.

"It was around 1959/60 when we started getting really into the R 'n' B. After the first wave of real rockers, we started getting the next wave doing watered down versions of songs – we wanted to hear the originals. We discovered Atlantic Records, started going down to Violet May's record shop in Sheffield and she'd say have a listen to this, John Lee Hooker, Muddy Waters or something. We wanted to know where all this great stuff was coming from."

As he readily admits, Dave Berry's subsequent success was thanks in no small way to the healthy Sheffield club scene that flourished with the Rhythm and Blues explosion of the early sixties. The legendary 'Club 60' was opened by Terry Thornton, fellow Sheffield muso, showcasing the best in both American talent and rising UK acts. When Thornton moved his operation to a new site on Leadmill Street, renaming it The Esquire Club, Berry and the Cruisers became a regular attraction there, along with Joe Cocker and his band – at that point their glorious stage name was 'Vance Arnold and the Avengers'. But still the next stage proved elusive.

"Joe looked like being left by the wayside. We all had those periods – I did for about nine months when really nothing was happening for us. I was starting to get the feeling that I'd let people down before we actually got signed. We did the London thing – played the '2i's' coffee bar. From that we got booked to play in Hamburg. We were working all over the country as well before we started making records."

Finally, it was Mickie Most who saw the band play in Doncaster of all places, and signed them to Decca. "They were actively looking for new bands that were making a stir in their part of the country and thankfully we fitted that."

The first three singles by Dave Berry and the Cruisers were naturally R 'n' B covers starting with Chuck Berry's 'Memphis Tennessee'; Dave had taken Chuck's surname so why not one of his biggest hits? "The first three or four records did okay but it never really took off for us, so someone suggested I try something different, what about this song, 'the Crying Game'? I really didn't want to record it at first, I didn't want to be like Cliff, singing ballads – I was more into clinging hold of my R 'n' B credibility. I wasn't being moulded into a pop singer as such; it was just a trial that worked incredibly well."

'The Crying Game' is a truly great record, to my ears at least, but it was Berry's stage performance that punters tended to remark upon, delivered with a mysterious panache that marks him out as the missing link between Gene Vincent in the 1950s and Alvin Stardust in the 1970s. He often sang half-hidden behind a curtain, his microphone stand, his upturned collar, anything. At least it looked like it was meant to be mysterious – it could have been he was a bit shy or even just taking the Michael. Dave's honest enough to say it wasn't completely pre-planned. "That act developed over the years. It was a little bit tongue in cheek to be honest. But there was this central support pillar in the Esquire club, right in the middle of the stage. So I decided since it was there, I might as well use it, hiding behind it as I sang. And I started wearing a single black glove to emphasise my hand movements. I would encourage these visuals working with the floor managers and cameramen on TV shows, using the lighting and the shadows cast across the set. The only thing you'd see on screen at the start of the song was my hand. It was a very televisual act for the time."

And TV pop really had stepped up a gear or two by the time that Dave was strutting his stuff for the camera. *Ready Steady Go!* had quickly become a flagship show for ITV from 1963; the BBC answered the growing teenage demand for pop music with *Top of the Pops* at the beginning of 1964 – opinion was divided as to which was the cooler option of the two shows but maybe the latter should get the vote by virtue of staying on the air for forty years longer than the former.

By the mid-sixties, Sheffield was one vibrant musical city. With the Esquire Club now nationally famous, the Black Cat Club and then the Mojo Club (originally The King Mojo) opened and received similar acclaim over the next few years. The local entrepreneur behind these rocking joints was Peter Stringfellow - yes the very same, a man who could make Jimmy Savile look like a conservative dresser. But anyway, thanks to Stringfellow and Thornton - and others - a platform for Sheffield talent was in place, and that talent was plentiful.

Can Dave Berry recall a sense of competition existing between Sheffield bands and artists? "It was more a work situation with colleagues who could be competitive at times. The only time I can remember it getting a bit 'bitchy' was in the early days. Jimmy Crawford had one top twenty hit at the end of 1961 but as soon as the Beatles broke, he was old hat, left behind. Jimmy was the big star in Sheffield – because he had a rich grandmother, she was buying the band new gear and a new van and what have you. It did get bitchy I suppose. Because most musicians had to save up or get gear on H.P. if they could."

Also watching enviously as Jimmy Crawford made at least a little splash would have been Vance Arnold, a.k.a. Joe Cocker. But Joe himself did have some moderate success around the same time as Dave Berry. His first big break was getting a support slot in 1963 with the rising stars of British R 'n' B, The Rolling Stones; the second should have been the release of his debut single a year later, a cover of the Lennon/McCartney song 'I'll Cry Instead', now under the banner of Joe Cocker Big Blues. But unfortunately for 'The Cock', whilst Berry built on his initial breaks, his own recorded debut didn't make enough ripples and the ex-apprentice gas fitter would have to wait a little longer for his more lasting moment.

Dave Berry's own chart career spanned three years, and included three top five hits together with a handful of lesser hit records. But as his profile was waning in the UK, it kept growing over on the continent, especially Belgium and Holland, where to this day he is still a regular on TV and radio. And in the forty years since his heyday there have been several timely 'credibility boosts' to keep Dave in the public eye.

He received a reverential name check in the Bob Dylan documentary film *Don't Look Back* in 1967; the Sex Pistols covered his 'Don't Gimme No Lip Child' ten years later; and in 1992, the Oscar-winning British film *The Crying Game* relit Dave's fire worldwide. Though Boy George sang the version of the song that appeared over the end credits, Dave's original version of The Crying Game features during one scene, and there's also a club scene where, Dave happily recalls – giving the film's pivotal twist away – "the transvestite character effectively does my act!"

And whilst many of Dave Berry's live appearances these days inevitably involve Sixties Revival Tours, a more recent development suggests this Sheffield lad still has friends in cool places. "I've opened up for Van Morrison many times in recent years. I've known him from the beginning of his career when he first came over from Ireland – he just asked me what I was doing on a certain date and I was only too happy playing support to him doing all the old R 'n' B stuff. I ended up doing the Albert Hall with Van. That was one of the highlights of my career as far as I'm concerned."

It can't be bad for a musician in his late sixties to still be enjoying his career as much as he obviously does. Not that he looks that old – more like our old friend David Bowie's older brother. It's good to encounter a musician whose enthusiasm has not been soured by the cynical nature of the music industry… though his parting shot on the subject is "it's a weird business this, y'know".

You'd guess any raw young talent plucked from our part of the world and dropped into the deep end of the burgeoning pop music industry would have felt the same back in early sixties. Take Pauline Matthews from Bradford – did I say music was exclusively a man thing in Yorkshire? I wasn't lying because it wasn't until ten years after signing her first recording contract that Pauline really made her mark as Kiki Dee. But as a young lass, our Pauline had been signed up to Fontana as early as 1963. She was just sixteen, working on the counter of Boots the Chemist by day, singing with a band in a Leeds ballroom at night, when, the story goes, a rep from the Philips electronics company, taped her performance from the balcony. The rough tape apparently made its way through the company up to the head of Fontana Records, Jack Baverstock, who hearing a powerful voice with no little soul, promptly invited Pauline down to London.

No sooner had she signed to the label than she was given a new name and Kiki Dee was born. Within two months, she'd released her first single, the first of many over the next three years for Fontana. However, her success was limited to just reasonable sales and critical acclaim over in Italy of all places. But being still a young girl, she was effectively serving an apprenticeship, most tellingly you'd think as a backing singer for Dusty Springfield, the biggest female star in the UK at the time. It could have been the kiss of death when Kiki Dee was officially nominated as one of the artists most likely to break big in 1966 – she was even introduced as such by presenter Cathy McGowan as she stood in the audience on *Ready Steady Go!*. Our Pauline all but delivered with a top-notch version of 'Why Don't I Run Away From You', but in the finally reckoning, 1966 wasn't her year after all. Though, as a consolation, we did win the World Cup. Stardom was still around a fair few corners for the 'belt-it-out bird' from Bradford, as Kiki Dee might have been referred to at the time. But probably wasn't.

While the likes of Dave Berry, Joe Cocker and Kiki Dee were working, and often struggling to build up a career from grass roots level, a pair of twins from Leeds were fast-tracked to full-on pop star media attention, cashing in on the obvious demand for pretty-boy pop. No disrespect meant but Paul and Barry

47

Ryan were as near to a manufactured act as you could get at this time. The novelty of good looking twins who could sing was too good an opportunity to miss. In fact it was a sure fire hit. They were Bros years before the brothers Goss saw their first hair gel. The brothers were perhaps destined to get a gilt-edged crack at pop stardom – their mother was Marion Ryan who'd had her own music moments in the 50s and had become something of a pin-up when she became a fixture on British TV shows. Their step-father was one Harold Davidson, UK tour manager to amongst others, Frank Sinatra and Judy Garland. It is said that Davidson strong-armed Decca into giving the Ryan boys a deal and turning them into instant heart-throbs.

It was the mid-sixties, and though The Beatles were still top dogs, Beatlemania, with the girls screaming for their favourite one of the Fab Four, was now a thing of the past. British pop had a new pin-up every week, whether it was the dreamily handsome Mick Jagger or the savagely cute Keith Richards. But the Ryan twins were two pin-ups for the price of one (always a good equation to Yorkshire folk). Their early records also reflected the fact there was now a big market for watered down beat driven music that could easily stray into ballad territory – Tom Jones managed to find the right balance but it wasn't long before Englebert Humperdink turned the clock back a good ten years and made middle-of-the-road profitably fashionable again (if you didn't know better, you'd wonder whether Englebert was from Cleckheaton himself, with a name like that. I checked – he wasn't – he was born in India).

So the time was right for an act such as Paul and Barry's – everyone else was cashing in, so why shouldn't a couple of lads from Leeds? But, though their first four singles registered around the Top Twenty of the charts, the Ryans hardly set the music world alight. When the next four struggled to make the big Top 40 at all, a wise man might have guessed something was less than right in the camp. With the stress of the business taking its toll, Paul Ryan suffered a nervous breakdown and so an enforced sabbatical was the obvious, indeed, inevitable development. Their last single released as brothers, 'Claire' only just crawled inside the Top 50, and their future as recording artists of any note appeared uncertain to say the least.

Not only that but it was now 1967, and things were changing man… sorry, changing, man. And once again, the source of the change came from over the pond. Yet another new attitude, admittedly just an extension of the last new attitude, was adopted by any young person old enough to have a good time, but young enough not to have responsibilities to worry about. What place or even chance now for the Yorkshire hopefuls still paying their dues on the circuit?

The times they were a-changing. Bloody 'ell – we were just getting used to the way it was.

Chapter Three

Free Love? Well, I'm Not Paying For It.

B atley and San Francisco - the twin towns that never were.

But in 1967, it was all happening in both Batley and San Francisco, believe me. But for some bizarre reason, it was the Californian city that got all the headlines.

There was a big change in the air, with the 'beautiful people' meeting up to listen to music, share the vibe and have some chicken in a basket. Yes, the world famous Batley Variety Club opened its doors in March 1967 bringing that little bit of 'Vegas' to the most unlikely of locations; Batley was slap-bang in-between Leeds and Bradford, just a mile from Dewsbury. And it still is.

Some may have seen it as just a glorified working men's club, but this was the big-time entertainment as far as many West Yorkshire punters were concerned. 'Build it and they will come', was the progressive thinking behind it; entertainments entrepreneur, Jimmy Corrigan was the man with the dream. And build it – on the A653 Bradford Road - he did. And lo and behold, come they did – not only your Tom Joneses, Shirley Basseys and Bee Gees's's's (don't worry, there was and still is only one Bee Gees) but more exotic international stars like Louis Armstrong, Eartha Kitt and The Grumbleweeds.

Apart from putting Batley on the map, the Variety Club was at least weeks ahead of its time; most cities across the nation had a similar entertainment 'Mecca' by the end of the decade; in Yorkshire alone, Sheffield had the Fiesta, and even Wakefield had its Theatre Club.

To be fair, they never tried to make out that the Variety Club was a 'young persons' establishment; punters under 30 weren't barred but either you liked that kind of thing or you didn't, i.e. you were old before your time or you weren't.

Meanwhile, over in Frisco, as we in Normanton liked to call it, the 'Summer of Love' was nigh. In what's still seen as the defining moment of the 1960s, the Californian city was the epicentre for the Hippie movement, with 100,000 young Americans coming together as an anti-establishment statement that started a counterculture revolution, not only denouncing capitalism and war (the Vietnam conflict was threatening to rage out of control), but embracing free-living and free-loving. Not just a big knees-up then? Of course it wasn't that straightforward - counterculture revolutions never bloody are, are they? The liberal partaking of drugs and even more liberal sexual attitudes meant that the dreaded 'hippy' was a threat to the fabric of society, according to the powers that be.

And if that was the attitude of the establishment in the States, you can bet your kaftan that it was just as bad, if not worse here in the UK. Blimey, we'd only just got used to the idea of a permissive society and young chaps wearing their hair past their collars. Communes and love-ins?... In Castleford and Leyburn?!

And what about the music? As the language that brought hippies from across the world together (not to mention some 'good shit') the music went a bit dreamy and psychedelic, laid-back and as free of 'downers', 'bummers' and 'drags' as it's possible to be. The movement gave birth to open-air music festivals as we still know them. So next time you're stuck in a quagmire of a field, soaked to the skin, drinking a beer that cost six quid, watching a distinctly mediocre band out of boredom, wondering where what you're doing there, blame the Hippies – they started it.

The Monterey Festival kicked it all off musically in San Francisco with Jefferson Airplane, Jimi Hendrix, Grateful Dead and The Who all writing their place in open-air pop history. Which is all very well, I hear you say, but what about our Yorkshire popsters? Surely it meant sod all to them.

You'll be surprised. Hopefully. The most high profile White Rose artist to 'turn up, tune in and drop out', was a singer last seen struggling to make a name for himself outside Sheffield. As unlikely as it seemed at the time – there was probably a hefty wind from several thousand Sheffielders doing a simultaneous double-take as the artist formerly known as Vance Arnold popped up on their TV screens – Joe Cocker became a massive star in 1968, thanks to the new 'love your brother' philosophy, and perhaps more importantly, recording an inspired choice of song.

Still together and certainly at the cutting edge of the new revolution were The Beatles. They themselves gave the movement an instant anthem with 'All You Need is Love' in that same Summer of Love in 1967. But it was Joe Cocker who took one of their less-celebrated ditties and turned it into an equally potent anthem. 'With A Little Help From My Friends' featured on the 'Sergeant Pepper' album released later that year, but sung by Ringo, it was, by Beatles standards at least, something of a sing-a-long filler.

The following year, Cocker took the song, slowed it down with a new bluesy time signature, and with his voice as raw as ever it was, gave the lyric a new soul slant. The production verged on the 'epic', complete with Soul Sister backing vocals and highly memorable Jimmy Page guitar licks. The end product, sorry 'happening', reached Number One in the UK, staying in the charts for an incredible 13 weeks – that's three months, a full quarter of a year, man.

Though he'd seemed to have re-appeared from nowhere, Joe Cocker had hardly been idle since being dropped by his first record company as his first stab at stardom came to nowt. He'd formed the Grease Band with equally respected blues muso, Chris Stanton, and carried on doing what he always did best, singing the blues, and living the sometimes inadvisable life of a blues singer. But the guy who had looked in danger of being left behind in the nicotine smog of Sheffield's live circuit, finally cemented his place in pop history with his iconic reading of a Beatles song – remember, his first single covering a Beatles tune flopped – and then put the proverbial cherry on the groovy cake with a show-stopping turn at Woodstock in 1969.

When old hippies talk about the sixties, they always end up referring to Woodstock as the high point of their scene – the two are synonymous with one another. While several million people claim to have been there at Woodstock, only thirty-odd acts can actually claim to have played there. And one of them was our celebrated ex-apprentice gas fitter from Sheffield. They say that if you can remember the sixties, you weren't there – though he's enjoyed many career highlights since, it's to be hoped that Joe Cocker can remember at least some of the period between the autumn of 1968 and the summer of 1969, surely the time of his life.

Life since has been up and down, to say the least, for our old Cocker. The early 1970s were marked by the excesses of life on the road; the infamous 'Mad Dogs and Englishmen' tour saw Cocker return home to Sheffield with a big drink problem, not to mention bouts of clinical depression. But after a troublesome decade where health problems inevitably restricted the performance side of things, the 1980s saw a revival in the singer's career thanks in no small part to his duet with Jennifer Warnes on the worldwide Number One, 'Up Where We Belong', taken from the movie, *An Officer and a Gentleman*. America continued its love affair with our Joe from that point on, and there he's stayed, living and working, though he did pop back to pick up an OBE in 2007.

Exhibit B in the 'Yorkshire Blokes becoming World-Renowned Hippies' discussion? The court calls Arthur Brown. Sounds just as much an anonymous Northerner as Joe Cocker, doesn't he? When actually, he was the self-proclaimed 'God of Hellfire'. From Whitby.

Actually born Arthur Wilton – not really any less rock 'n' roll a name than 'Arthur Brown' in my book (i.e. this one) – this slightly deranged son of North Yorkshire, who like so many of the county's early pop stars, spent a hefty period of his childhood in Leeds, took a distinctly different route to pop immortality, shunning a promising academic future for one on the wilder side of modern music. He studied law and philosophy at the Universities of London and Reading but discovered the bohemian lifestyle of the capital's jazz set and dropped out to follow his true calling of 'Rock Madman'. He enjoyed early acclaim following performances in Paris during the time of the French Student riots but returned to these shores in 1967, finding himself still in the ranks of the unknown. But that too could have been so very different, so very quickly; Arthur became one of two lead singers with a new soul group, the Foundations, with Clem Curtis. Of course, in the tradition of 'too many cooks', something had to give, and our man graciously stepped away leaving Clem and Co to make their mark on the charts with 'Baby, Now That I've Found You' and 'Build Me Up, Buttercup', amongst other hits.

No matter, Arthur had an agenda of his own, a very un-Foundations-like agenda. He developed a quite amazing stage-act, The Crazy World of Arthur Brown, that appeared to owe as much to voodoo and the dark arts as it did to Rock and, indeed, Roll. Not only did he paint his face in a manner more akin to a very bad Hammer horror film, he wore a metal helmet, an adornment of which he was very fond of setting alight with the aid of lighter fluid. Of course there were many occasions when this led to the rest of him being set on fire, and on one such occasion, onlookers in the audience put out the flames with a torrent of beer – if you had to go out in a literal blaze of glory, what a way to go. The music itself was a hard-edged variant on the psychedelic rock of the time, as pioneered by the likes of the early Pink Floyd. Much of that was dreamy, trance-like, and of course 'far-out'; Brown's musical contribution was more nightmarish, adrenalin-inducing, and probably further out than was actually advisable.

Building up a cult following, in the days when a cult following wasn't a euphemism for having 23 fans, Arthur was snapped up by The Who's management team. They immediately put the likable nutter into the studio, released the stand-out track from the sessions as a single, and hey presto, a Number One Pop Star was born. In retrospect, 'Fire' was progressive rock before it's time, and Arthur Brown was Alice Cooper before the American rocker had even considered the potential of face-paints and theatrics.

That chart-topping single may have been both the start and the finish of his mainstream career but his ensuing rock career has not been without event or colour. Though he doesn't automatically sound completely in line with the 'peace love and understanding' mood of the time, Brown was embraced as a refreshing detour within the hippy scene. A long standing favourite in the Brown repertoire was a song that could only be a hippy anthem – 'Give Him a Flower'. And the fact that he toured the States with both Frank Zappa and Jimi Hendrix surely reflects his high standing in the movement. Hendrix even wanted Brown to front his side project, Band of Gypsies, but the singer with the flaming helmet (ouch) was otherwise committed. Some would say being 'committed' was surely only a matter of time where Arthur Brown was concerned (getting arrested and charged in Italy for exposing himself in public sounds very rock 'n' roll for anyone else but disappointingly normal for Arthur).

Though the rest of the man's career could easily fill another chapter or three, Brown's profile was never as high again. He's spent the last forty years flitting from musical project to project, crossing the Atlantic whenever the project required, discovering 'alternative' religion, surviving a brain haemorrhage, and generally cramming as much relative weirdness into life as possible. We probably shouldn't be that surprised since he hailed from the creepy, gothic coastal town of Whitby.

Arthur Brown's legacy from those heady days of the late sixties is perhaps the first wave of heavy rock acts that heralded the arrival of the 1970s in the UK, with the likes of Black Sabbath and Deep Purple at its forefront. Ozzy Osbourne and 'Sabs' in particular owed Arthur a great debt of gratitude, certainly in terms of style and presentation as much as their music.

It was very nearly a hat trick of Number Ones for acts hailing from God's own county in 1968. And yet again, the purveyors of the record that should have been *Top of The Pops*, were just as unlikely as both Cocker and Brown but for a different reason. Remember Paul and Barry Ryan? When Paul retreated from the pop frontline after his nervous breakdown, the prospects for an ongoing career for either himself or his twin brother were less than rosy. But they came back with a 'Plan B' that could, and may well have been borrowed from the Beach Boys.

After Brian Wilson suffered his own supremely bonkers breakdown in the mid-1960s, it was decided that the rest of the Beach Boys would tour with a live show whilst Brian sat in the sanctuary of his sand pit composing new material for their return, where upon, he would weave his remarkable aural magic in the recording studio. Though you could hardly call him another Brian Wilson, it seems that Paul Ryan could write a decent song too. Heavily influenced by composer Jimmy Webb, whose 'MacArthur Park', a big sweeping drama of a song, had been a top five single for actor Richard Harris, and undoubtedly by the Tom Jones's instant classic, 'Delilah', Paul came up with the highly ambitious 'Eloise', and got twin brother Barry to provide the lead vocal on its recording. The result was little short of a revelation, and spent 12 big weeks in the UK singles chart, kept off the top slot only by the mighty combination of Mary Hopkin, Joe Cocker and Hugo Montenegro, 'The Good, the Bad and the Ugly'.

Sorry, that was the name of Hugo's record, the theme from the Clint Eastwood film of the same name, not a cruel observation of those three artists. Well, not in that order anyway.

The Ryans had come back with a bang, but unfortunately, and maybe understandably given the quality of 'Eloise', they couldn't follow it up. The Damned had a big hit with their version of the song nearly twenty years later, just to prove what a fine pop song it was. But like so many acts of the sixties, any future success lay on the continent for Barry Ryan, with brother Paul remaining firmly in the background; he sadly lost his battle with cancer in the early 1990s.

What of the county's foremost female pop battler, Kiki Dee? Turning 21 in 1968, she was still more notable for the vocal appearances she had made as backing singer for other artists than those on her own records. Although... her single release in November of that year did bring an unexpected portion of attention, thanks to the B-side rather than the A-side. 'On A Magic Carpet Ride' became a Northern Soul favourite, a development that may have given Kiki a welcome credibility boost but propelled her only slightly nearer to pop star status. The fact is Northern Soul fans were almost exclusively drawn only to records imported from the States, with the only real contribution of the nation's Northerners being confined to the role of listening to, and of course dancing in a health-threatening fashion to the records.

Kiki Dee's situation wasn't helped by her record company's decision to collect together a seemingly random selection of her previous recordings and release the collection as Kiki's debut long-player; the singer was far from impressed and refused to promote the record. That was effectively the end of the Deester's relationship with Fontana but no-one involved could have predicted what would happen next... Kiki Dee signed a contract with Tamla Motown in the summer of 1967. *The* Tamla Motown? Affirmative! She became the first white UK artist to sign for the famous label – surely full-blown success was imminent now for the Bradford chanteuse?...

Two other notable Yorkshire musicians had spent almost the whole of the decade beavering away, learning their craft, and patiently waiting for that ever-elusive big break. A name to drop in his home city of Leeds, Jeff Christie had, not unlike Kiki Dee, been seemingly on the verge of tasting true success for years. Jeff was the prodigious talent behind The Outer Limits, a Leeds-based band who sound like they should have been at the vanguard of the new trip-to-be-hip psychedelic movement, but were actually far straighter than that in a melodic three-minute-pop-song kind of way.

Like everyone other sixties contender, Jeff had served a music business apprenticeship from an early age, gigging with his bands from the outrageous age of 13. "I actually wanted to be a flamenco guitarist when I was a kid. My mother had been a classical ballet dancer – she instilled into me all the classics. But I was a bit like any kid wanting to rebel against their parents. I went to see a Flamenco performance in Leeds around 1956, and the whole thing blew me away, but the guitar-playing in particular. I was learning classical piano up to that point, but after that I wanted to learn flamenco guitar. But rock 'n' roll quickly replaced that.

"I was lucky from an early age that I knew that I wanted to be a professional musician – I wasn't bothered about being famous. I saw the jazz and be-bop musicians playing, and Lonnie Donegan and the skiffle thing was very influential - it just looked like a great thing to do for a living. It was just a matter of deciding what kind of music I wanted to play."

So began a career in pop music. Each band of Jeff's evolved into the next with personnel changing gradually along the way rather than wholesale, until The Outer Limits came into being around 1965 and within two years became Yorkshire's band most likely to succeed. But until that point, Jeff Christie's songwriting output had been next to nothing.

"You've got to remember that young kids like me thought that writing songs was a highly specialised skill until the Beatles came along. I saw them

58

performing 'Love Me Do' on ITV's *Scene at 6.30* but I didn't get it straight away. Once I did, I realised we had to change – we had to write our own material to get a record deal, that was the way forward. The whole music scene changed drastically in the mid-sixties, it wasn't just the Beatles, it was Motown and the R 'n' B bands coming through. We'd failed one record audition because we didn't do our own stuff, only covers. I didn't even know if I could write songs at that point."

The Outer Limits' early claim to fame was that they were the British band chosen to promote the launch of the *Batman* TV series in the UK. After they got through the audition, the next step was to have the band dress as 'The Caped Crusaders' and play as a band. Due to some last minute disagreement, it never happened – that may have either denied Jeff and the band an early taste of success, saved them from an early grave, or both.

"There's a great saying – don't pray for the break, pray that when the break comes, you're ready for it. Apart from learning your craft, it's about knowing how to handle the success and fame when it comes along." It's a music business moral that Jeff Christie did well to heed, given later circumstances.

But the initial break didn't come easy, though The Outer Limits had encountered few problems building up a live following – there was a relatively vibrant local scene going on around the Leeds area. "There were so many places to play in those days. We were the top group in Leeds at the time with The Dawnbreakers, who I suppose were our big rivals. They took my bass player and they got a record deal first, but they folded when it didn't happen for them. I carried on sending demos down to our agent Drew Harvey in London until finally he heard the song and said, 'that's the single.'"

'Just One More Chance' was released as the Outer Limits' debut seven-inch on Decca's Deram label. It created 'a buzz', putting them on the nation's radio airwaves but not on the charts.

"It was officially 'bubbling under' the charts in those days, getting lots of radio airplay not least on the hip and trendy *Radio Caroline*, and *Radio London*.

It really looked like it was going to be our breakthrough. It made a dent but didn't quite achieve what I hoped it would achieve. But the funny thing is, it got us on the Jimi Hendrix tour, an amazing achievement. It was like touring with royalty – apart from Hendrix there was Pink Floyd, Amen Corner, The Nice, The Move – if anyone on the tour hadn't already made it, they'd find success after."

It was the last package tour of its kind in the 60s and from all accounts like going on a school trip on acid. It confirmed Jimi Hendrix as one of the stars of that era. But it was also the tour when the legendary Syd Barrett finally lost it – he left Pink Floyd shortly after. There are tales of sex, drugs and knife throwing aplenty but from the Outer Limits point of view, it surely put them on the brink of making it.

All looked good as the follow-up single, 'Great Train Robbery', had everything going for it – it was catchier than its predecessor, it was produced and released on the label owned and run by the Rolling Stones manager, Andrew Loog Oldham, and the band's profile had already been hoisted high courtesy of the Hendrix tour. The only thing it didn't have going for it was a title without any degree of dodginess; with great predictability, the BBC was at the time very sensitive about anything even slightly controversial or contentious, so 'Great Train Robbery', coming just a few years after the actual misdemeanour involving Ronnie Biggs, Buster Edwards and Co, wasn't an automatic addition to the *Radio One* Playlist.

"I've since been told that BBC wouldn't play that because it was too 'political'. It was a fictitious lyric about a train being held up in America – you can get a song out of anything if you try! It was supposed to go out on Andrew Oldham's Immediate label, which carried a great deal of kudos. For some reason – still don't know why – he created a label called Instant and put it out on that instead."

When the single sank without trace, Outer Limits' chances went with it. A cynic might view it as snatching defeat from the jaws of victory; whichever way you want to put it, the writing was on the wall for Jeff and his boys. "The group had had enough and I just couldn't keep it together. We were all fed up about the money situation – well, the lack of it. It's like being married to three or four people and you can only be democratic to a point. There was always some jealousy and resentment even without money problems. It's just human nature."

Outer Limits' big chance had come and quickly gone, and perhaps songwriter Christie knew it. In a bizarre piece of P.R., Jeff Christie agreed to a Yorkshire TV film crew following the band as they headed toward the inevitable decision to call it a day. *The Death of a Pop Group*, a mini-documentary, ironically gave the band the kind of coverage that they had craved and had indeed needed to make a success of things. But this really was as 'Ronseal' a moment in Yorkshire Pop History as you can imagine, doing what it said on the tin, witnessing a band going through their swansong and biting the bitter dust of failure.

"I can't remember whose actual idea it was. We'd been on *Calendar* (Yorkshire TV's regional news programme) and played the YTV Christmas party in the past. Whoever it was, they just realised they had a ready-made TV programme in front of them. It was a reflection of the frustration we felt – having had two great records and been on this major tour with Hendrix and all those other bands, we felt let down. The general feeling around us was, this is a great band, why haven't they made it when others are?"

Crippling debts and the ever-increasing cost of recording and touring provided the basic bottom-line answer but other contributory factors, voiced by the members of the band, included a regrettable lack of support from record company, radio stations and music-loving public alike. It's not insignificant that Jeff Christie was the most prepared to put the bitterness behind him. "At the end of the documentary, the reporter asked what each member was going to do now and I just said I was going to keep going, trying to break through. I wasn't sure how. It had been my life that band, mutating out of different bands since I was 13. I was tired of all the stuff that goes on when you're in a band. I was the engine of the band, making people turn up for rehearsals and do

61

things right – that's probably why I carried on driving things through and got success in the end, because I had tunnel vision. I was not going to give up."

It's easy to say that this could be any band anywhere at the time but you do get the feeling that Christie and his band mates fully expected to make it, if not big, then moderately large. The fact that they were Leeds' Great White Hopes for much of the second half of the sixties makes their fate all the more significant for Tykes in general, and this book in particular.

Jeff Christie however was not to be thwarted; though he knew Outer Limits' number was up, he was adamant that his wasn't. He would carry on writing songs, if not for his own pop vehicle then for other artists. His determination would eventually be rewarded.

Meanwhile, around the same time in 1969, over in Humberside… Mick Ronson had returned home after his latest stint down in London that had once more left the guitarist totally potless, wholeheartedly disillusioned with the music business and seemingly destined to remain a legend only in his own town of Hull.

A talented musician with great ability on the piano and cello as well as guitar, Ronson's musical career had started in earnest in The Mariners around 1963, quickly followed by a spell in The Crestas fronted by the splendidly named Johnny Hawk. (These 'Crestas' are not to be confused with the aforementioned 'Cresters' who hailed from Leeds around the same time – a bit like 'The Beatulls' who should not be confused with… well, you get the picture). While he played out the dream on Hull's stages at night, 'Ronno' was employed by the council's Parks Department by day. When The Crestas fell apart, he decided to take the deep plunge and take his guitar and amp down to the capital. He was about to turn professional with his next band The Voice before divine intervention (well almost) changed his plans. The other members of the band were members of a religious cult, and decided to buy a small island in the Bahamas and take their religion with them, as you do.

62

Deep in debt, Ronson returned to Hull to start again – this time taking up with established local band, The Rats, helping them to build up a good live reputation both on home soil and abroad. Though the band themselves never quite fell into the category of serious contenders, Mick Ronson became known as a player of some quality, getting invited to play on the occasional session for other artists also skirting around the periphery of making it. It was one such excursion down to London that changed the course of his career.

Invited to play on tracks for another Yorkshire artist called Michael Chapman – born in Hunslet, very folky, very singer-songwriter, not very 'pop star' - Mick Ronson first came onto the radar of one Tony Visconti, a respected musician himself, soon to be an even more respected record producer. Mick did his thing and returned to Hull, The Rats, and his day job with the Parks Department.

It was around this time, in summer/autumn 1969, that Tadcaster's favourite grandson – remember him? - was getting his first taste of chart success with a record that was almost the perfect overture for his stellar career in the first half of the next decade. You can safely say that 'Space Oddity' marked David Bowie out as one to watch.

Mick Ronson was apparently marking out a rugby pitch when John Cambridge, The Rats' old drummer delivered the news that he was being recruited for this bloke David Bowie's new backing band, and Mick himself, having been remembered by Bowie's bass player Tony Visconti, was required down in 'The Smoke' to audition as guitarist for said band.

Having had a bellyful of London, Ronson needed some serious persuasion. You can imagine his dilemma, can't you? He could stick around and probably be in charge of re-seeding the bowling greens up in Hull. Or... he could give this fella – what was his name again? - Derek Booley a chance and go play some rock 'n' roll down in the biggest, baddest, most-happening city in the country.

Who knew? With the wind blowing in the right direction, the 1970s could just be a brave new world for everyone...

63

Chapter Four

It's Glam Up North.

The sixties went swinging into the seventies and never swung back, and what do you know, conscription, rationing and prohibition all returned in one cruel package. You'd think that was the case, the way some people talk about the 1970s in relation to the hallowed decade that preceded it. Granted, it must be dispiriting to think you've already had it as good as you're ever gonna have it, and it's all downhill from thereon in. I was a mere child at the time but from what I have since gleaned, the 60s must have been a hard act to follow. From the aspect of music, so much happened in those oft-celebrated ten years, too much even. But in its very own way, the 1970s – the time that taste forgot, yes, yes - had more surprises up its sleeve than the sixties.

From our point of view, Yorkshire had ended the 1960s distinctly on the up. After a couple of sensaaaational Number Ones by 'local' solo artists, all we were wondering now – well, not me personally as I was too busy playing with my soldiers, but someone must've been wondering – was when were we going to have a full group of 'long-haired Jessies' (thanks Mam) from around our way making a meaningful impact on the crazy world of pop music?

It was a good question because it's at this point in pop music history that the opportunity really did offer itself with bells on. In amongst the landmark events of 1970 was one significant development that ended one era and opened up another rich with possibilities.

While the world watched the Vietnam War drag on with no end in sight after 11 years, and the UK saw a new Tory government ushered in - this in the age when the two major parties seemed to take turns every four years - the music world acknowledged the official end of the three-year-long Summer of Love as it mourned the death of Jimi Hendrix, the Che Guevara of the electric guitar, a true icon of sixties.

Less gloomily, The Who released 'Live at Leeds', possibly the best live album ever, and yes, it was that same Leeds, the one in Yorkshire, the classic gig being recorded in the city's University refectory. Black Sabbath released their debut album, perhaps the first heavy metal album - though not every one would agree that this was an event worthy of celebration. And the very first Glastonbury festival took place with T. Rex headlining with 1,500 hippies turning up and laying down the foundations of an institution that no-one could possibly have predicted would prosper to this day - no one told them that The Summer of Love was over.

But the real headline news, and perhaps a demise more mourned than the death of Hendrix, was the disbanding of The Beatles, who had dominated the music scene since 1962, continually raising the bar in the process. With the 'Fab Four' out of the way, perhaps the bar would be lowered somewhat, but more positively, there would be the opportunity for other artists hitherto denied. There was certainly a vacancy or two in pop's echelon. Couldn't Yorkshire at least play a part in the next exciting chapter of pop?

Following his acceptance to take his 'axe' (his guitar, mate, his guitar) down to London for an audition, Hull's Mick Ronson got the gig with David Bowie, and was eventually joined by fellow Yorkshiremen Trevor Bolder and Woody Woodmansey in the band, named at this point, The Hype. The Tyke trio's first contribution appeared on 'The Man Who Sold the World', a less acoustic, more rock orientated effort that proved to be the platform for Bowie's most successful period, creatively and critically. Ronson's guitar sound – owing much to Jeff Beck apparently - became much imitated itself.

The band secured a recording deal of their own, independent of Bowie, but their only true taste of success came with Tadcaster's favourite grandson, playing on subsequent classic albums, 'Hunky Dory', 'The Rise and Fall of Ziggy Stardust' and the 'Spiders from Mars', and 'Aladdin Sane'. Supremely talented as he was in the general musical sense, Ronson was also the man behind the lush string arrangements on Bowie's albums, and, sticking another feather in his occasional fedora, he also co-produced Lou Reed's seminal 'Transformer' album, even playing piano on the wonderful 'Perfect Day'.

It's tempting to say that, if anyone made Bowie look perhaps better than he was - apart from the opposition - it was Mick Ronson. But surprisingly, your man decided against using his Humberside sidekick after 1973's 'Pin Ups', and so Ronson naturally took a crack at a solo career, with some success too. 1975's 'Slaughter on Tenth Avenue' went Top Ten in the album charts - it featured a wonderful version of Elvis's 'Love Me Tender' – and the follow-up, 'Play Don't Worry' also charted, complete with the best song that Bowie never sang, 'Billy Porter'. By now, Ronson had taken up with Ian Hunter, as lead guitarist in the last days of Mott the Hoople, then adding his musical might to Hunter's solo work, not least on the hit single, 'Once Bitten Twice Shy'. Though his own time as a solo star came and went – he'd realised it wasn't really for him - Ronson remained wildly in demand, both as a player, and as a producer for many subsequent upstarts (Rich Kids, Morrissey, Wildhearts), up to his death in 1993. However, he'll always be best remembered as Bowie's 'musical rock' in his glam years. And he was better looking than 'Ziggy' too – no make-up required.

We really should stop talking about you-know-who – message to self, he wasn't from Yorkshire, live with it. And besides, in 1970, Bowie – doh! - and his band were still waiting in the wings. So where were the bands from Yorkshire capable of stepping into the Beatles' shoes/boots/sandals, and setting the music world alight, well for a month or two at least?

Step forward our old friend, Jeff Christie, and his band, er, Christie. We'd last heard of Jeff setting out as a songwriter-for-hire after his once highly-fancied band Outer Limits bowed to the financial inevitable and called it a day in front of the TV cameras in 1969.

"I decided I was just going to keep writing. By that time I knew a lot of the big names – I'd worked with them. And in those days you could still get to them without too much trouble. There was no point taking songs to bands who wrote their own material but there were still plenty who didn't. Even the fact that Batley Variety Club was just down the road was good – there was no problem getting backstage to talk to artists like Gene Pitney or Roy Orbison.

"I was writing during the day and playing a cabaret club in town at night, trying out my new songs. I was really quite driven. I sometimes wrote with specific people in mind; I wrote a song for the Tremeloes called 'Tomorrow Night' which I thought was very 'them'. They said it was exactly what they were trying to get away from. And so I played my tape of other songs and they started to look at their watches. The tape came to 'Yellow River' – it was part of the swamp country rock stuff I'd been experimenting with. The Tremeloes listened, started harmonising and that was it. They wanted the song.

"They recorded the backing track but then, for whatever reason, they decided to pass in the end. They obviously regretted that decision because it could have extended their chart career by years. But by the time they passed, their publicist Brian Longley had heard my demo and decided this was a hit record… what was wrong with me singing it myself? The Tremeloes had just followed my original basic arrangement of the song, and I could sing it fine."

You know you've written a potential chart-topper when one of the top managers in the business offers you money to delay your release so one of his clients can put their version out first; such was the case when Tom Jones's manager Gordon Mills wanted his man Leapy Lee to get a head start with his 'Yellow River'. In subsequent years, the song has been covered many times, most notably by R.E.M. and Elton John. But back in 1970, Jeff Christie had a more pressing matter to attend to. "I'd written this song that was going to be a hit and I didn't have a band. Brian introduced me to two guys, Mike Blakely, brother of Alan from the Tremeloes, and Vic Elmes – we went on the road with that line-up for a while."

But what should have been a golden era in Christie's career was soured by the bad blood between Jeff and the Tremeloes camp, the inevitable resentment this brought into the Christie set-up with its Tremeloes connections, and last but not least, the fact that Jeff didn't reap the rewards you'd expect from penning such a successful song. "It went Number One all over the world but let's put it this way, a lot of other people got rich. I really don't know where the money went. I didn't even know about *Yellow Pages* using 'Yellow River' for their ad campaign until it was already running. They didn't even need permission from me, and it ran for a long time."

'Yellow River' hit the top spot in 26 countries and got to number six in the States. You'd think that Jeff would have made more than the 'few quid' he says he made. Amazingly, he's not bitter about the experience. "I'd achieved my dream, to have my music played all over the world on radio, TV, etc, as well as performing my songs on a global platform. My original dream as a kid was to be a professional musician and that's what I'm still doing. I'm thankful for that - it's heart warming when thousands of people around the world still tell me how happy my music has made them, and continues to do so through internet sites such as *YouTube*. That means a lot to me."

Nice man, nasty business.

In the same summer of 1970 that Jeff enjoyed his finest pop moment, a rock classic peaked at Number Two in the UK singles chart, and subsequently topped the charts of 20 other countries. The success of 'All Right Now' transformed Free from promising young blues band into big-time rock band. The voice of Free – and he was actually nicknamed 'The Voice' by the music press – was one Paul Rodgers from the parish of Middlesbrough. This fact digs up a bone of contention – is Middlesbrough in Yorkshire or not? Stick with me here. I, personally, had always viewed the big old gas yard as being part of the region generally referred to as 'the North-East', not Yorkshire. And most 'Smoggies' I have met go to great pains to deny even a connection to the county. Yet Yorkshire was officially part of their postal address right up until the early seventies, and it remains the town's ceremonial county, specifically North Yorkshire. It's clearly a generational issue, as 'Boro' folk under a certain age would much rather count themselves as Teessiders, Welsh, Satan's offspring or anything other than Yorkshiremen.

Clearly then, it is my sworn duty to put two fingers up to those detractors, nay defectors, and claim Paul Rodgers as one of our own.

By the time 'All Right Now' had catapulted Free to international acclaim, Rodgers was already a relative veteran of the blues-rock scene, having played with several local bands from his mid-teens before moving down to London and forming Free with Kossoff, Kirke and Fraser in 1968. As is often sadly the way, with big success came big problems; Rodgers and Andy Fraser's working relationship deteriorated whilst Paul Kossoff struggled with the drug addiction that would eventually claim his life in 1975.

By that time, Free were no more. Though they'd followed up their breakthrough 1970 album 'Fire and Water', with three more well-received albums, and three more chart singles, the band fell to pieces in 1973. Which was more than a pity since they were, by then, being referred to in the same respectful rocking breath as Led Zeppelin.

Rodgers wasted little time getting his next venture off the ground. Together with Free drummer Simon Kirke, King Crimson bassist Boz Burrell, and Mott the Hoople guitarist Mick Ralphs, he formed Bad Company. Since the new band were immediately brought under the wing of infamous Led Zep manager Peter Grant, it's little surprise that they achieved the kind of massive trans-Atlantic success that Grant's main charges had been enjoying for some years. Best selling albums on both sides of 'the pond', were accompanied by occasional sorties into the singles charts, most memorably with debut seven-incher 'Can't Get Enough', and the mucho-macho 'Feel Like Makin' Love'... yeah, baby!

Truth is, Bad Company became the archetypal American stadium rock monsters and did most of their business Stateside as the years went on. Rodgers it was who instigated an unscheduled sabbatical in the early 1980s, before there were any serious casualties of the inevitable excesses. But by the time the rest of the band were ready to resume rockin' duties, 'Rodgo' had taken up with little-known guitarist Jimmy Page and formed The Firm; the 'supergroup' venture surprisingly flopped in relative terms. Not that our man was put off from undertaking another similar collaboration – next time the musical partner being ex-Faces and Who drummer Kenney Jones. The Law – as they called themselves – fared no better that The Firm, so 'The Voice' returned to the bosom of the Bad Company family.

And so it was until some bright spark – one with shoulder length tight-curled hair called Brian, perhaps? – came up with the idea with the idea of putting the Freddie Mercury-less Queen on tour with a new vocalist. Guess who got the gig? If I was really mean-spirited I could offer the opinion that Paul Rodgers undid all the good work he'd done in days of old by getting involved in what appeared to be a blatant flog-a-dead-horse exercise. But I'm bigger than that.

As of summer 2009, the Rodgers/Queen arrangement is no more; the singer was last heard of touring the States with a reformed Bad Company. Could be worse. One of the great British singers of blues and rock, at least The Voice of Middlesbrough hasn't sold out completely, releasing a covers album of

Gershwin and Porter songs or something similar. There's still time, mind.

Back down at the other end of the county, in the indisputably Yorkshire city of Sheffield, another Christie was making his big move in 1970. Tony Christie was no relation to Jeff – born Anthony Fitzgerald, he's decided on Christie as a new stage name on seeing a 1960s movie starring the screen darling of the time, Julie Christie. After paying his dues in bands and duos throughout that decade, Christie the solo act became an established star in the variety clubs of the region. He signed a deal in 1969 and that's when the harder work of making Tony Christie a recording star started. MCA brought in the recognised formula songwriters of the day – Mitch Mitchell and Peter Callander - and the first fruits of success came in early 1971 with Las Vegas, as 'cabaret' a song as you're likely to hear, a cheesier-than-stilton paean to the place but chart-worthy nonetheless. Much better, in a low-fat cheese kind of way, came further chart hits 'Maria', and 'Is This the Way' to 'Amarillo', the former of which actually placed higher in the charts at number two. Three hits in a year established Christie as a voice to be reckoned with, but it was a couple of more years before he had, to these ears at least, his finest moment with the theme tune to TV show *The Protectors*. 'Avenues and Alleyways' is quintessential Tony Christie for me, and should have surely led to our man having a pop at a *James Bond* theme tune, alas not to be.

Many unkind critics dismissed Christie as the poor man's Tom Jones - I know that from having a bar-room brawl with Mick Hucknall. Okay, when I say bar-room brawl, I actually mean having a chat over a pint and a game of pool in the pub just around the corner from where the band I was playing in were rehearsing at the time (The Danny Boys – should've been big). Displaying what we thought was impeccable taste, the band's drummer, Vinny, and myself elected to put 'Avenues and Alleyways' on the pub's jukebox and that Hucknall fella – obviously not yet gallivanting around Monte Carlo chasing Catherine Zeta Jones - dismissed your man as, you guessed it, the 'poor man's

Tom Jones'. We weren't having that. We argued our man's corner admirably and if I remember correctly, scored an honourable draw in the debate. I'm sure I won the ensuing game of pool, and Vinny nicked and necked Hucknall's pint. God knows what happened to the ginger ragamuffin. Though I do recall him duetting with Tom Jones.

As for Tony Christie, he hasn't stopped working since his early seventies heyday. Though his recording success has continued abroad, notably in Germany, some periods have seen a perhaps reluctant return to variety club land. But like his fellow Sheffield-er before him, Dave Berry, Christie has had some welcome boosts in his later career, the first of which was the endorsement of one Jarvis Cocker in the late 1990s when the Pulp singer wrote a song especially for the old warbler – 'Walk Like A Panther' – which actually made the Top Ten of the charts under the name, Tony Christie featuring The All Seeing I, a quirksome electronica trio of local repute.

Better still, Christie's old favourite 'Amarillo' was resurrected for Comic Relief in 2002 by comedian Peter Kay and an extended stint at Number One naturally paved the way for a new Greatest Hits compilation. More recently, latter-day Steel City crooner Richard Hawley has tried to do for Christie what Rick Rubin did for Johnny Cash and Neil Diamond, recording a well-considered set of covers with the singer and giving the tracks a contemporary production treatment. The added significance of this development lay in the collection's title, 'Made In Sheffield', where each song was a ditty written and previously recorded by that city's pop luminaries, from the Human League's 'Louise', to the Arctic Monkeys 'Only Ones Who Know', through to 'Coles Corner', written by Hawley himself.

One singer who you'd never look at and say 'Yorkshire Pop Star' was Robert Palmer, he of 'Addicted to Love' fame with its famous Bouncing Bosoms video (though some unkind people were of the view that the singer himself was the biggest tit on show in that video). But a Tyke, through and through, he indeed was, having been born in Batley, the land of variety, lest we forget, with much of his childhood spent in good old Scarborough. Palmer cut his performing teeth in the late 60s, very nearly playing in the same band as Mick Ronson at one point. But he really came to the fore early the next decade as one of the lead vocalists with post-hippy rhythm and blues combo Vinegar Joe, his fellow vocalist being none other than Elkie Brooks, one Northern bird with one ballsy voice. But alas from Lancashire. Let's be honest here, Palmer in the context of being a co-singer in a relatively obscure combo means next to naff-all in our ongoing quest. His time would come later in the decade as a solo artist, and would be of even more significance to us when *MTV* took over in the next decade, ushering in the age of the video, replete with Bouncing Bosoms.

But try to forget Bouncing Bosoms for now. Did someone say Northern bird with ballsy voice? What about one coming from the right side of the Pennines? At last, finally and indeed, of course, it was never in doubt, Kiki Dee became a star. She was last seen slumming it at Tamla Motown, where she recorded just the one album before a disappointing parting of the ways.

Someone who deserves at least some of the thanks for giving our Bradford lass a significant leg-up after ten years of toil, is none other than Elton John. The Rocket Record label was one of the many worthwhile creative ventures that 'Reg' involved himself in before he started the rather tiresome evolution into Liberace, and Rocket finally gave Kiki the T.L.C. she'd craved since first getting signed aged 16 by Fontana; the label released her first successful singles, 'Amoureuse' and 'I've Got the Music in Me', and then the chart-topping duet with Elton himself on 'Don't Go Breaking My Heart'. Amazingly, the record was not only Kiki's first (and last) Number One, it Elton John's first UK chart-topper too. What seemed, to many folk, to have been an overnight success for Ms Dee, was in fact anything but for West Yorkshire's own Pauline Matthews.

Like most young fellas of 11 or 12 in those times, the world and its wonders came to me through the telly. For every TV moment of magical epiphany, such as Bowie singing 'Starman', there were a thousand more of utter mundanity. But I watched all the same – you didn't want to miss anything, did you? My theory was that ITV aired *Opportunity Knocks* on a Monday night because there was never anything worthwhile to watch on a Monday outside of *Coronation Street*. Hughie Green's talent show was an early example of 'car crash TV', so of course I watched it. Most of the acts were crap, fact. Peters and Lee were crap as far as I was concerned but respect was due as the hubby and wife duo won the viewers' vote for a record seven weeks in a row. Lenny Peters was from 'Darn Larndun' but Diane Lee was a Sheffield girl; the duo's first single 'Welcome Home' duly went to Number One in 1973, and the buggers were never off the box for the next few years.

Another goggle-box regular in these innocent times was singer and poet, Jake Thackray. He appeared on TV shows such as *That's Life*, telling stories of Yorkshire life through music in a fashion that no-one of my tender years had heard before. In retrospect, the Leeds-born minstrel could have stepped out of one of Chaucer's works, with his bawdy tales sang in nervy baritone. Even if I couldn't understand the cut of his wit at such a young age, I looked on in fascination, as it seems did the likes of Jarvis Cocker and Morrissey. He really should have been a pop star.

My other obsession was football, and still is, so I demand that attention is drawn to a certain Top Ten of April 1972. As became the norm for football clubs reaching the FA Cup Final, the Mighty Leeds United team became recording artists and reached the heady heights of the Hit Parade with a double A-side; that success owed much to the songwriting and arrangement talents of Les Reed, a Whites fan with true musical pedigree, having co-written numerous chart hits, including the peerless 'Delilah' for Tom Jones. On the occasions that Leeds have played Stoke City in recent years, you can hear Stoke fans singing their adopted theme-tune, 'Delilah' at one end of the ground, while the United fans launch into the anthemic 'Leeds Leeds Leeds' at the other – how many songwriters can lay claim to being responsible for such a carry-on?

Honourable mention here too for Sheffield's Paul Carrick who in the early 1970s was setting out on a long-term career that has beeped loudly on the radar on many occasions, but no louder than in 1975 when his band Ace took their place in the One-Hit-Wonder pile with their sublime debut single, 'How Long?'. Carrick's dulcet tones not only graced our charts but also the top reaches of the US Billboard chart. His subsequent career as a solo artist and a guest vocalist with the likes of Squeeze and Mike and the Mechanics has established a soulful voice more recognisable than his face – a compliment to Paul Carrick's talent I'd say.

So all was looking rosy in our rhubarb patch. We were really getting somewhere with some of our long-suffering wannabes becoming back-slapped somebodies. That possibly sounds less than substantial and more than a little superficial but in an industry capable of being frighteningly fake, fickle and other words beginning with F, it was an achievement to be proud of for the individuals concerned. But it was rather perverse too. The likes of Tony Christie and Kiki Dee were finding fame at a time when a new variety of pop star was taking over the charts, airwaves, and pin-up magazines. And we're not talking about bland American entities like The Osmonds and David Cassidy here.

Though they'd both made sizable dents in the charts previously, Marc Bolan and that other bloke beginning with B, each started carving a deep niche in the modern music stage circa 1971. With foil, sequins, and mucho glitter in evidence, some bright spark coined the phrase 'Glam Rock' and a bandwagon was created, perfect for jumping on. Slade were doing fine without it but since it was there, why not? Sweet, Mud and Suzi Quatro were understandably packaged to cash in on the times, bubble gum pop dressed in satin, drapes, leather and make-up. Glam rock was as trashy as bubble gum much of the time, but much more fun than a Spacehopper – who could stay on those things for longer than three bounces? Me and my mate Pete Walker even wrote our own glam rocking tune a la 'Blockbuster', in his Dad's shed, with upturned bucket for a drum and a one-stringed guitar. Our opus 'Maniac', boasted a chorus of 'Maniac… yes he's back. Maniac, maniac'. If only we'd had another guitar string.

Glam rock was escapism almost on a pantomime level – with the nation entrenched in times of economic unrest, strikes and power cuts aplenty, the sparkling pomp of glam was a welcome distraction. But apart from the cheap tack, there were also Roxy Music, and later Cockney Rebel who joined Bowie and Bolan in the more credible ranks of the glam circus, with a more subversive element running through their act, not to mention a retro-modern nod towards literature and cinema in their armoury.

Surely it was time for a White Rose representative to join the shiny, sparkly parade? If a set of ex-skinheads from Wolverhampton like Slade could ride the wave, one of our own could do the same – we wouldn't have minded whether they were lining up to join those credible ranks of the scene or they were 100% trash.

Registering high on the close-but-no-cigar scale were Sharks, a band featuring sometime Sheffield resident Chris Spedding on guitar and Hull-born warbler Steve Parsons, aka 'Snips', on vocal duties. Spedding was and still is a highly respected 'axe-for-hire', and artiste in his own right – 'Motorbiking' was his one big hit in 1975. He was so nearly a Rolling Stone, was almost definitely a Womble, donning full furry suit on *Top of the Pops*, and player/producer on more high-profile recording sessions than space allows here, some more significant than others. But this really was Spedding's band, his own shot at stardom, and Island Records' Great White Hopes of 1973, heavily championed not least for Snips's idiosyncratic delivery, and equally quirky song lyrics. But it wasn't to be, despite having more than one bite at the cherry. An acclaimed tour support with Roxy Music at their glam-tastic height, and a flight-case full of kindly reviews were all that this band really had to show for all their promise.

Bugger. All we bloody wanted was a moderately successful local band setting out on a career lasting long enough to lay claims to a back catalogue of records, preferably deemed collectors items rather than bargain-bin fixtures.

Cut to 1975, Normanton Grammar School… yours truly has a new 'rough book' to decorate/deface in the celebrated Rock-obsessed schoolboy manner, with the names of bands or artists scribbled thereon in felt-tip pen. My mates, classmates and fellow rock fans go for the predictable 'Led Zep', 'Black Sabs', 'Purple' and even, oh no, 'Yes'. More specific in tribute, they go for the guitar heroes of the day, Gods of the Axe, if you like… Clapton, Page, Blackmore and Iommi. Not me. No siree. It's either Ian Sharp, Jez Slack or Chris Mitchell who look over at my very own Rough Book masterpiece… "Bill Nelson? Who the Fuck is Bill Nelson?!?"

I'd found my first local hero. I can't remember exactly when and how I found out that Be Bop Deluxe were from just down the road in Wakefield, but as soon as I did, I needed to know everything I could about them. Top of the list was the fact they were led by singer-songwriter, and more importantly, shit-hot guitarist, Bill Nelson.

Of course, I knew then that I would sit down in a York city centre pub over thirty years later with that same Bill Nelson and discuss just how he came to be my first real musical hero. And it quickly becomes clear that Bill's is a familiar story – he became a 'pop star' more by accident than design. "I never wanted to be a professional musician or went looking for it."

Bill Nelson's Dad, Walter, was a jazz musician, playing in the many dance halls of Wakefield, so there was always plenty of music in the Nelson household even before Bill heard Duane Eddy and decided he wanted to be a guitarist. "I started playing with bands around 1963, bands influenced by the Shadows more than anyone else. One of the bands was called The Teenagers - I was the only actual teenager in the band and the leader was over thirty."

But painting was the young Nelson's other great love and he attended Wakefield Art College fully intending to pursue a career of an artist. Then chance took him down the road to music at the end of the sixties. "I just walked past an old building in Wakefield where the kind of West Coast music I'd been listening to was blasting out of a first floor window. I went to investigate and found out it was a recording studio – Holyground studios. Next thing, I'm recording my own set of songs."

The result was 'Northern Dream', a long-player which featured a photo of Bill in full Hippy uniform and headset, strumming an acoustic guitar sat on a set of terrace steps. I was less than excited by the cover when I secured my rare copy many years later but the significance of the content shouldn't be underestimated. "John Peel got a copy and sent me a letter saying he'd be playing it on his show on a certain date – I thought he meant one track but he actually played the whole LP! Next thing, I'm getting all these labels wanting to sign me up. EMI wanted me alone as a singer-songwriter but I'd just got Be Bop together. They were old friends and people who I'd played around Wakefield with."

And of course, by the time Be Bop Deluxe hit the road, 'Glam Rock' was stomping its platform boots to the max. But I'm pleased to report that Be Bop was certainly no flash in the glam pan. Actually despite first impressions, they weren't glam at all. "We'd started doing the glam thing with make-up before we signed to EMI, but there was more than an element of having a laugh about it – we even stopped off at a chip shop on the way back from Hull, and deliberately kept all the gear on just to see how the locals reacted. But we weren't really glam. The label persuaded us to keep that image for the first album even though it wasn't really us; even the back of the album photo was us caked in make-up glam-style, and one of the band had been ordered to keep out of the way at the back because they thought he looked more like a bus-driver than a pop star."

But if the record company didn't want to change the look, they made it clear they wanted Bill to at least think about changing his band personnel. "I stayed loyal to the guys who started Be Bop with me and we toured, most significantly, with Steve Harley and Cockney Rebel who were big at the time. Just seeing how professional they were made me think that EMI had a point." Come the second album, Bill took the tough executive decision, dropped his original band-mates and took on the musicians - Charlie Tumahai, Simon Fox and Andy Clark - who were to become the steady Be Bop line-up.

The band's early experiences with the record producers hired by the label left a lasting impression on the young Bill Nelson. The producer of debut album, 'Axe Victim' was "possibly an acid casualty was having bad trips all the way through the sessions when he wasn't falling asleep". For the second album – 'Futurama' - EMI brought in Queen's producer Roy Thomas Baker; "he built this makeshift throne and got the tapes rolling with a theatrical cry of 'rolly-wolly, takey-wakey'…"

Despite the idiosyncrasies of producer 'Bakey-Wakey', Futurama featured the track, indeed single, that quickly became the band's signature tune. 'Maid in Heaven' sounded like the perfect slice of melodic rock back then, instantly catchy, with more guitar riff-age than seems possible in two minutes twenty seconds. And it still sounds startlingly good even today. It was an early high point for Bill and the band – "I sat back and couldn't think of anything I'd add or take away. It was spot on – a perfect bit of rock, if you like."

The engineer on that album was 'spot on' too. John Leckie is possibly best known for his later work on albums by the Stone Roses and Radiohead. But his first producing job was for Be Bop Deluxe, co producing 'Sunburst Finish' with Bill Nelson. It was a track from that third album that gave Bill his first long-awaited success in the singles chart. Though he reveals a lack of affection for 'Ships in the Night' these days, the memory of its unexpected success is a good one. "We never expected to be doing Top of the Pops and getting introduced by Jimmy Savile! It felt like a triumph."

By 1976, Be Bop, rightly or wrongly, were seen as part of the progressive rock scene – due to Bill's regularly featured guitar virtuosity - lurking at best on the pop periphery. So scoring a hit single really was a novelty – we were more used to hearing Be Bop on Alan Freeman's Saturday afternoon show.

"We were always more about albums than singles – after the glam rock label we were called 'Prog Rock', 'Heavy Rock', even 'Heavy Metal'. But I thought 'Art Rock' was about the best label. There was always a pop art thing with us. I used to say that I wanted to make pop music that's the equivalent of Andy Warhol's soup cans – y'know, it looks like a soup can, but you can't get any soup out of it. We had more in common with Bowie and Roxy than the other rock acts of the time. It was about taking facets of popular culture and transposing them into a different context."

Did someone say 'Prog Rock'? Progressive is something it usually wasn't – it tended to go forward at a rather slow rate thanks to ten-minute guitar solos, meandering aimlessly in the musical ether. Much of this overblown self-indulgence had its roots in free-form jazz, where players improvised until they dropped. One respected guitarist with his musical roots in jazz and his geographical roots in Yorkshire, was, and still is Doncaster's John McLaughlin. A supremely talented musician, McLaughlin has played with Miles Davis, 'sessioned' for the Stones, and has collaborated with some of the world's finest musicians, jazz or otherwise in a career knocking on 50 years. But my own personal experience of him is his Mahavishnu Orchestra, playing tracks that could, and possibly did go on for hours. I'm probably not worthy of passing opinion on a talent as respected as Macca's; however for the purposes of this book, I will anyway. He's perhaps the most revered musician to get a mention in these pages but he really wasn't, and isn't a pop star. I'm sure he'd concede that.

On the subject of opinions, esteemed DJ and broadcaster Mark Radcliffe rightly referred to Bill Nelson as the first 'non-macho guitar hero', and the tag says much about the pleasingly unaffected Yorkshireman. Even as a fan, I always viewed him as something of a reluctant pop star. "I didn't really have a strategy… if I did it was one that changed inside my head quite regularly. I got into this because of the music and I felt that always had to be the bottom line. A couple of times I did compromise in a small way, but generally I don't feel I compromised the music because of anything the record company demanded. I couldn't see any point in being a human jukebox and just doing what other people wanted me to do. But I realised that I had to engage with the business because I'd made that commitment to it. I wanted to continue to have music at the centre of my life and so I needed to maintain that commitment."

Perhaps the reason that Nelson stayed grounded was because he continued living in Yorkshire for most of the Be Bop era. "Because I did travel a lot, it was always nice to come back to Yorkshire. There's something in the soul of Yorkshire for me, the people – there's a lot of nostalgic romance and earthiness that's always appealed to me."

Be Bop Deluxe were my first live gig experience in 1976, supported by The Steve Gibbons Band at Leeds Grand Theatre. My sister Kathryn took me, and she also got Bill's autograph via his brother Ian who was on the same course as her at Huddersfield College of Music. It's natural that I've got a soft spot for Bill. To me and many other fans, Bill Nelson's Be Bop Deluxe delivered on several fronts. But they weren't the Yorkshire band that enjoyed frequent visits to the singles charts, appearances on *Top of the Pops* and multiple weeks on the *Radio One* Playlist in the mid-1970s. That band was Smokie.

Having gone through more name changes than *Spinal Tap*, Smokie were called 'Kindness' when they signed to RCA, were dropped by RCA, then were signed to Decca Records in the early seventies by the man who passed on the Beatles. It's perhaps little surprise then that the allegiance never bore fruit, and it'll no doubt be a comfort to Macca and Ringo that they never got signed by the man at Decca – their career would have turned to crap...ask Smokie.

But luckily for the Bradford band, they had a second chance. It came courtesy of Chinn and Chapman the songwriting team that had been responsible for much of the trashier end of the glam rock canon, writing smash hits for the likes of Sweet, Mud and Suzi Quatro, to name the more credible artists. The pair managed to get the Yorkshire quartet signed to Mickie Most's RAK label and it was they who suggested their new name – Smokey at first, but changed to Smokie after the great Smokey Robinson threatened legal action if they didn't change the spelling at least. A bit harsh perhaps but some might argue he should have threatened action if they released a record under any name.

But release records they did, and very successful they were too. 'If You Think You Know How to Love Me' was Smokie's first hit in 1975, making the top three of the singles chart. Five more Top Tenners followed, most notably 'Living Next Door to Alice'. Nothing remarkable about it when it charted in 1976. But when it was re-recorded and re-released in 1995 with comic additions from Roy 'Chubby' Brown, they became the first band to get a song containing the word 'fuck' in the UK Top Ten. Oh how we laughed. It almost made you hanker for Smokie's original brand of soft country-tinged pop.

But in 1976, something wonderfully foul was festering nicely in the pond at the bottom of pop's garden. Not that Smokie would have noticed or cared about what was about to crawl out. Bill Nelson for one did notice and did care. Mick Ronson too. And though he may not have realised it at the time, half guitar-hero/half Womble, Chris Spedding produced and beefed up the guitar tracks on a demo by the band that would change music in the United Kingdom forever. That band was Black Lace, sorry... no, that band was The Sex Pistols.

Chapter Five

Never Mind The Sex Pistols...

Scruffy young pillocks gobbing on you, eff-ing and jeff-ing in public, and generally making a deeply unpleasant racket. Then punk came along and walking down Normanton High Street on a Saturday afternoon was an even more unsavoury experience.

Strange to think that Yorkshire's biggest hit during the punk period was 'The Floral Dance' by the Brighouse and Rastrick Brass Band. Then again, maybe not strange at all. As was the form with anything new and different, Yorkshire in general didn't get punk until months after everyone else in the country. And even then, Yorkshire in general didn't get punk, full-stop. Yes, we saw the front of the tabloids, and watched the news – 'Utter Outrage on Local London TV Show'. So what? It didn't mean anything to us... until we heard the music. My own introduction to the rabid rabble was, as usual with any such cultural development, via the telly. A sensational-before-its-time advert for the now defunct *Revellie Weekly* carried a brief insert of The Sex Pistols 'singing' one of their jolly tunes. 'Oooh no!' I said, pulling a vaguely disconcerted mug in front of my Mam and Dad. 'Oooh interesting!' is what I was actually thinking (though obviously not with a camp Kenneth Williams intonation; I was a young Tetley Bitterman on the verge of shaving, for goodness sake).

On reflection, punk was both a very un-Yorkshire coup and at the same time a rather Yorkshire one too. The former because on the whole we traditionally gave any new trend emanating from London curiosity at best, and short-shrift if at all possible. A dose of acceptable corporal punishment was what these 'Johnny Rottens' needed – 'a clip round t'ear'ole' was the trusted Yorkshire method of dealing with an anti-christ/anarchist.

But then again, a set of young people telling it how it is, in a highly visceral manner and to hell with the consequences was surely the very lifeblood of our county – displays of recklessly frank expression leading to outbreaks of casual violence could be found on every other Yorkshire bus or in many a Yorkshire chip shop any day of the week, never mind the pubs and clubs on a Saturday night.

The post-war boom in the UK was all but forgotten in late 1976 as the Labour government fought an increasingly futile rearguard battle against inflation, and its partner in crime, unemployment. The Winter of Discontent was not far away with matters coming to a head in late 1978, an economic low which precipitated Margaret Thatcher's ascension to power. It's an understatement to say that by the mid-seventies, The Establishment no longer had the respect it had come to expect as a given. In fact it was becoming patently obvious that parts of it were rotten to the core; young people were now well aware of the culture of corruption and lies thriving in the corridors of power. Cynicism and disaffection provided the perfect fuel for a glorious backlash – punk.

It wasn't until 1977 that I really got punk and I can pinpoint the moment. I recall the absolute adrenalin rush of hearing 'God Save the Queen' for the very first time in its full-on glory on my brother's stereo. Could this be the same brother who had been a Grateful Dead-Head in the late sixties? Yes indeed but Pete got it straight away even though he was a rather ancient 25 by then. Very few of my mates got it – Derek Raspberry possibly, and Phil Lunn perhaps (he did buy The Damned album) – but very few wanted to get it. Most of them were very happy with Genesis and Queen, thanks very much.

By that time, I'd started buying the *New Musical Express* regularly, and sometimes one of its inky rivals, *Sounds*. While those two immediately plugged into the new zeitgeist, *Melody Maker* dragged its heels, playing safer with the old guard. It was through reading the *NME* – as it became known – that I found out that the best way to taste punk was go to one of the numerous gigs featuring one of its practitioners. Well yes, but er, 'hello'... I was a 16-year -old living in seriously behind-the-times West Yorkshire. Luckily, I also found out the alternative was to listen to John Peel's weeknight show on *Radio One*. I had heard of Peel but only in rare and lonely despatches. Why would I want to be tuning into the radio at ten o'clock at night when there was perfectly good rubbish on the telly? Now I had a reason.

Okay, in reality it was hardly Anarchy in the UK, but it was certainly as near to a youth revolution as we were going to get, certainly in Yorkshire. I hadn't realised how conservative (with the smallest 'c' possible) we were until I saw the general reaction of the county's populace to the threatening menace that was punk.

But if it didn't succeed in demystifying the politics of the day, punk demystified the music of the day completely. You didn't have to be Rick Wakeman to make a record – you didn't even have to be Rick Wakeman to wear a silly costume. One cheap guitar and one sturdy bar chord was all it took to throw up a song, and a session with a pair of scissors was all it took to get your outfit. Still, you had to be a very brave young thing to walk through the streets of Wakefield even daring to look different.

Yorkshire can lay claim to at least two milestones in the brief era of punk. The Clash played their debut gig at the Black Swan in Sheffield (now known as The Board walk) in July 1976, supporting the Sex Pistols. The Pistols had just finished recording their demo with Chris Spedding, one of the few established musicians to champion the Pistols from the word 'go'. And in a neat piece of symmetry, the Sex Pistols played their last ever UK gig in Yorkshire, at Ivanhoes club in Huddersfield on Christmas Day 1977. Me and my mate Derek said we'd definitely go. But Christmas Day was Christmas Day, and besides, there'd be other opportunities. Yes, course there would…

But who were Yorkshire's Sex Pistols, the county's Clash? In fact, who were the first punk band in Yorkshire? An extensive five-minute trawl across the Internet suggest it could have been either S.O.S. or Abrasive Wheels, both in the accepted three-chord punk bombast mould, and both from the cutting-edge Metropolis that was, and is Leeds. The first Yorkshire punk(-ish) band I heard however, on Peel's show, was The Mekons. That's not to say I knew they were from Leeds when Peely played 'Where Were You?' And that's not to say they were the first Yorkshire punk act to be played on his show.

The fact is, apart from one member of the band, The Mekons were neither from Leeds nor Yorkshire; they were students at Leeds University. For the first time in our story, musicians from elsewhere in the UK play a big and justifiable part. In days of old, the Yorkshire Cricket rules would probably apply – if they're not born in the county they can't play for the county.

But this is different; these people were responsible for starting a 'scene' in Yorkshire – our first! Well, I say 'scene' but perhaps it was just a pocket of activity. In 1977, Leeds-based students formed an important collective within the scheme of punk; The Mekons, The Gang of Four and the Delta 5 – with their various offshoots – created a bona fide scene in Leeds. It transpires that the middle suspect(s) of that line-up set the ball rolling.

When the Gang of Four's Andy Gill and Jon King came up from Kent in 1975, there wasn't even the merest hint of a music scene in the area, never mind in Leeds. The scene that developed was completely based around a bunch of friends who were on art courses at Leeds Polytechnic and University.

The Gang of Four were formed in 1976, with Gill and King on guitar and vocals and Dave Allen and Hugo Burnham on bass and drums respectively. And though, as Andy confirms, they weren't an actual 'punk band' as such – "it was a very catch-all phrase" - they immediately adopted the punk ethic. So, according to their guitarist, 'The Four' were the first punk band in Leeds, "very closely followed by the Mekons. We'd rehearse and our mates, the Mekons would ask if they could use our instruments when we'd finished.

"We thought that the best way to get gigs was to have all your own gear – and I mean everything. We cobbled together a PA system, building speaker cabinets out of old wardrobes. We got the speakers themselves from an old army surplus shop in Leeds - these speakers had apparently been mounted under the wings of planes to broadcast propaganda."

The set-up very quickly became that of a 'collective' – "everyone from the GoF and the Mekons put in a bit of money and we managed to buy a little mixing desk between us, 'borrowed' a couple of microphones, shall we say, and between us we'd got a PA. Hugo, the drummer, had a transit van – there you go, up and running."

The very first Gang of Four gig was in May 1977, when they themselves booked the Corn Exchange in Leeds, because as Jon King explains, they had no other option if they wanted to play live. "There were no venues in Leeds that would allow us to play. We booked it ourselves and promoted it ourselves. Even the university wouldn't put us on."

That may be the case but a few weeks later, an enterprising young Leeds resident, John Keenan, started promoting punk gigs at the Polytechnic and by the end of the year had established the 'F Club', a weekly event at first but by the end of the seventies, putting punk and new wave acts on three nights a week at whatever city club would have it. But before there was a specific punk platform in Leeds, the Gang of Four would "turn up at various venues in

Yorkshire and just ask if we could play. It was the right time when people were open to that DIY aesthetic. If you sit on your arse and wait for people to come to you and say come and play a gig, it's not going to happen. You had to get in people's faces to get things moving."

Their big break, according to Andy, came courtesy of one of punk's non-elitist elite – "The Buzzcocks were on a national tour, and we just turned up with our PA, found their manager Richard Boon who'd never met us, and said what about us setting up our PA in front of yours and we'll play a short warm-up for the Buzzcocks. He said fine and we did it. He phoned us up next day and asked if we wanted to do the rest of the tour. Next thing, Siouxsie and the Banshees were ringing up asking if we wanted to support them."

The band quickly became known as much for their political edge as their jagged but highly danceable funk-rock – well, they were named after the quartet charged with treason at the end of China's Cultural Revolution - so it seems fair to assume they'd have a manifesto when they started. "It would be ludicrous to pretend that when you start out you've got everything fully formed. As you get more serious about it, and start working at it, that's how you come to form what it is you're trying to say. People sometimes forget that the band had a lot of humour in it. They thought we came over as quite dour."

Was being in Leeds of any importance at the time or could it have been anywhere? "Leeds had a strong influence on the way we were and the way we sounded. A lot of the city was made up of slums that were falling down, a bit of a bomb site. It was also a time when the far-right was having a field day. There were Nazi rallies marching around the city and violence in the air."

Jon King puts their situation then into a pop perspective – "at that time, if you weren't a band in London, you never got noticed and you never got reviews. We were very committed to being a Leeds band even though we didn't come from Leeds. It'd have been convenient if we'd re-invented ourselves as a southern band but we wouldn't do that. We were lucky really in that it gave us the chance to find our own thing and our own place."

Despite preconceptions perhaps stoked by the press, Andy, Jon and Co were interested in being successful in the populist sense – "we weren't trying to make music that was inaccessible. Though we had an art background, we didn't want to get into that elitist aspect of the art world that felt like you had to learn a special language to understand what was going on with our music. Our agenda always involved a dialogue with aspects of popular music. There were aspects of what we did that weren't instantly consumable and a bit difficult. But there was always a relationship to rock music, funk and even reggae – they were always present in what we did."

The 'Damaged Goods' EP eventually sold around 100,000 copies but says Jon, "we were totally robbed blind by Fast Product, (the Edinburgh independent label who put the record out) – with licensing, Bob Last must have made a quarter of a million out of it and we got literally nothing". But given their political leanings, did Andy or the others see signing for a major record company like EMI as a sell-out? "It was something we wanted to do. There's this attitude that if you make a political criticism, the implication is that you're on the right side. We recognised that there's always a certain degree of complicity in whatever you do. Being politically correct can only exist in an imagined utopia. We wanted to be on EMI and the symbolism of that was something that we embraced. The music wasn't about being in an avant garde ghetto, it was about being accessible. The idea that a GoF record was rubbing shoulders with a Cliff record was good as far as we were concerned."

The debut album 'Entertainment' came out to almost unanimous acclaim but even now Andy really doesn't know who their audience was, and Jon struggles with that too – "what I do know is our audience wasn't a student audience. It was more your clubbing audience – teenagers or people in their twenties who didn't mind going out, who enjoyed new music, maybe trouble-making kind of people who enjoyed having a bit of fun. Even now I find it puzzling that we weren't considered to be a draw on the college circuit. We were more a club and theatre band, very rarely played the universities."

Sad to report that despite the band's willingness to embrace Leeds, that great city was more than reluctant to adopt the Gang of Four as its own. "Of all the places we played, I think Leeds was the place that we drew the smallest audience. It's not really a big music city like Sheffield. I think there was quite a lot of resentment – when we first on the front of the *NME*, the reaction was almost universally hostile from the people in Leeds. Even when we were selling out two nights at Hammersmith Palais, and having our first album placed in the top 500 albums of all time by *Rolling Stone*, we still couldn't get a gig at Leeds University. I don't think any bands benefited from being a Leeds band at that time. They never got big local audiences. We could go to America, be very well thought of, then get back to Leeds and be ignored. That has its own kind of pleasure to it. But I quite like that about the Yorkshire mentality because it's not pretentious and it's grounded. At the time I thought that the North was definitely a better place to be."

Of course, it would be a crime to talk to the Gang of Four without getting their version of events when they played 'At Home He's a Tourist' on *Top of the Pops*, or rather, when they didn't. Jon King eventually reveals a dark consequence of this sorry episode. "We got zero airplay on radio, apart from Peel obviously, but to everyone's astonishment we went up in the charts. The rule was that if your song went up you'd be invited to go on *TOTP* but if it stayed in the same chart position, you wouldn't. So we were automatically invited on the show but of course we had to re-record the song as was the way at the time. They said, it's a family programme, so you can't use the word 'rubbers' – remember the Number One that week was 'Ring My Bell' by Anita Ward. We decided to play the game and replaced 'rubbers' with 'packets'. In the end that was the only thing we re-recorded. Then of course on the show, you mimed to your re-recording in the TV studio. We decided that in terms of performance, we weren't going to move – our thought was not to look like any of the other bands on that show. The producer was really pissed off that we weren't going to 'do anything'. So they picked on the changed lyric saying that 'packets' still had the same meaning as 'rubbers', could we change it again to 'rubbish'. We told him to go fuck himself. That was his plan – he was making his light-entertainment point. We walked out and that's how Dire Straits got on for their first appearance in our place, even though 'Sultans of Swing' hadn't moved that week."

Aaaaghhhh! Talk about a sting in the tale?! Should we blame the Gang of Four or that BBC producer for the rise of Knopfler and the Straits? ('The Knopf' was a journo at the Yorkshire Evening Post during the seventies by the way, and he recorded his first demo tapes whilst resident in Pudsey).

It wasn't the Gang of Four's last experience of BBC censorship; 'I Love a Man in Uniform' was banned in 1982 because of the Falklands War. Jon King's got no doubts – "we were so outside that cosy media club – we were outsiders, and definitely objectionable to those kinds of people. I hated them all".

So there you have it, the Gang of Four were 'outsiders', committed to being a Leeds band, and were ringleaders of the first (and maybe only) music scene the city has known. Surely they qualify as honorary Yorkshire Pop Stars?

Their pals, The Mekons, who also had their early records released on Fast Product, including the debut 'Never Been In A Riot' (a wry retort to The Clash's 'White Riot – you didn't really get riots up in Leeds), were never as vital or visceral as their chums Gang of Four, and never had the same commercial success, but similarly, they carved out long careers in music. Jon Langford has proved to be something of a renaissance man, gaining recognition not only as a musician – he was one of The Three Johns, another Peel fave in the early 80s with their agit-rock – but also a successful artist, DJ and writer. Sally Timms, the only Leeds-born protagonist in that late seventies crowd, is a highly respected alternative country singer over in the good old US of A. In fact, The Mekons are still active over in the States, making music in a left-field country vein. The Gang of Four – or King and Gill at least – are still high-profile in the UK and Europe, and are regularly referenced by anyone from the mega-big Red Hot Chilli Peppers to UK indie darlings Bloc Party.

The third member of that old Leeds trinity, Delta 5 came slightly later than the other two bands with the three womenfolk of the outfit – Julz Sale, Ros Allen and Bethan Peters apparently forming a pop group 'for a lark'. All had close connections with The Mekons, not least Ros who had played bass with that top ranking combo. Whilst a unique feature of the Deltas was they incorporated two bass players into their sound, the content of their songs was a different kind of politics to GoF and the Mekons – emotional politics, or 'relationships' to put it basically. Though they did end up signing to a major label offshoot – PRE – it's the early Rough Trade singles that are best remembered, particularly their debut, 'None of Your Business'.

But if you think that's the end of the punk/new wave bands from Leeds with a girly slant, then you'd be sadly wrong. It this was one of Pete Frame's Rock Family Trees, we'd be tracing a line from the aforementioned S.O.S. through to another quite-good-but-never-quite-good-enough combo called The Butterflies, and finally on to Girls at Our Best. Though the Delta 5 boasted three female members, 'Girls…' only had the one, vocalist Jo Allen. But at least they were all true locals, well vaguely; Jo came from the rather posher Wetherby up the A58. They too were Peel favourites, which I suppose all these bands have in common. But unlike some of Peel's faves, Girls at Our Best came very close to making that crossover into the mainstream, courtesy of Jude's model looks attracting the attention of glossy magazines. Just as they were ready to… they split.

This is all very well (or would have been had some of these bands really made it as chart acts) but how was the punk philosophy affecting our more established 'musos'? But Bill Nelson for one wasn't fazed. "There'd always been an alternative scene. I was always aware of that underground, and I was always interested in experimental music, John Cage, Stockhausen and all that minimalism stuff. It was all very much a part of the avant guard art scene. So punk just seemed to be another generation trying to pick up on that. The idea to empower people was great. But the music often disappointed me. It didn't

92

really break any barriers at all. I actually wrote an article about the Sex Pistols and punk in general for the *NME* – apart from the attitude and Lydon's singing style, the music itself was just Chuck Berry. Pub rock really. The only thing that distinguished it really was the media view, the hype of the movement's confrontational aspects. Musically it was very conservative. Tom Robinson wrote a reply the week after, saying don't be against us, come and join us."

The kind of experimental music Nelson found far more interesting had actually been happening a lot closer than he could have imagined. Deep down in the underground of Sheffield, Cabaret Voltaire were playing around with industrial sounds long before the Human League had even beeped their first beep.

As early as 1973, Richard H Kirk, Stephen Mallinder and Chris Watson were experimenting with 'industrial electronics', but it has to be said without a great deal of recognition or acclaim. That could have something to do with them not actually playing a gig until 1975; when they did, they got bottled off. It was only when punk provided a forum for brave, new and different sounds that their bleak soundscapes were looked on as a serious music form and they given the chance to commit their sounds to vinyl. As Kirk has said since, "the Cabs started the trend, all the others followed". If punk suited the grim decay of cities like Leeds and their surrounding suburbs, the industrial punk initiated by Cabaret Voltaire more than suited the grimmer industrial decay of Sheffield. Kirk and his pals were students of the Dada movement – from whence they plundered their name. The fact that Kirk himself was studying to be an artist when he got shanghaied by music has faint echoes of Bill Nelson and probably a million other pop musicians before and since.

Dubbed 'Noise-art Terrorists', the idea behind Cabaret Voltaire was to 'create a bit of antagonism' via their music. Their approach was punk before punk was gobbed up onto the Great British Public's consciousness; looking back on their early gigs, Kirk admitted the idea was just to get a reaction, "any reaction was good as far as we were concerned. And anything other than people being disinterested was better than being ignored".

The Cabs finally made it onto vinyl, first via a Factory Records 'sampler' compilation, then in their own right on Rough Trade Records. But by that time, another Sheffield band had crept up on the rails – though the Cabs had been around a lot longer, the Human League had a record out first.

The Human League, in Phil Oakey's words, "were *more* punk than punk", with the celebrated rudimentary of playing the guitar replaced by the even more rudimentary of producing a noise from a synthesizer with one clueless finger. Their story has become a well worn path now, and has nothing to do with waitresses in cocktail bars. Computer operators, Martyn Ware and Ian Craig Marsh had been fannying around with synthesizers for a while, finally arriving at their crossroads – or at least their first one – in 1977 when third member Adi Newton left The Future (as they were known then) starting his own synth driven combo, Clock DVA.

Ware and Marsh had been told in no uncertain terms by the major record companies that they'd never be signed without any marketable songs in their locker. Obvious really. Equally obvious was the need for a strong vocalist and focal point to add to their Kraftwerk-esque sound. In their minds, that could only be one man… Glenn Gregory. Eh?! Surely some mistake. No – Glenn was the man they wanted but at the time he was the man they couldn't get. His frontline involvement would come later. Step forward second-choice, Phil Oakey, an old school chum of Martyn Ware's – "he already looked like a pop star" was Ware's assessment. He had the haircut and the make-up, a reasonable voice - The Human League was born, the name lifted from a science fiction war game. Of course.

But it wasn't until mid-1978 that they made strides and waves. Fast Product Records – did they have some kind of monopoly going on? - released the debut Human League single to rave reviews; 'Being Boiled', featuring a fascinating Oakey lyric concerned with dodgy Buddhist behaviour, sounded like nothing else at the time, and was at odds with the all the other post-punk output flooding the pop market. Like all significant pop acts, they polarised opinion – David 'Tadcaster' Bowie saw them and hailed them as the 'future of pop music' whilst Johnny 'No connection with Yorkshire whatsoever' Rotten heard The Human League and dismissed them as 'trendy hippies'. Mind you, they had by that time added Adrian Wright on stage visuals, thus becoming a modern day Pink Floyd on stage at least, so your man had a point. The Undertones even immortalised their name with an affectionate dig in their Top Ten hit 'My Perfect Cousin'.

After support slots with the likes of Siouxsie and the Banshees and the granddaddy of punk, Iggy Pop, 'The League' (as Peter Powell would call them) released the seminal 'Dignity of Labour' EP and the major labels came running. That's when the problems first started, for Ware and Marsh at least.

Virgin won the band's signature, and immediately insisted on a more commercial approach for the Human League's next single, with traditional instrumentation drafted in alongside the band's trademark synths, a move that Ware was, quite rightly, so opposed to that he in turn insisted on it being released under the pseudonym, The Men. The single, 'I Don't Depend on You' bombed and the band was allowed to return to their original style. But that disco tinged single, complete with girl backing vocals was, prophetically, a sign of things to come for Sheffield's newest pop stars. But things were going to get worse before they became better.

If the fact that relations in the band between Oakey and Ware were deteriorating at this time wasn't bad enough, worse was the rise of Gary Numan, whose 'Are Friends Electric?' seemed to creep up from nowhere and snatch the electronica baton from the Human League. The decade ended in relative turmoil for the band as Ware and Marsh shaped to exit. Smart money had been on resounding success for the Human League; suddenly you were wiser saving your money.

By the end of the seventies, there was plenty of opportunity for anyone prepared to try something new. Step forward once more, Bill Nelson. "I thought it could open some doors even for me and Be Bop Deluxe. I'd got the idea to do another band anyway around that time but the management had talked me out of it, persuading me to do one more album as Be Bop and then think about it. So we did the 'Drastic Plastic' album. I was trying to be a bit more minimalistic about what we were doing but still keeping it sounding like Be-Bop... we cut back on the virtuoso stuff with a bit more of a sci-fi story line going on. It was a struggle, not least as the band weren't okay with it as individuals."

Bill parked Be Bop Deluxe up for good and quickly swung back out in his new vehicle, built for the times, Red Noise. "EMI were a little puzzled as to why I'd gone in this direction but they went with it. But in America we were signed to Capitol, and they thought I'd lost it completely. They sent copies of the Red Noise album, 'Sound on Sound' out to US radio stations and asked for feedback. The general response was – *what is this shit?* It was funny because I thought what we'd done was really accessible, energetic and defined.

"Shortly after that EMI were taken over by Thorn Lighting and the company started getting run buy accountants. There was an inevitable trimming of the roster – they kept mega-sellers like McCartney and Kate Bush but got rid of bands like Red Noise and Wire. I was without a deal, so set up my own label."

And so began the rest of Bill Nelson's musical and artistic life. His initial solo efforts very nearly signalled a return to the charts – 'Do You Dream in Colour?' sounds vibrantly current nearly thirty years on. His subsequent prolific output has marked him out as an enduring artist rather than a fleeting careerist. He was an in-demand producer in the 1980s but less-than-satisfying experiences with the likes of Gary Numan probably prompted the man to concentrate on his own music, which has to be said, has been in a more personal vein since he started writing and recording for himself, and not a record company. And whilst unlikely allies such as Dude-turned-Druid Julian Cope have voiced their fondness for Be Bop Deluxe, Bill's worldwide fan base have stayed tuned into his every musical swerve to this day, even setting up an annual Nelsonica

Convention, now coming up for it's tenth anniversary. "I've just turned 60 and I do wonder how much time I've got left – so it's only natural to take stock and see what you've done. You want to try and understand why you've arrived where you are. You need to revisit where you've been, rediscover what sent you in a certain direction. I started playing jazz music when I first taught myself guitar in my teenage years and I suppose I've come full circle."

In reality, punk as the threatening anti-establishment entity that had started out as – or had been perceived to be – didn't last for very long. By 1978, the Pistols died a sudden death at the right time, just as they were in danger of becoming a parody of themselves, and much of what remained felt like mischief-making at best. Appropriately, the press now talked about the 'New Wave', a more general, gentler term for the glut of new acts that had ridden into public awareness on the back of punk's initial bombastic splendour. Sting was no more a punk than I was a lion tamer (but, as I always say, a job interview's a job interview).

By 1978, the competition as such was Disco, most of it thankfully coming over from the States as the home-produced stuff was dire; the fact that most UK disco music stayed within the confines of the nations variety clubs could justify their existence alone. But disco was a good thing – the plush production of your Bee Gees and Chic records providing a perfect contrast to the dozens of home produced guitar-driven efforts being turned out on independent labels every week. And that, fellow-music-fans was punk's finest legacy, the establishment of a thriving independent record scene that lives to this day. The *NME*, *Sounds* and *Melody Maker* all had their own 'Indie' charts that further galvanised the growing alternative music scene. Yorkshire's most renowned indie label, Warp, didn't come into being at the end of the next decade playing a massive role in the dance scene of the 1990s.

And it was punk that kicked off my own glittering music career, i.e. I bought a cheap electric guitar, a fire engine red Futurama and I think I paid my mate

Hodgy the grand sum of £16 for it. I didn't have an amp to play it through but that was a minor point. The ambition now was to form a band.

But there were members of the extended Ferguson family who had beaten me to it. My cousins Neil and Tony had long been proud owners of guitars – and amps! Now they'd taken advantage of the times and put out their own record under the name, The Donkeys. I wasn't too taken with their choice of moniker but that didn't matter – as soon as their single, 'What I Want' got played by John Peel (and more than once), that was it… I made sure everyone knew they were my cousins. It didn't matter that the song itself was distinctly 'Power Pop' in nature. And did I mention that Peel played it?

And when they got to support Stiff Little Fingers on tour, they'd arrived in my eyes. I'd just moved to Manchester, somehow getting on the Economics course at the Polytechnic, and obviously when the tour came to town, I had to be there. My sister Kathryn even came over – we were only on the guest list weren't we? By the time we got into the old Polytechnic Union building, The Donkeys had finished their set but we went backstage to have a drink with Neil and Tony, completely missing the Stiff Little Fingers set. So we didn't actually get to see either band play. No matter, we'd actually got to 'lig' backstage with our cousins, the pop stars. Okay, The Donkeys never set the world alight but they did light my performing touchpaper; if they – two working class lads from Normanton, West Yorkshire – could do it, I could do it.

As punk petered out, and the millions of new wave acts were sieved out into the performers of true and lasting quality, a new sound hit the airwaves and clubs – well not new at all really. But ska was new to many of us and the Two Tone sound was a breath of fresh air. It was the first high profile multi-racial music the UK had cooked up in my lifetime. Yes, there were multi-racial communities all over Yorkshire, not least in the Leeds and Bradford suburbs, but it felt right that Two Tone was born of another unfashionable part of the country, the Midlands. Madness were the exception of course, but their springboard to success was still Jerry Dammers' Coventry based label. Any other part of the country trying to emulate what Two Tone did would have seemed ridiculous and pointless, I think – that movement belonged to the Midlands. (Though the young, Birmingham-born Roland Gift was first spotted singing with Hull ska band Akrylykz, and remembered by Andy Cox and Dave Steele when they were recruiting for their post-Beat band, Fine Young Cannibals). Apart from enjoying the music, we could all rejoice in the fact that Two Tone couldn't have done what it did without punk's legacy of 'do-it-yourself-and-two-fingers-up-to-the-establishment'.

Leeds received a more tangible legacy from punk in the form of the Futurama Festival (no relation to my beloved guitar), an annual musical event that ran well into the 1980s. The man behind it was 'Mr F Club' himself, John Keenan. The first Futurama – 'the world's first science fiction music festival'… huh?! - held at the city's Queens Hall, featured John Lydon's Public Image and Joy Division. Its significance to the development of punk's offspring would become clear in years to come.

That punk ethic had a lot to answer for, and not only in the quarters you'd expect. While some of us were listening to John Peel, pogoing in private as well as in public, others were listening to Tommy Vance, head-banging in Halifax, and moshing in Mexborough. Oh yes - don't knock the Rock, cock!

Chapter Six

Rockin' Like A Bastud!

Come on, hands up who had a mullet haircut, or at least a 'feather cut', an early incarnation of that sartorial abomination that is the mullet, back in the pre-punk days of 1976? That's me and 90% of Yorkshiremen aged between 40 and 55 then. Hands up who still had one by 1978? I'm out – I can provide proof, your Honour - but look, there are a whole lot of hands still held aloft in South Yorkshire.

That indisputably, highly accurate survey proves perhaps several things. Firstly, take note Nicky Clarke, we in Yorkshire surely invented the mullet. Secondly, not every young fella in the county was inspired enough by punk to cut off his shameful neck-warming mop. And lastly, South Yorkshire was at the epicentre of the new heavy metal revolution that took place in the wake of punk rock.

Well, I say heavy metal – what I actually mean is the ass-kicking acronym NWOBHM, or to the blissfully ignorant, the New Wave of British Heavy Metal. We all knew that though, didn't we? There were plenty of rockers, old and new, determined to dig their heels in, respond to punk in a language it could understand by saying 'fuck off', and carry on listening to meandering seven-minute album tracks by artists as dangerous as their dad in a cheesecloth shirt and fur-lined moccasins. But there was a happy medium. Apparently. And this is where NWOBHM – or 'nuh-wobbum'- comes in.

Old rock had been born of the Blues, or more specifically the R'n'B explosion of the early 1960s. Example… Led Zeppelin was spawned from the last version of the Yardbirds who had started their career covering the Blues classics of Howlin Wolf, Bo Diddley and Muddy Waters.

Come 1977, punk had, at the very least, suggested that upping the tempo of the most ordinary of guitar riffs would result in a vigorous energy around which you could build an entire bloody song. The new heavy metal crew took note, apparently 'kicked out the blues' and toughened up the sound, producing, ahem, 'pure metal, made for metal fans'. Yeah! Rock like a bitch, and all that.

At the vanguard of this rockin' revolution was Motorhead, led by that most handsome of chappies, Lemmy, late of Hawkwind. However, the Lemster's band of rockers didn't immediately wow the rock fans of the nation; it wasn't until Yorkshire's new rockers joined the fray that the serious head-banging really started, en masse.

It's strange to think that while the likes of Cabaret Voltaire, Human League, Clock DVA et al were all happily beeping away in Sheffield, a rock band in that same city were making the first moves of a career than would see them became one of the most successful bands in rock history. I kid you not. Atomic Mass were formed in 1977 and if they'd kept that as their name there's probably every chance they'd have headed back down Oblivion Road within weeks. As it was, a change of personnel brought more than one significant change to their fortunes as their new 18-year-old vocalist, Joe Elliot, suggested 'Deaf

Leopard' as a smart new handle. It has been said that they eventually modified the spelling to 'Def Leppard' to sound less like a punk band. Eh?!

Personally, I'd suggest one of two real reasons for this change; either they were looking for the most Led Zeppelin-esque name imaginable for the band, or they didn't want any potential fans to think they were unfashionably literate by spelling the two words correctly.

Yeah whatever, because 'Def Lep', like 'Led Zep' before them, were given vital radio airplay by none other than John Peel when a copy of the band's debut EP (an extended play seven-inch comprising of three tracks) landed on the desk of our favourite DJ. I'd wager that the Champion of Punk wouldn't have dreamt he was giving a leg up to a group that would become the kind of Trans-Atlantic Mega Band he loathed with a passion. And, it has to be said, it's hard to imagine Peely playing any track called 'Getcha Rocks Off' in 1979.

Def Leppard were even considered leaders of the new wave heavy metal thingy for a while before those Johnny-Come-Lately's, Iron Maiden, took over the mantle. Not that Def Lep would let that bother them. They had bigger fish to fry than little grey old Britain – it was quickly clear the band had set their sights on success in the arena of Stateside Stadium 'Rawk'. The second track on their debut album was rather tellingly titled 'Hello America'; what a giveaway. Geoff Barton, the lead rock writer of Nuh-Wobbum supporting *Sounds*, and the man who apparently coined the seriously annoying phrase, even took the band to task when that track was released as a single, claiming that 'The Defs' had been taken over by the big-business side of the music industry far too easily, and much too early into their career. The band denied this and promised to take the matter up with their record label, Phonogram, but Barton was obviously onto something.

It was the enrolment of Mutt Lange as producer for the second album, 'High 'n' Dry' that officially put Def Leppard on that hundred-dollar-bill paved highway. Lange had previously weaved his knob-twiddling magic on AC/DC, giving the Aussie rockers a sugar coated stadium-sized sound that wowed the head banging dudes of America. Joe Elliot explained the 'Mutt Method' thus – "Mutt had come and seen us opening for AC/DC at a gig in England. And he saw something. He saw a lot of bad things, but he could see something, otherwise he wouldn't have worked with us. And he said… 'I think I can polish this lot up'. So we brought Mutt on board for the second record, and the difference versus the debut is just ridiculous. What he did is he stripped our riffs down. He'd tell Pete or Steve to take certain notes out and make it easier, rather than musical". Yeah, right, whatever.

Incoming guitarist Phil Collen's view of the developing Leppard sound is probably/hopefully more insightful. "When I joined, all the songs were written already for 'Pyromania', so I just had to play solos on top, basically, and do a bit of singing. Just my impression of it was, I had never heard anything quite like it, because it was an absolute hybrid – a rock hybrid. We were still a rock band. When I heard a lot of American bands… they had very sweet vocals, very high. We weren't, we owed our thing to punk, and that's where we come from, you know, 'Won't Get Fooled Again', 'Holidays in the Sun', 'God Save the Queen'. That's where we were singing from, only we could do it in tune."

It's maybe the only time that The Who song has been referred to as a punk track, but we know what Phil meant, don't we? Well even if we don't, with Mutt Lange onboard, and with the added help of *MTV*, Def Leppard went unimaginably mega in the 1980s, with 'Pyromania' and its follow-up, 'Hysteria', shifting by the skip load, no offence meant. Both albums went 'Diamond' in the States – selling 10 million copies each – and propelled them into an elite group of five artists who have also achieved such sales figures with two long players, The Beatles, Pink Floyd, Van Halen and yes, Led Zeppelin being the other members of that exclusive club.

But the band had to leave their original heavy metal fans behind to get that obscenely big. And the glossy bubble gum-rock sound that became their trademark, courtesy of the Muttmiester, has been copied by American rock bands ever since, a sound that Joe Elliot himself has described as "a cross between AC/DC and Queen".

But outrageous success was not without more outrageous adversity for 'the Leps', indeed tragedy. Having already fired one guitarist in 1982 because of his alcohol abuse, they lost another one – Steve Clark – to an accidental overdose of drink and drugs in 1991. And in-between, their drummer Rick Allen lost an arm in a car accident on these shores in 1984. But, hats off to him, the drummer learnt to play his part on a specially modified kit and has been in charge of the stick ever since.

These days they might not be as massive as they once were, but without doubt Def Leppard take the prize for Yorkshire's Most Successful Pop Act of All Time – over 65 million albums sold worldwide and still rising. They're even in the *Guinness Book of Records* for playing a gig on three separate continents within 24 hours; whoever was driving the transit that day deserved first pick of the groupies, or at least the sandwiches. Strange to say but they're probably the most revered Tyke act on a global level, though certainly not in the UK, but if shifting global units is the criteria by which success is measured – and unfortunately it is – no one comes near them.

That's not to knock them, or at least not much. The original members of Def Leppard were very much working-class lads from Sheffield. Glam-rock obsessed lead-singer Elliot was still working as a storesman in a local tool-works in the early days of the band, having turned his back on a football career after training on schoolboy forms with Sheffield United. It seems that if he wasn't going to live one dream of every working class boy and make it as a professional footballer, he was going to live the other one, making it even bigger in a rock 'n' roll band. Getting kicked to bits at Bramall Lane on a cold January afternoon or getting treated like royalty for singing a few ditties to a stadium full of dollar-packing punters – it must have been a tough call.

There must have been, and probably still are dozens of rock bands still toiling around the Yorkshire pubs and clubs, with fine names like 'Flaming Nora' and

'Bison'. Actually, these are band names me and my pals have conjured up in our frequent rock musing sessions down the pub over the years but you do hope and pray there are bands somewhere that have had the same flash of utter inspiration and have actually adopted these fine handles (I've since found out that there was actually a ska band in Yorkshire that adopted the name Bison in the last few years, which is just wrong. They've now split up, so the name's back up for grabs, you rockers!)

There most definitely was a band called Son Of A Bitch – there had to be though, eh? - just down the road from Def Leppard, and indisputably Barnsley's own new heavy metal pioneers, as it were. Son Of A Bitch – ring any bells? Course not. They too made the wise move of picking out a new name when it was perhaps pointed out that they were in danger of hindering their own progress by keeping their current one.

They hit on Saxon. Fronted by Peter 'Biff' Byford, the Barnsley boys struck their first Metal hallmark around the same time as Def Leppard in 1979. But it wasn't without a struggle at first. They were either ignored or dismissed as a band out-of-time by most record A&R men who were looking for the new Police or Boomtown Rats, until EMI's Peter Hinton recommended them to French producer Claude Carrere who was looking for talent to record on his new Carrere label. Their eponymous album, released in 1979 was followed a year later by the long player that broke Saxon big-time. 'Wheels of Steel' spawned two top-selling singles, in the title-track and '747 (Strangers in the Night)', records that put Biff's brigade on 'Top of the Pops' at a time when rock bands hardly got a look-in on the show.

In an interview with The *Guardian*'s Roy Wilkinson at the beginning of 2009, Byford recalled the DIY nature of Saxon in their early days; not dissimilar to the likes of the Gang of Four, they made their own PA speakers, and actually lugged their gear around in an old van previously, and conspicuously owned by the local Tripe merchant. Biff, perhaps more begrudgingly than Phil Collen from Def Leppard, admitted the band owed punk a debt of gratitude, saying "punk was definitely important… it just created a different mood – like when Def Leppard put out their own EP. We actually supported The Clash in Manchester in 1977. I bumped into Joe Strummer about five years ago. I couldn't believe it but he actually remembered the show. He said they'd been jamming our song '747' in their dressing room."

Mmmm, right… I wanted to speak to Biff myself for this book, and I really tried to make it happen, as did the PR company assigned to Saxon affairs. If '747' is the song that became their biggest hit single in 1980, was it really there in the band's repertoire back in 1977? If so, how come it didn't go on their first album instead of their second? I would have liked to ask your man that.

But, despite months of courting his PR company via email, I never got to speak to Biff. Which is a shame for another reason – I wanted to ask him about his teeth. I have it on good authority – from a friend who edited *Kerrang!* actually – that Byford is a long-time denture-wearer. Nothing unusual or wrong with that really. But apparently, Biff is, or was known for having a set of 'singing teeth', and a set of 'photo teeth', each of which he swaps around for the appropriate task (a bit like Worzel Gummidge and his heads if you like). Slightly amusing, yes, but much more amusing by all accounts when the rest of the band, in the past at least, chose to garnish the said dentures with mustard without Biff's knowledge. You can imagine the resultant heavy rock snarl when the Biffster popped the top set of his 'photo teeth' in (next time you see an old piccy of Saxon, and Biff's snarling at the camera…). I was keen to broach this with the man himself, keen as mustard in fact.

Like Def Leppard, Saxon are very much your South Yorkshire working class lads made good. Byford, for example, had even worked 'down t' pit' for a spell before the band took off. But when they did take off, Saxon enjoyed very reasonable chart success for a metal band all through the 1980s, with three more Top 40 singles to add to their initial pair, and seven Top 40 albums in the wake of 'Wheels of Steel'. Times got leaner for the band in the UK during 1990s and fortunes continued in the same vein into the new century. It wasn't a complete surprise then when they agreed to get involved with Harvey Goldsmith's reality TV show *Get Your Act Together* in 2007, the intention being to revitalise their career. The experience did Saxon no harm whatsoever; the single featured in the show, 'If I Was You', went to Number One in the Rock Charts of ten countries, giving the veteran Rockers their most successful single for over ten years. Newly refreshed, they embarked a World Tour in the summer of 2009 and look set to continue rocking for the foreseeable. Reports of a new concept album titled 'Dentures of Doom' however remain unfounded.

Though Saxon have never had the same ridiculously massive Stateside commercial success enjoyed by Def Leppard, they were right there on the frontline when heavy metal became hip in the late 1970s. When I say 'hip', it's obviously from a relative perspective. Punks were never going to think British heavy metal was hip, per se. And that's probably down to the look – apart from the hair, the metal look was still regulation denim jackets adorned with embroidered band-name patches, stonewashed flared jeans and maybe even, gulp, cowboy boots. Even if you were a punk who liked a metal track, you'd never even think about dressing like you liked it – chances are you'd thrown that uniform in the dustbin two or three years before. Not that I had it in the first, let's make that clear.

People elsewhere, for some reason, thought that all young Yorkshiremen dressed like heavy metal fans – since Yorkshire was the least hip and happening place in the country, all the young people of the province must obviously like the least hip and happening music available, i.e. heavy metal. I know this because I was resident in Manchester by this time (if you remember), mingling with trendy young students from all corners of the nation, and even beyond.

This is not the chip on my shoulder now, believe me, but I quickly came to realise that to many, Yorkshire was a cultural joke. It's easy to understand where they came from given that the Luddite attitude of older Tykes had become the staple material for comedians and sketch-writers. Monty Python have much to answer for. Yes, Yorkshiremen knew what they liked and liked what they knew, and all that. Heavy metal was proof of that; it was an outdated music form with a ridiculously outmoded macho, sexist attitude. Amazingly, some people even said it like it was a bad thing.

Seriously though, or nearly, there was something refreshing about the New Metal; rock bands making three-minute, radio-friendly singles was actually little short of revolutionary. Iron Maiden seemed to be guaranteed a place in the singles charts with every release from their debut in 1980; ten years later their 'Take Your Daughter to the Slaughter' amazingly went straight to Number One on its release. But contrary to popular opinion, Flight Lieutenant Dickinson and his crew of fellow Southern Softies didn't surge to the front of the movement until 1982.

Oh, I can't carry on dissing 'Dicko', can I? If he'd have been born twenty miles north-west of his actual birthplace, Bruce Dickinson would have been a headline act in the story of Yorkshire Rock and provided us – and most importantly me, the writer – with several pages of entertainment. Though the voice of Iron Maiden spent much of his childhood in Sheffield, he was actually born in the Nottinghamshire town of Worksop. And of course, apart from being a Metal screamer par excellence, the man has become something of a renaissance man, earning his stripes as a TV and radio presenter, author, tournament fencer, and literally earning them as an airline pilot. But... the detail missing from the C.V. is, most significantly, 'Yorkshireman'.

If Saxon and Def Leppard were Premiership new heavy metal outfits, Vardis were at least top of the next division, always seemingly pushing for promotion but not quite achieving it. Vardis were led impressively by Wakefield's Steve Zodiac – of course everyone from our area knew the Zodiac's of Wakefield. Okay, so that wasn't his real name – it was lifted from the Gerry Anderson puppet series of the 1960s, Fireball XL5. But it's a better stage name than most, showing at least the hint of a sense of humour often at a premium in Rock circles in these pre-Spinal Tap times.

Formed in 1978 around the considerable guitar skills of Zodiac, an Edgar Winter lookalike without the albino eyes, this local trio were at first known as Quo Vardis. But they dropped the 'Quo' bit for obvious reasons. Though Stevie Z was the main man in every way, the member of the threesome of most interest to yours truly was Alan Selway, who played bass in the Vardis frontline. Al Selway?! He lived in the next street from me in Normanton! More Pete Walker's mate than mine, he could have bloody joined our shed-band back in 1973 but at that point he was obviously hiding his light under a bushel, or at least his Fender Precision bass under his bed.

With a distinctive sound at the time, Vardis's first commitment to vinyl was the '100 MPH' extended-play, reflecting their high-tempo, high-energy riff-ological approach to the genre. They were a lot nearer Motorhead than any of the other bands of the metal new wave, playing a suped-up brand of boogie with a healthy dose of glam stomp thrown in for good, or rather badass measure.

Labelled marvellously as 'Wakefield's Electric Warriors', one observer of the Rock World described Vardis as being responsible for the 'democratisation of UK Rock'. Erm... yeah, nicely put. And Zodiac went all Sandie Shaw, actually playing barefoot on stage. A self-confessed Marc Bolan fan, your man displayed a nice line in self-deprecation, declaring that heavy metal was 'just entertainment' before he told *Sounds*' Des Moines in 1980 that they wanted "to get a different angle - and try to be original. If you don't want to try to be original, then you shouldn't be doing it. Unless you're just in it for a living, which I'm not. Like, I think Motorhead are originals . . . I've seen them, and I could quite happily have banged me head to them all night". And given a severe haircut, Zodiac could well have been a hero for a different set of fans – "like, we used to be billed as 'high energy rock', even during punk - in fact, I was always being asked to join punk bands - but I was into heavy metal so much, and wasn't going to change."

With the reputation as a startlingly vibrant live act, the support of the rock music press and his two (bare) feet firmly on the ground, Steve Zodiac and Vardis could and should have been big. So what went wrong?

All was going well after two well-received albums (though *Sounds* reviewed their second album as 'flat as a witch's tit' – hang on, weren't Witch's Tit a band from Rotherham?), they even opened the 'legendary' Heavy Metal Holocaust Festival in 1981, their fan base was growing more than steadily. And that Peel of Rock and Metal, Tommy Vance, positively loved them.

Then came that rather difficult third album – oh yes, or in Vardis's case, oh no. In their less-than-infinite wisdom, Vardis decided to stray away from the tried and trusted metal instrumentation and introduced piano and saxophone. Whoops. They might as well as have gone the full Spinal Tap nine-yards, and started playing free-form jazz.

In the immortal words of Tommy Cockles, they went from being the talk of the town to being the whisper of the village. Vardis never quite regained their promotion form and Steve Zodiac finally broke up the band in 1986. The ultimate reason appears to be rather vague, merely stating that Zodiac quit because of 'disagreements with people in the music industry'. Both he and Selway are reported to be in the teaching profession these days, with Zodiac teaching music in London, and my fellow Normantonian teaching Audio Engineering in New Zealand. But did they make their mark on rock 'n' roll? Hell, yes! Vardis are looked on now as a pioneering metal band, cited as a major influence by no less than Metallica. Blimey.

Question: how near is Saltburn-by-the-Sea to Middlesbrough? Yes, we're back on this again. It's very close, is the answer, within 12 miles to be more precise. And like its larger industrial neighbour, Saltburn has a Teesside postcode these days with North Yorkshire merely its largely unwritten ceremonial county, but I have no doubt that, in truth, the little seaside town is Yorkshire through and through. And why's that? Because Saltburn's most famous son, David Coverdale, never misses an opportunity to publically flag up his Yorkshire roots, and I don't mean the greying ones of his crazy rock 'n' roll barnet either.

Coverdale first strutted his cock-rocking stuff on the national, even world stage back in 1973 when, as a complete unknown, he took over as lead singer of Rock Titans, Deep Purple no less, from the departing Ian Gillan. Allegedly, their first choice to replace Gillan was, you guessed it, Paul Rodgers. But in the end, Coverdale got the gig. According to my mate Keith from Stockton, his appointment was greeting back in the Teesside area with some amazement – 'Coverdale?... He couldn't shout 'coal' down a back alley!'

The singer's previous experience had been as a member of North-East bluesy soul outfit, The Government, then briefly the pleasingly titled Fabulosa Brothers, and finally local rock combo, Magdalene. But of course, becoming the voice of one of unquestionably the biggest bands on the planet quickly propelled Coverdale to Rock God status, a position he understandably capitalised on when Purple split up (for the first time) in 1976, by forming his own band, Whitesnake, who almost immediately went colossal in the UK. It took a few years before Coverdale and his ever-changing backing band went globally colossal, thanks mainly to the onset of *MTV* and the law of any rock video having to feature a scantily clad 'rock chick' or five.

They accidentally-on-purpose strayed into the highly lucrative territory of soft rock – 'Poodle Rock' as it started to become known not least because of the ridiculous, but entertaining hairdos on show - retaining the rock raunchiness that was required of a band calling itself Whitesnake (rumours that 'Bigknob' was another band name considered, remain unconfirmed). In a moment of pure Spinal Tap-ness, Dishy Dave said "People saw my lyrics as sexist when I thought they were sexy". Coverdale invited his fans to 'come and shake with the 'Snake' – classic. How could we resist?"

Well quite easily actually. The 'Snake were not really my cup of tea, as is possibly patently obvious, but in the scheme of things, I quite like that Coverdale bloke. Why? Look through some of his interviews on the Internet, and as well as coming over as less than precious, possessing a self-effacing sense of humour, the man's not averse to referring to his Yorkshireness, even occasionally dropping into the dialect. Again, I tried to talk to the man himself, but yet again my requests came to nowt. I was actually frustratingly close to securing an interview with Def Leppard's Joe Elliot, but as with Biff Byford, I ended up empty-handed. These rockers are elusive to say the least – most of them chose to flee their British nest long ago.

Aye, and there's the rub... balanced against this evidence suggesting that David Coverdale deserves to be honoured as a Yorkshire Pop Star, is the fact that he applied for and gained U.S. citizenship in 2007, actually giving him a dual UK/US citizenship status. Consequently, the man with his shaking snake, in my book at least, is only half a Yorkshire Pop Star, end of. Still, better half than not at all…

Regardless of such outrageous controversy, Yorkshire's starring role in the ongoing evolution of British Rock is beyond question. Love it or hate it, heavy metal is still one of the most popular modern music genres in the world, Western or otherwise. Even in the pre-*MTV* period, heavy metal bands knew how to behave like stars, even when they were just playing to an apathetic set of pub regulars. I know – I remember witnessing such a spectacle. They could teach a thing or two to these punks looking to actually stick around for longer than the gob stains on their leathers.

But some of those punks already had the chops to do it for themselves; all they needed now were the career opportunities.

Chapter Seven

Thankfully Not Being Kevin Rowland, It Doesn't Apply.

I really liked Dexys Midnight Runners, and on occasion, loved them. Loved the first single, 'Dance Stance', and obviously loved it even more when 'Geno' went to Number One. Then the album came out. 'Searching for The Young Soul Rebels' was a classic, I agree. But erm… what was that track all about? You know the one – 'Thankfully Not Living in Yorkshire It Doesn't Apply'.

Cheeky twat. He was having a 'go', wasn't he? What was it - something about keeping him away from Leeds? Okay – so in that fine city, some people did walk around with frowns on their faces and you did get in the odd scrap, but come on Kev, neither Birmingham nor Wolverhampton were hardly a laugh a minute in those days – in fact, are they now? Neither has ever been the British equivalent of Paris, Rome or Madrid in my experience, teeming with tortured poets, artists and musicians, each spreading deep and meaningful humanity

113

through their art. If you'd bothered to stick around in the White Rose County for a bit longer, Kevin, you'd have found a few soul rebels and passion a-plenty, cocker.

He was just miffed I think. Before they hit on the idea of the decidedly anti-fashionable stevedore outfits – donkey jackets and woolly caps – Kev's fledgling Dexys appeared on stage wearing the kind of clobber that would have made Boy George blush. Their dandy threads, avec lace, silks and what-have-you, together with their made-up faces were perhaps months, if not years ahead of their time – 'New Romantics' took up the look at the start of the eighties and never got bottled off the stage like Kev had. Maybe he of the tawdry 'tache knew what was coming and was jealous; a new glossy era of pop was just around the corner with, amazingly, Yorkshire at the centre of it.

When pop commentators look back on the early years of the 1980s, the phrase 'like punk never happened' inevitably gets wheeled out at some juncture. The truth is, the eighties, musically at least, were exactly as they were because punk happened. Punk re-invigorated a tired, sterile pop culture and hundreds, nay thousands of youngsters who would never have otherwise dreamt of performing, recording and posing for the cameras, suddenly realised that this pop business was far from rocket science.

There was a delicious juxtaposition at work in UK youth culture at that time. Public Enemy Number One was Margaret Thatcher, closely followed by her government hoods, systematically stripping the towns and cities of industrial Britain of their livelihood and dignity, and in turn depriving the young people therein of their immediate prospects of work, prosperity and happiness. You can almost hear the swirling icy wind that brings in the first few bars of The Specials' 'Ghost Town', just thinking about it.

Then on the other hand, there was the shiny new pop sensibility of the post-punk generation, with music and pictures serving up sheer escapism on a grand scale.

The main players in this scenario were young people who had first had a go in those halcyon days of 'learn three chords and form a band' in 1977. The ones who rose to the top from this legion were the clever punks who were most prepared to dress outrageously and resort to the shock tactics of punk if all else, i.e. the music, failed - Adam Ant, Boy George, etc.

In 1978, a new glossy pop magazine had hit the shelves from a rather unlikely source. Smash Hits was ostensibly your dumbed down pop mag before dumbing down was even invented. Strangely, its founder was Nick Logan, the highly respected ex-editor of the *NME*, who would go on to bring monthly style bible The Face into the publishing world. The content of Smash Hits was firmly aimed at record-buying teenagers, not least because it published the song lyrics to the Top 20 chart singles, ideal for when you wanted to sing along in front of the bedroom mirror. Not that I myself did that, obviously.

But by its very nature – full-colour gloss, superficial interviews with an onus on frothy entertainment rather than insightful information – Smash Hits could have been beamed up from the glam era of ten years previously. It was irresistibly entertaining.

There were acts born to be on the cover of Smash Hits, and undoubtedly several more put together with the glossy mag in mind. If you knew nothing of their history, you'd be sure that The Human League fell into the second camp. But weren't they lying in a critical state in the emergency unit of Saint Pop's Hospital at the end of the seventies?

The upshot of the aforementioned Ware/Oakey friction was that Martyn Ware and Ian Craig Marsh broke away to do their own thing, leaving Oakey with the haircut and the name... at a price of 10% of future profits. A wise bit of business by Ware and Marsh, or what?

Oakey had the image and all-round technician Adrian Wright alongside him, but bugger all else. So did he go recruiting down a cocktail bar? No – he went down a well-known Sheffield Club called The Crazy Daisy, and saw two local lasses dancing in a rather ordinary fashion – 'you were dancing in a rather ordinary fashion when I met you two' doesn't quite scan does it?

Nevertheless, it proved to be a moment of inspiration for your man – he roped in Joanne Catherall and Susan Sulley as backing vocalists for Human League Mk 2. His most important recruitment though, less referred to for some reason, was that of Jo Callis, erstwhile guitarist with The Rezillos. Rotherham born Callis was a highly talented musician with a top-notch pop sensibility, having had hits in both singles and album charts with the cartoon-esque Edinburgh punksters.

Together with the obligatory respected producer, Martin Rushent, the band put together a pop masterpiece for the times, both catchy in a sing-along chorus kind of way, and danceable with an irresistible electronic pulse rhythm running throughout. 'Dare' was the classic album that spawned numerous sparkling singles, topped off by 'Don't You Want Me', the track that Oakey actually didn't want released as a single yet sold nearly one-and-a-half million copies – a scale of success that's hard to imagine in an age when five thousand downloads guarantees a place in the charts. The accompanying video was seen as ground-breaking; shot on film rather than videotape, the promo was like a mini-drama within a mini-movie.

Though the make-up wasn't dispensed with – Joanne and Susan doubtlessly enjoyed bitching about Phil's lip-glossing technique – the lopsided haircut was. It was replaced by an oddly normal cut that revealed that Oakey was indeed one handsome dog. As a band, the second incarnation of the Human League was nigh on visually perfect for the day. And aurally, they set the standards for any other electronic acts looking to storm the charts.

But what of Oakey's old colleagues, the two computer nerds who had actually started the whole thing off? Martyn Ware and Ian Marsh had wasted no time in both creating a new agenda and finding a new singer.

Glenn Gregory, you may remember, was apparently in line to be the face and voice of the Human League before ugly old Phil Oakey got the gig. The man himself explains – "me, Martyn and Ian were in bands previous to the Human

League and I always used to end up being the singer. They were mostly made-up bands who never actually played. We had one called 'VD Kay and the Studs', and put up loads of posters with this band name on saying *'Dr Who* – out now'. But there were all these people thinking 'great there's a Sheffield punk band', and going into shops asking for a record that didn't exist."

One previous band that definitely did exist, the wonderfully named Musical Vomit, even numbered the bloke who ended up playing drum-playing Vernon in *Coronation Street* actually on drums – life imitating art-in-the-future, if you get what I mean.

But back to VD and his Studs… "we eventually got a gig at a local art college supporting The Drones (sizable Manchester punk band of the time) and we thought 'fucking hell, we better get something together!' We got two of the guys from Cabaret Voltaire, two from a band called 2.3, and we went on stage and did a 20-minute version of the *Dr Who* theme with me screaming and wailing. We refused to get off the stage because we were having such a good time but The Drones wanted to come on. The crowd loved it so we went into this impromptu song called 'The Drones want to come on now' – their manager kept coming on stage, and we kept kicking him off. It was great.

"It was just after that gig that I decided to move down to London again because the music scene was hotter down there and I'd started taking photos for the music papers. And it was almost that same weekend that Martyn and Ian decided to form the Human League. Had I not gone down to London – and Phil (Oakey) would agree with this – I would have probably ended up being the original singer with the Human League, because, by default, I just used to end up being the singer of whatever we were doing."

Glenn followed the progress of his old Sheffield pals closely from down in London, putting the band up in his flat when they played down there and always taking the photos at their London gigs.

Fast forward three years… "I had to go back up to Sheffield to take pictures of Joe Jackson live, and I met up with Martyn. He was asking too many questions…

Was I happy in London? Was I happy doing what I was doing? What this was leading to was the fact that he and Ian were splitting from the Human League, did I want to come back up to Sheffield and be the singer with whatever project they did next? That was the Friday… I was back living at me Mum and Dad's in Sheffield the following Tuesday."

Things moved unfeasibly fast for Heaven 17 – the name lifted from 'A Clockwork Orange' - and before they knew it, they really were the hippest new band, not just in old Sheffield town, but in the UK. "It was all very quick – I'd say we'd recorded 'Fascist Groove Thang' within about two weeks. It was like, 'it's fucking great that – let's have another one of them!' But you've got to remember when that single came out, it wasn't a particularly nice time, there were skinheads back on the streets and right wing movements on the rise. We genuinely kind of feared for ourselves when we put that out - we thought we might get firebombed or something!"

Lyrically, 'Fascist Groove Thang' took a timely swipe at the sway to the right in both British and American politics, and the frightening rise of the extreme right on the streets of Britain. Heaven 17 had made a record of relevance both musically and politically.

"After it came out, we stayed up all night and went down the train station to buy the music papers when they came in early the next morning. It was like 'bloody hell, it's 'Record of the Week' in *Sounds*!'… and 'bloody hell it's the same in the *NME*!'. We were just gobsmacked, y'know - Paul Morley, full of prose, exalting us!"

They'd certainly hit the ground running and if anything, the instant success diverted Ware, Marsh and Gregory away from their original manifesto. "The main thing was that Martyn and Ian didn't want to be a band as such. They'd toured a lot with the Human League and it cost them a lot of money, and in their view wasted quite a lot of time. It wasn't moving them forward. I think that was part of the reason for the split – Phil wanted to go more mainstream, I think. Martyn and Ian wanted to set up what would be basically a production company (British Electric Foundation) – it was going to be almost like their own little record label, with them writing and producing. The people at Virgin were totally cool with that."

But before BEF could make its own mark, Heaven 17 had a debut album to make, and what an album it was, blowing away the electronic powder puff of the New Romantic competition with funky grooves supporting a wry observation on the crass nature of Thatcher's new British vision, and indeed the capitalist world at large. "We recorded 'Penthouse and Pavement' in the same studio, at the same time as Human League were recording 'Dare' – it was the old Human League studio that they co-owned. We worked shifts, taking it in turns, one week you'd work nights with the other band recording in the days, and the next week you'd swap over. And Phil was sleeping in the room upstairs from the studio. People think the split was really acrimonious, but it was more that daft things were said, sometimes in a jokey way – Martyn and Phil were both intelligent headstrong people, and they did clash from time to time. But two very good albums came out of all that. The record company (Virgin) were laughing – they got two bands for the price of one."

There must have been a competitive edge between the two camps? "There was a total competitive edge between Phil and Martyn. Phil has since said to me that, at that point, he just wanted to grind Martyn and Ian's noses in it. I wasn't as bothered about it, but each of them wanted to prove that they were the best."

For the record, 'Penthouse and Pavement' came out before 'Dare' in 1981, and quickly became the album to have in your collection. Glenn admits that they 'stumbled' into the style that served them so well, writing songs in a synth stylee, but then adding the more traditional guitar, bass and drums. But what about the political element of the lyrics that distinguished the songs on 'Penthouse'? "There wasn't any pressure to have that content and edge - that's just what we were like and what we were doing. A lot of the second album was the same. It wasn't contrived. Later on, you did think 'oh fucking hell – I wish

I could write a song about going to the park with me bird.' We had a veto on certain words in songs – like love, dream, etc. Writing emotional songs about relationships becomes very difficult when you can't use certain words. 'Let Me Go' was about as emotional as it got for us – it's a love song but there's no mention of love in there."

But the 'instant success' of 'Penthouse and Pavement' was only half the story. Once they were able to rein Heaven 17 in a smidgen, the trio started thinking about other projects with BEF, the most noteworthy of which was 'Music of Quality and Distinction', an album of various vocalists covering other people's songs and getting the BEF production treatment. It was actually a novel idea at the time with such collaborations being something of a rarity in 1982. "Virgin loved the idea – they were still a bit indie themselves, pretty punk. They were brilliant when we set about getting hold of the singers – it was like 'my auntie's friend knows his hairdresser, I'll get his phone number."

It turns out that they couldn't afford James Brown, but they got the likes of Billy McKenzie, Sandie Shaw and indeed, Tina Turner. "We went to Hollywood to meet up with Tina, and at the time she was doing pretty poor venues, some Vegas gigs and what-have-you. It was like 'bloody hell, we're in Tina Turner's house!'" The collaboration, resulting in 'Let's Stick Together', rescued and reinvigorated Turner's career, propelling the singer into the most mega-successful period of her 80 years in showbiz. Or something like that.

All good stuff, but undoubtedly, all this other BEF activity served as support to Heaven 17. Their high point of popularity came with the 'Temptation' single, featuring added vocals from the fabulous Carol Kenyon. Reaching Number Two in the charts, Glenn Gregory agrees was one of those 'It Doesn't Get Much Better Than This' moments – "there's a point at which you think you are David Bowie... yeah, I'll write 'The Lodger', then I'll star in films, and I'll have me pick of supermodels. But of course it doesn't quite pan out like that."

But this era was very much the Return of the 'Pop Star'. Was the Smash Hits-type pop ethic at odds with where they'd come from? "Yeah – we were never completely comfortably with it. I look now at some of the photos we were in and think how did they get us to do that? More to the point, why did we do it?! But that's just the way it was going at the time so to swing against it was quite difficult."

Was it indeed like punk never happened or did punk philosophies remain intact? "Without punk the Human League would never have existed, so neither would Heaven 17. But punk was really just rock 'n' roll; electronic music was actually 'the new thing', making the most of technology. And of course it was the *MTV* age now – so rather than spending a hundred-and-fifty grand on going live, you stupidly used to spend the same amount on one video! Technology was changing, not just in terms of the instrumentation of a band but the way that people viewed and listened to music."

It was a good way into their existence before Heaven 17 actually performed live though. "We were seen as very cool and hip – we actually played Studio 54 in New York just before it closed. John Lydon came to see us then though he didn't let on – he's a friend now. But he said he liked what we were doing from the early days." Ah, the butter-loving Mr Lydon/Rotten, and the same man who dismissed The Human League as 'art school trendies'.

It's amazing to think that although the city itself was hardly a social hive of activity in the early 1980s – the Leadmill had only just opened - Sheffield was turning out other fine pop acts on a regular basis at this point. It pains me to say it, as a Yorkshireman from the Western sector, but Sheffield always seemed to have that faint whiff of cosmopolitan sophistication that set it apart from the rest of the county.

Apart from the admirable Cabaret Voltaire, themselves heading towards a more danceable brand of electronic experimentation, there was the similarly industrial Clock DVA and the pop-ier Comsat Angels. The former, Adi Newton's constantly experimental band, never quite crossed the great divide from critical acclaim to commercial success. The Comsats were coming more from the Joy Division school of pop with a danceable melody shining through their bleakness. Strangely, Robert 'Addicted to Love' Palmer had a hand in their career, encouraging Island Records to sign the band, then co-producing their first album for the label. Sadly, despite beavering away for over ten years and getting through nearly as many record labels, the Angels never made the big breakthrough either.

But more significantly at the start of the decade, a local band called Vice Versa made the remarkable transition from punk also-rans to the perfect pop package, renaming themselves ABC. The catalyst for this was indisputably the entry into the fold of one Martyn Fry; he'd gone to interview Vice Versa for his fanzine and ended up becoming their new frontman. Fry was strictly speaking a Mancunian who lived in Sheffield, but his band mates were all bona fide locals, born-and-bred.

What Fry brought to the band, apart from a decent voice and a nice line in rhyming couplets, was a single-minded thirst for doing things right with a view to making it big. As Fry told the BBC's Pop Britannia, "we were really trying to be pop stars. Pop was a revolutionary idea after punk. We wanted to be on *Top of the Pops* – we wanted to be popular. The gold lame suit was an audacious move – it was about looking into pop and rock mythology, Elvis etc. We wanted to be identified as *pop*."

After the debut ABC single, 'Tears Are Not Enough', tested the water and charted, the album 'Lexicon of Love' pulled out all the commercial stops and 'defined the aesthetic of post-punk pop'. Fry had specifically picked out Trevor Horn to produce the record, Horn having been the talented ears behind the chart hits of featherlite pop-duo Dollar, and of course late-seventies one-hit wonders, The Buggles, of 'Video Killed the Radio Star' fame.

Horn revealed the thinking behind the ABC's debut long-player to the BBC: "it was intended as a dance record. The guys went to a club in Sheffield – they wanted to make a record that would get played in their club and people would dance to it."

The result was a typically plushly produced affair, replete with gorgeous string arrangements – courtesy of Anne Dudley – providing the perfect platform for the irresistible smart songsmithery of Fry. Choc-a-bloc with potential Top Ten singles, just three were plundered and to good effect, making ABC perhaps the pop act of 1982. Alongside Billy McKenzie and the Associates' wonderful 'Sulk', 'Lexicon of Love' had to be one of the albums of the year.

Fry was there among the new breed of intelligent, clued-up pop stars of the day. There was a tongue-in-cheek element to ABC that made them almost impossible to dislike, and it was indicative of the times. 'It was a more innocent age' said Fry, "far less corporate – with self-made stars like Boy George and Adam Ant".

It has been said that ABC should have perhaps held back a couple of those 'Lexicon of Love' tracks for their follow-up, because it was always going to be a tough act to follow. For whatever reason, Fry and his associates chose not to employ the considerable services of Trevor Horn for 'Beauty Stab' – it has since been opined that Horn's contribution to that glorious debut has been over-stated, but the fact is that the old Buggle became *the* producer-in-demand because of 'Lexicon of Love', and the subsequent work of ABC has forever been measured against the lofty standards of that record. The second album would have been seen as a fine effort had it been by anyone else, and there have been many top tracks from ABC since. But none as good as those on that bloody 'Lexicon of Love'. It must be a burden.

But in a way, the quality of the music was, at this stage of the proceedings, in danger of becoming less important than the quality of the video that accompanied it. The dawn of *MTV* meant that image and packaging was more important than ever. In some cases, both single and video were first class, and the former could live without the latter – ABC's promo for 'Poison Arrow' was directed by film-making enfant terrible Julian Temple and very good it was too, but the song was better.

But, at the risk of sounding irritatingly worthy, videos provided the

123

opportunity for blatant exploitation… 'Bouncing Bosoms' again anyone? Ah yes – Robert Palmer! Be honest, if you think 1980s pop videos, it's difficult not to think of that particular video. But you'll always think of the video before you think of the song. 'Addicted to Love' cemented Palmer's place as coffee-table blue-eyed watered-down soul-singer for the middle-class music listener. It's hard to hear any trace of soul in the hits that the man's best remembered for, but trust me, he did have a fine soulful voice. Once his record company saw the gap for another slick, smooth operator whose records would fit nicely between Rod Stewart's and Bryan Ferry's, the Robster was on a sure-fire winner. He even looked like he went to Ferry's tailor for his suits, but the tailor didn't need as much material for pint-size Palmer.

The fact that this Yorkshire singer was on higher-than-highly respected Island Records should be enough to tell you that he must have been a talented chap despite how annoying his later career became – forming a 'supergroup' with members of Duran Duran?… Do me a favour. But fair play to him, Robert Palmer enjoyed a highly successful global pop career up to his death in 2003. Not bad for a mere lad from Batley.

If you bought a Robert Palmer record during the eighties, there's every chance you bought a Chris Rea record too. In fact I'll bet my Dire Straits box set on it. We can add Rea to the 'they're-from-the-North-East-but-they're-still-Yorkshire' list. But it's fair to say that the Middlesbrough singer-songwriter has had a rather odd career in a quite literally uneven way. It's hard to pick out a definitive purple period in his thirty odd years in the music industry but his sales figures reveal a highly successful career by most musician's standards.

The son of an Italian ice-cream retailer, the young Chris Rea's main claim to fame in his early music career was that he replaced our great mate David Coverdale in a band called Magdalene after the old snake-shaker was poached by Deep Purple in 1975. Once he'd gone solo and got snapped up by Magnet Records, Rea's career got off to a flying start as far back as the post-punk days of 1978. The lead single from his debut album went Top 30 in both the UK and the USA; many, myself included, would argue however that he's never made a better record than 'Fool (If You Think It's Over)'. The album was titled 'Whatever Happened to Benny Santini?', a reference to the stage name that Rea's record company had originally wanted him to adopt. After the album sold rather well in the States, it looked like the Boro boy was going to be a big star Stateside. But actually, it all went a bit a quiet in the early 1980s for the gravel-voiced performer. His standing in Europe was building nicely but he couldn't buy a hit at home, let alone in the U.S.

Fortunes improved with the 'On the Beach' album in 1986, though the title track didn't trouble the singles charts compiler first time round. It was 'Let's Dance' (nothing to do with the Bowie song) that promoted Chris Rea to a higher profile, TV appearances, sustained radio-play and the charts of both varieties. Though he's perhaps best known for his only Top 10 single, 'Road to Hell', it's the success of his albums between 1987 and 1998 that saw Rea become a major act. The fact that he's sold over 30 million albums worldwide means he's something of a dark horse in the Successful Yorkshire Pop Star stakes – largely unfancied, but a good 'stayer', and perhaps worth backing for a place at the line.

So while Sheffield was perhaps the most fashionable local source of hit-scoring pop acts, in the early-eighties at least, the rest of Yorkshire did most definitely make a telling contribution too. Whilst some of the less forward-thinking areas were still busy discovering punk, some of its expatriates were definitely in the thick of it, a-moving and a-shaking.

For the first time, Halifax figures in the story. Tom Bailey, the main man in the Thompson Twins, was born in Halifax, but was brought up in the Chesterfield area. Actually a classically trained pianist – true apparently - Tom taught music in a Sheffield school prior to his pop career taking off. I recall seeing the Thompson Twins supporting The Teardrop Explodes back in 1980, when there were seven of them in the band (at least) and the music they propelled at the drunken student audience bore next to no resemblance to the formulaic pop tunes the down-sized Twins offered up two or three years later.

If any band was shaped and packaged to look the part for the video age, it was the Thompson Twins – a white guy with red mullet, a blonde woman dressed as a man, and a black dude with dreads. If that doesn't sound like a winner, put a skunk on my head and call me Limahl. Ten Top 40 hits inside three years, half of which went Top Ten, is a pretty impressive record, even if they never sounded like the real deal to these ears. Apparently, Tom Bailey was once shot at in the Khyber Pass; I didn't much rate the Thompson Twins but I didn't think they were that bad.

What about Leeds? Big city, bright lights, efficient bus service… surely something was bubbling under? There was – but it was a rather un-Yorkshire act in every way. Not least because it was, yet again, a pair of bloody students, studying in Leeds, who made it big in a Number One fashion.

Soft Cell was perhaps the original electronica duo, maybe even the template for electronica acts of the future, with one member pressing the knobs and plonking the keys, and the other adding vocals. 'Flat as a fart', said my Mam when she first heard that voice. It was hard to disagree at times – Marc Almond really wasn't the greatest singer in the world; he may not have even been the best singer in Soft Cell, but since Dave Bell kept his gob firmly shut, we'll never know.

There was something more than slightly sleazy about Soft Cell, and not just their chosen image and subsequent packaging. 'Non-Stop Erotic Cabaret' was the album, yet there was something unsettlingly un-erotic about Almond – or 'The Walnut' as my mate Mick creatively christened the fella. Whatever, it has to be said that their version of 'Tainted Love' still passes the test nearly thirty years on. It was the biggest selling British hit single of 1981 and the record that turned an interesting club act into a chart-topping pop stars. The only mistake they made with 'Tainted Love' was putting another cover version on the B-side, namely 'Where Did Our Love Go?'. Had they thought to put one of their own compositions on there, they would have actually received some royalties from a record that sold millions all over the world.

Almond and Ball developed their act whilst studying at Leeds Polytechnic school of art, and like the Gang of Four before them, are worthy of special mention in our extended analysis of all things Pop and Yorkshire, because their residence in the Leeds at the time undoubtedly contributed to the music they made. Almond lived in a less-than-salubrious bedsit in the nearly notorious suburb of Chapeltown, and worked in the cloakroom of the trendy new Leeds venue of the time, The Warehouse, the club where Soft Cell actually made their live debut in 1979.

But Almond had a history in the Leeds area way before his student days; though born in Southport, he spent much of his youth in the leafy Leeds suburb of Horsforth, not entirely happy days by his own account, but certainly they informed much of the lyrical content in his songwriting. Urban myths aside – you know the one – Almond and Ball deserve their place in the Yorkshire Hall of Pop Fame. They shone brightly, in a red light in the bedroom window kind of way, for just the right stretch of time before calling it quits.

The art departments of Leeds University, and Leeds Polytechnic as it was, proved to be a great source of raw pop star material in the late 1970s. Members of Scritti Politti, including the decidedly un-Tetleybitterman-esque lead singer, Green Gartside, had been students in Leeds back then but had long left the city before they embarked on their poptastic career in the 1980s. The late Frank Tovey also figured in these ranks before making his mark on electronic music as Fad Gadget. Described by *Sounds* as 'the bumbling but talented Dr Who of electro-pop', Tovey was a true entertainer, prone to giving himself the tar and feather treatment on stage, or even worse/better, stripping naked and covering himself in shaving cream. Inspired.

In the same way that lazy observers of music like to lump every new act of 1977 into the punk bracket, any electronic sounding act of 1981 is somehow seen as New Romantic. If that was accurate, Sheffield would have been the New Romantic capital of the world. It wasn't – it didn't want to be. Was the New Romantic movement confined to London? If Birmingham's Duran Duran were part of that scene, no it wasn't. But did we in old romantic Yorkshire have any true part in it?

Hell, yes! Look at the personnel involved on Visage's 'Fade to Grey', one of the records credited with kick-starting the New Romantic thingy - two members of Ultravox are implicated. So Midge Ure is really a Yorkshireman? No, of course not. But the really talented member of Ultravox was. The man who played that violin break in 'Vienna' was born and bred in Huddersfield. Yes, Billy Currie had been a founding member of Ultravox along with original vocalist John Foxx back when Midge still had enough hair to forge a quiff and front Scottish teen-sensations, Slik.

Ultravox – not unlike the Human League – were pioneers of accessible British electronic music during the punk period, putting three albums out and working with such production luminaries as Brian Eno and Connie Plank. Currie even guested on Gary Numan's breakthrough recordings in 1978/79. But it really wasn't until 'Vienna' that Ultravox and Billy Currie entered the nation's pop consciousness. It's an oft-quoted fact that the single was kept off the top of the charts by 'Shadapp You Face' by Joe Dolce. That nugget of info' was funny until I realised that abomination had stopped another Tyke from claiming a Number One. Vienna – it finally means something to me.

This little pocket of pop history may have had its London boys staking their claim for supremacy but to my mind the best moments belong to Sheffield and Yorkshire. It's with a beautiful symmetry then that the three main protagonist factions got back together in 2008 for… muted fanfare… yes, a Reunion Tour. These are two words that have been known to strike dread into the stoutest of

Rockin' Bobbin! Ronnie Hilton went from working in a Leeds sewing factory to being, arguably Yorkshire's first Pop Star.

Coming down the line from Halifax, Don Lang brought Rock 'n' Roll into 1950s living rooms with his 'Frantic Five' on 'Six-Five Special'.

All hail the musical genius that is John Barry, from the dance halls of York to the Hollywood silver screen via the Hit Parade of the early 1960s.

From gas fitter to Woodstock legend... he might not remember much of the sixties but Joe Cocker remains one of Sheffield's biggest pop exports.

No it's not David Bowie! Coming out Sheffield's R 'n' B scene, 3 Top Ten singles turned Dave Berry into a bona fide pop star in the mid 60s.

Double Vision... from a showbiz background, Leeds twins Paul and Barry Ryan had their big moment when the latter wrote 'Eloise' for the former to record.

Flexing his plecs... Hull's Mick Ronson was Bowie's onstage sidekick and musical rock throughout his mega-successful early 1970s Glam period.

After years of toil, Bradford's Pauline Matthews finally made the big time as Kiki Dee thanks to a Number One duet with Elton John.

Star of Glastonbury 2009, Sheffield's Tony Christie is a musical survivor, with much more than 'Amarillo' stored in a forty-year back catalogue.

'Yellow River' by Leeds band Christie was not only the first Yorkshire chart topper of the 1970s, it got murdered every night by several cabaret bands.

Hats off to 'em. Be Bop Deluxe, led by Bill Nelson (holding guitar) put Wakefield on the modern music map for the first time in the early 70s.

Now on the Stateside alternative country scene, Leeds-based students The Mekons first came to the fore as John Peel favourites during the punk era.

Magnificently moody, indisputably influential. 'Honorary' Yorkshire band Gang of Four spearheaded Leeds's contribution to the punk revolution.

Yorkshire bands don't come bigger than Def Leppard; the Sheffield rockers went mega in the 1980s thanks to MTV and stadium rock.

Son of a Bitch! Well Barnsley rockers Saxon actually, featuring the famous singing teeth of Biff Byford. But alas here, he'd forgotten his photo teeth.

Suave, sophisticated and from Batley, Robert Palmer enjoyed the most successful period of his career with the advent of the music video in the 1980s.

Fronting the ever-changing line-up of Whitesnake, David Coverdale was plucked from North Yorkshire obscurity to become vocalist with Deep Purple in the mid-70s.

Agadon't! Here in the days before they slimmed down to a pineapple-pushing, tree-shaking duo, Black Lace were Ossett's priceless gift to pop.

Neither a gold suit nor a Look of Love in evidence with Martyn Fry here, but Sheffield's ABC positively sparkled in Pop's resurgence in the 1980s.

Modelling for Habitat, it's Human League Mk 2. Sheffield's Phil Oakey and his new colleagues struck immediate pop gold with their landmark album, 'Dare'.

Are they having a laugh? Sisters of Mercy must take much of the responsibility for turning Leeds into Goth Rock Central in the 1980s.

Tainted fact: Soft Cell were technically a Leeds duo, but students Marc Almond (left) and David Ball were originally from Southport and Blackpool respectively.

What, no dancing girls? Ware and Marsh quit the Human League, added Gregory, and gave Sheffield another electronic success story, Heaven 17.

A bit of a Cult... Before he hooked up with Billy Duffy and went 100% rock, Bradford's Ian Astbury (in hat), led 'Goth Rockers' Southern Death Cult.

London 0 Hull 4?! Everybody's favourite Marxist Christian a cappella act of the 1980s, The Housemartins.

Still going strong, Leeds's The Wedding Present succeeded The Smiths as the Indie music fan's favourite band at the end of the 1980s.

Different Class. Sheffield's Pulp were well into the second decade of their existence before 'Common People' made a star of Sir Jarvis Cocker.

Keighley's biggest chart act, sorry, only chart act was Terrorvision, a laddish Britrock tonic in the mid-1990s era of laddish Britpop bands.

Not quite the Resurrection, John Squire's Seahorses again brought sleepy old York into the realms of sexy young Britpop, featuring a trio of local musicians.

Lass Power! Melanie Brown - or 'Scary Spice' - was Leeds's contribution to the worldwide pop phenomenon that was the Spice Girls.

But there are only five of them... with their quintet of hit singles, York's Shed Seven had more Top 40 successes than any other chart act in 1996.

Come and have a go... Out of Armley (no, not the jail), agit-popsters Chumbawamba became unlikely chart stars in 1997 with 'Tubthumping'.

Tune! Coming out of both the Dance Revolution and Leeds, Jez and Tim of the Utah Saints were greeted as pioneers of sampled dance music.

The Peters and Lee of dance music? Sheffield-based duo Moloko went Top Ten via the clubs of Ibiza at the end of the last millennium.

Back to Reality TV... Bradford's Gareth Gates became an 'overnight success' thanks to Pop Idol.

Guitarist-for-hire Richard Hawley stepped into his own personal spotlight with celebrated solo albums in the 'Noughties'.

Whatever we say they are, that is what they're not. Sheffield's popular beat group, and award show pranksters, the Arctic Monkeys.

Back of the net! Leeds band Kaiser Chiefs' success started with a glorious award-winning 2005 at the vanguard of the press-spun 'New Yorkshire' movement.

We're Jarman... Only Wakefield's second chart-infiltrating band, the new-improved Cribs are still determinedly punk, still determinedly independent.

He could have been a contender, and could still be; as the politicised voice of Reverend and the Makers, Jon McClure is already a Sheffield Star.

Strictly for the birds... Rothwell's Pigeon Detectives came out of the shadows of the Kaiser Chiefs with an extended run of Top 40 hit singles in 2007.

music fans, and often with good reason. A few years ago I myself was persuaded to go and see none other than Kevin Rowland and what were now his Dexys Midnight Strollers on one of these tours and – joking aside – it was hard not to regret that I hadn't seen them in their pomp when Kev was young and fit enough to sing every song at the tempo they were recorded at.

The Steel City Reunion had been touted for years, with obvious reservations stopping it happening until ABC, The Human League and Heaven 17 finally agreed the time was right. It was an unqualified success for all concerned, Glenn Gregory included. "It was great – I loved it. I thought the Human League were fantastic, a great show. I've always loved the Human League though. Honest."

Born of a period when style-obsessed pop acts straddled thin lines between glamorous, pompous and ludicrous, it's pleasing to report that the likes of 'Love Action', 'Temptation' and 'The Look of Love' have stood the test of time.

Detractors referred to the sounds coming out of Sheffield as 'synthetic pop' – where were the guitars? They were all in West Yorkshire, matey. As the alternative music scene became the mainstream, a new pop, or rather 'rock' underbelly had to be lovingly fed and stroked. Goth rock… like synthesizers never happened.

Chapter Eight

Paint It Blacker.

Hey, we liked our slogans in the 1980s, didn't we? Slogans on T-shirts, on record sleeves, on badges. The Musicians Union persisted in giving out stickers encouraging everyone to 'Keep Music Live', this despite the Human League Mk 1 having perverted the sentiment gloriously in their early days by displaying the alternative legend, 'Keep Music Dead' on stage. And whilst we had one highly successful band giving us 'Frankie Says Relax', we had Wham! saying 'Choose Life'; personally, I don't know how I'd have got through that period without those two nuggets of advice. On a more political level, the badge to wear in 1984 said 'Coal Not Dole', a show of support for the miners as they took on Thatcher's steamroller of a government.

Then there was 'Punk's Not Dead', a statement of defiance that in translation could only mean there were still some people dressing like punks, behaving like punks, and making music like punks, as though it was still 1977. If you still cared enough to think about it further, you could take that to mean that there were some people who had only just got the punk thing, or had only just got the opportunity to do the punk thing. A better badge would have read 'Punk's Not Dead… It's Just A Bit Poorly'.

While synthesizer-driven music was dominating the mainstream music scene, there were other movements giving continued endorsement to guitar bands. From Liverpool, there was 'Merseybeat the Sequel', spearheaded by Echo and the Bunnymen, Teardrop Explodes and Wah! Heat. From Glasgow, there was Postcard Records, with Orange Juice, Aztec Camera and Josef K representing 'the Sound of Young Scotland'.

And finally, and in many ways, most grimly, there was Goth Rock – possibly 'The Sound of Miserable Yorkshire'. Whilst the scenes from Liverpool and Glasgow between them nodded towards classic influences like The Velvet Underground, The Byrds, and 60s psychedelia, goth owed more to The Doors, The Stooges and even Leonard Cohen. Doom and gloom – what better place to be miserable than Yorkshire, the home of misery? There were times when this dank, dark music made Joy Division sound like Abba.

But at least it was what you could call another genuine 'scene' finding a home in our neck of the woods, even if it was deep down in the darkest, spookiest corner of the woods. Southern Death Cult, Sisters of Mercy, The March Violets, Red Lorry Yellow Lorry and Danse Society all carried the flag bearing Yorkshire's White Rose – actually if they had carried any flag, it'd surely have been a big black one bearing the face of that Keith Richard lookalike, The Grim Reaper.

To be fair, there were non-Tyke acts at the vanguard of the goth movement; hailing from the decaying crypt that is Northampton, was Bauhaus, arguably the first goth rock band, instantly supplying the movement with its first anthem 'Bela Lugosi's Dead' as the 1970s crawled uncertainly into the 80s. But much more interesting was laugh-a-minute Australian oddball Nick Cave and The Birthday Party; despite their disdain for the dreaded goth label, their 'Release the Bats' quickly became a goth standard too.

Image wise, the goth look came partly out of punk, partly out of Hammer horror films - well, fair enough as goth was short for gothic. Siouxsie and the Banshees and The Cure were the two foremost bands who lived through and developed beyond the punk period, emerging with commercial success in the eighties, their own image becoming wilder and darker with the years – big deranged hair and garish make-up was, and still is de rigueur for a goth. A head resembling that of an unkempt vampire, ghoul or zombie was preferable, but at the very least the garments you wore on your body had to be black, always black. Goth 'haunts', like Le Phonographique in Leeds, tended to have the feel of a dimly lit cave; all you could see was white faces, 'pale and interesting' as my Mam used to say. Not that she went down many goth clubs.

Then there was the music itself. Southern Death Cult apart, the Yorkshire goth sound owed much to Joy Division at their glummest. But Ian Astbury's band had a much more dynamic tribal thing going on, with Native American rhythms rumbling on beneath an avalanche of guitars – but don't be fooled, the result was as menacingly dark as Adam and the Ants were amusingly shiny. Their debut, a double A-side 'Fatman'/'Moya' catapulted the Bradford boys to the top of the *NME* indie chart, whilst their live performances made them the new band to go and see at the beginning of 1983.

So I went to see them. Or rather a posse of us from the infamous Brundrettes Road commune turned up at Manchester Polytechnic Union to see what all the fuss was about. We walked in and headed straight to the bar to fight for service. As we turned back, drinks in hand, Prokofiev started to blast out from the PA. As we nervously strutted towards the back of the hall, everyone else walked trance-like the other way towards the stage. I felt like I'd walked into a sequel to *Children of the Damned… Children of the Goths* where the blonde haired little monsters of the original had been superseded by a legion of spotty Herberts who were keeping black hair dye manufacturers in business. I'll level with you - I felt scared.

132

But, it turns out that Southern Death Cult were worthy of the hype, with a primal energy born of 1977 but with a sound unlike anything else at the time. The undoubted star of the show was frantic-footed frontman, Astbury – we managed to get a close-up of your man after the gig when he came up to one of our posse, Shaf and asked for a light. He looked a lot bigger on stage, put it that way. Little did we know that we'd actually witnessed the last performance of Southern Death Cult.

Astbury sacked the rest of the band, hooked up with ex-Theatre of Hate guitarist, Billy Duffy and a brand new rhythm-section as all-new, all-improved Death Cult. It wasn't long before they realised the 'Death' part of the name still tied then to the dreaded goth movement – with their sound heading toward more mainstream rock, it was clear they craved a broader appeal. They finally stuck with The Cult as their handle, a move justified by the high profile afforded them with breakthrough album 'Dreamtime' and its lead single 'Spiritwalker'.

But it was with 'She Sells Sanctuary' in 1985 that The Cult went Premier League, in the UK at least, the single going Top 20, and the two subsequent releases from the Top Ten album 'Love' also charting. The follow-up album, 'Electric' consolidated their position as new rockers on the block in the UK, and made inroads in the States; 'Sonic Temple', the 1989 long player struck gold in the US and we'd lost them to *Rawwwkunroll* mega-stardom. Inevitably that was the point where all the in-fighting, law suits, a weekly turnover of personnel, etc, took over and suddenly The Cult could have been any American rock group. Bizarrely, Astbury even stepped into Jim Morrison's shoes with the remaining members of The Doors to tour as 'Riders on the Storm' in 2002. A far cry from the raw Bradford band that excited this punter at Manchester Polytechnic in the February of 1983.

In that early period, Southern Death Cult were a definite cut above – whilst the output from the rest of the goth combos could often be categorised as dirges for depressives, for the rest of the eighties at least, Astbury's outfit, whatever the name, whatever the personnel, were very capable of high-tempo exhilaration. No wonder he had wanted to take his band out of the goth ghetto and be recognised as a rock band.

Goth Rock was a natural successor to punk, evolving from its darker side, and for a time it was more commonly referred to as 'Positive Punk'. Not a great deal of positivity going on to my mind, quite the opposite in tone most of the time. Arguably it was even more akin to heavy metal, not just with respect to the music but also the faux devil-worship thing that seemed to be going on, even if it was just by suggestion via dodgy record sleeve designs.

And it wasn't long before the nation's goths had what appeared to be their own big private party, or even underworld gathering. The Futurama Festival was an annual musical event that started at the old Queens Hall in Leeds long before festivals became monster corporate events sponsored by beer companies and the like. It became something of a gothic orgy after its inaugural year in 1979 when Joy Division, as the undoubted stars of the whole event, set the tone for all subsequent Futuramas. In 1980, it was Siouxsie and the Banshees who stole the show. And by Futurama 3, the controls had been well and truly set to goth, with the Sisters of Mercy gracing the bill.

The Sisters, with an eventual tally of five Top Forty albums, and seven charting singles to their name, led the Leeds pack of goth rockers but rather disappointingly – and not for the first time – the main architect of their success wasn't from the local parish. Andrew Eldritch was from Ely near Cambridge, and he wasn't really called Andrew Eldritch either; he was Andrew Taylor, naughty boy. At least his original partner in crime was a Yorkshireman though – from the Hull area, Gary Marx, or Mark Pairman to his mum. Inspired by punk bands that they'd seen at the F-Club, the two students came up with a band name, nabbed from a Leonard Cohen song, and released a single on their own Merciful Release label, to reasonable success; "Andrew was always the one putting pen to paper and drawing up plans", says Marx – "I was more the throw-things-in-the-air merchant".

134

Expanding their ranks with a drum-machine, 'Doktor Avalanche', and bass player, Craig Adams, so they could go live with Eldritch's dulcet tones, the Sisters of Mercy played several times at the F-Club, getting support slots with The Clash amongst others. Then came a big break, making the bill of Futurama 3, held in Hanley for 1981. "Futurama was great for us because it grew out of Leeds, out of (promoter) John Keenan and the F-Club. Because we had our feet so firmly under that table it gave us an assumed status far beyond what the band had actually earned."

The Sisters of Mercy built up one of them cult followings before third single 'Alice' put them in the next category along, the 'bigger than a cult act' category, but still on their own independent label. Was it always the intention of the band to remain independent of the mainstream music industry? "In the first instance it was the only option – our music was never going to get any cheque books excited. In a relatively short space of time we had become a successful band in terms of singles sales and that brought great freedom. Then there was no desire to sign (to a major label) and no need – the failure of the top punk bands to work outside the status quo was still fresh in all our minds and we weren't the only ones happy to stick two fingers and a thumb up! To be honest, we attracted fans within the industry, often in quite senior positions, but they tended to prefer not to spoil their love of the band by actually working with us."

But as Gary adds, rather pointedly, "This was pretty shrewd as it turned out as the band didn't always part on good terms with ex-partners"...

It was signing a deal with WEA, and the import of a Bristolian Wayne Hussey, fresh from Pete Burns' Dead or Alive, that signalled the start of the band's problems, perhaps not covered by musical differences alone. Cutting out the tedious details, the upshot was that Marx departed the fold in the first instance, setting up Ghost Dance, closely followed by Hussey and Adams who formed The Mission. (Right honourable mention here for Craig Adams; not only did the Otley-born bassist play with The Sisters and The Mission, he has since turned up in incarnations of The Cult, Spear of Destiny and Theatre of Hate, not to mention The Alarm. Too late).

Meanwhile the eternally brooding Eldrich relocated to Germany, as you do, and started auditioning for new band-mates to put out records under the name The Sisterhood before Hussey and Adams could. He got one – Patricia Morrison, ex of the Gun Club – then changed his mind and re-cast his band completely with a new line-up that included Tony James, once of Generation X and later of pillocks par excellence Sigue Sigue Sputnik, and Tim Bricheno, from All About Eve. Detour – Tyke Alert!...

... Both Bricheno and All About Eve bass player Andy Cousins were from Huddersfield, birthplace of renowned violin player of 'Vienna' fame, Billy Currie. Though they had several singles in the lower ends of the charts, the band's most memorable moment came on a live edition of *Top of the Pops* as some less-than-bright spark forgot to turn the speakers on when the band were supposed to be miming to their hit, 'Martha's Harbour' – singer Julianne Regan's face was the very picture of muted bewilderment.

Back with the script of 'Andrew and his Sisters', the circumstances surrounding personnel changes in Eldritch's band become sillier and more tedious as time goes on. (In fact, tracing the whole timeline of Leeds bands of the period is one that even Pete Frame would rather have avoided). Suffice it to say that Eldritch fell out with everyone including record label East West, the Warner Brothers offshoot. It resulted in Eldritch and whoever he wanted to be in his band that month being dropped by the label – he and the Sisters haven't released any brand new material since 1993. The Sisters, have however continued to tour almost annually, still boasting an ever-enthusiastic fan base.

It's impossible to explore goth rock without continually crossing paths with The Sisters of Mercy – believe me I've tried. They became something of a model for other bands flirting with the genre. Most goth bands, it seems, had an intrinsic instability that meant there was a heavy turnover of personnel.

Does ex-Sister, Gary Marx think that was down to strong personalities clashing, single-minded ambition, or maybe even the brooding, often fatalistic nature of the music? "That's way wide of the mark – sorry but there wasn't even a hint of a Jim Morrison in the (Sisters of Mercy) camp. From my experience, every single member of a band tends to have a different idea of what equates to being successful and what they are prepared to do to reach that level – it's no surprise that personnel change. I sometimes think the only reason they don't is because certain bands achieve a threshold of financial success early enough to fend off all the other nonsense."

Okay, here goes then – how do you cope with someone determined to play the rock star to the full – or is that being unfair on Eldritch (Marx's old musical partner)? "You've not really got the man in focus at all there – Andrew simply saw more fun in acknowledging the lineage we belonged to than ignoring the fact he was a singer in a rock band."

Fair enough – I applaud the obvious loyalty inherent in that answer. But I was less enamoured to learn that, as far as Gary's concerned, there was no Leeds goth scene; "… certainly there was a wave of bands getting jiggy with the Duracells and blowing their rent money on fuzz boxes and drum machines, but the idea of a scene isn't really true for me."

Well, Leeds was seen as the epicentre for the 'Goth scene' – was that because of the place itself, the politics of the day, or both? "I think when we get into the politics of goth, we are in trouble – if you just focus on it being a scene in the North of England, a whole host of bands would come yelling from South of Northampton claiming heresy." Bollocks to Bauhaus, I say! Altogether now…

I myself grew up in Wakefield, and it certainly was a miserable place to be in the early 1980s – isn't it reasonable that people associate the dark, moody music of those times with the run-down Yorkshire cities and towns of that era? At last Gary and I agree on something – "a crumbling industrial base gives birth to a dislocated melancholy music. Dead right." Not absolutely right, but *dead* right – you can take the lad out of the goth band…

How does our man look back on that early 1980s period now, both as a musician involved, and a music fan? "Strangely enough I've found myself listening to a lot of early Soft Cell recently and I can easily picture myself back in the Warehouse when the Sisters were just about starting. I was a boy in a hurry."

Like the band set on their merry way by Marx and Eldritch (not to be confused with the band set on their merry way by Marx and Engels – they were more drum 'n' bass), The March Violets' sound was anchored originally by a drum machine and featured regulation swirling, echo-laden guitars. Their departure from the goth norm of the time was the dual vocal set-up of Simon Denbigh and Rosie Garland. All was rosy in the garden for the Violets for a good while – two well-received singles on Merciful Release before they appeared to fall from favour with Eldritch (hard to imagine, eh?), a couple more of the same on their own label, and then… personnel changes, and then…cue tolling bell… the beginning of the end.

What was it with these goth bands? Just when they're getting somewhere, everyone falls out and there's something approaching a purge – was the happy feeling of success just too much to bear, had they signed a contract committing themselves to continual misery?

It appears the boss of everyone – the 'Andrew Eldritch' if you like - in the March Violets was guitarist Tom Ashton. After ditching his two original front persons, Ashton's subsequent attempts to take the band into more commercial territory was clearly a very bad idea and led to the inevitable wilting and binning of The March Violets.

There was a reunion of the original line-up a couple of years ago for a successful one-off gig. More interesting though is, firstly, the fact that singer Simon Denbigh now runs his own independent label, called, inspiringly, 'Jazzwank', and the rumour that co-vocalist Rosie Garland has now changed her name to Rosie Lugosi and is now Manchester's foremost 'lesbian vampire poet'. Who'd have thought?

There are some band names that just trip off the tongue – Red Lorry Yellow Lorry less so. The Lorries (it would be nice to report this was yet another Peter Powell nickname but it was actually their fans' affectionate term for their cacophonous faves) were reluctant goths, that is, they never saw themselves as part of that malarkey, wisely preferring to be seen as simply 'a rock band'.

But their main man, or the Lorry driver if you will, Chris Reed had a familiarly morose voice akin to Lurch from the Addams Family, and their sound was pure archetypal goth. Their 'Spinning Around' single couldn't be more goth – twang-tastic riffs drowning in reverb, monotonous thudding and even more monotonous vocals. Like many others of the doom-laden rock persuasion (see how I avoided using the G-word?) the Lorries always registered high on the Indie charts with every release, but not surprisingly never troubled the compilers of the mainstream countdowns, despite the support of Beggars Banquet, technically a major label. It's ironic then that their fourth album for Beggars, 'Blow', a more mainstream, optimistic record, was a conscious effort to jettison the 'Goth' tag once and for all - the label saw fit to drop the band shortly after.

And the Leeds bands just kept on coming… It was, and probably still is unfair to casually throw Rose of Avalanche into our goth pit, but being from Leeds, using a drum machine and having a leaning towards the goth imagery means they're built for this chapter. Apart from Southern Death Cult, the Rose of Avalanche are perhaps the most credible act of the bunch, having been a very young outfit when they started out, with no university intellectualism nonsense to get in the way of them making what was really just rock music. Add to that, Peel not only played their records he gave them a session – he obviously really liked them.

That highlight was probably down to a rather decent debut single 'LA Rain' – terrible song-title for a band from Yorkshire but a well received rocker, which actually ended 1985 in fine style, taking the number 26 in Peel's annual Festive Fifty. Sadly, their rockin' career – more influenced by 60s psychedelic period than goth – never built on that, due in part to signing for the wrong independent label to record for, and also choosing the wrong crowd to support on tour, i.e. bigger, more pompous goth bands.

Another band that perhaps more ridiculously got sucked into the gothic Rock fold around the early to mid 1980s, was Bradford's New Model Army. Of course they weren't Goth! Post-Punk, Folk-Punk, Punk-Noir(?!) if you like or must. Though I prefer 'Crusty-Rock', in a New-Age, dog-on-a-string, big bottle of White Lightning, crocheted shoulder bag, roll-your-own kind of way. Only joking obviously, but all this pigeonholing deserves ridicule, though perhaps stopping short of being so offensive. Apologies.

Named after Cromwell's revolutionary army, Justin Sullivan's humanitarian collective were, and still are *rock*, pure and simple. The difference was that 'Slade the Leveller' (as our Justin chose to call himself in the early days) was belting our lyrics relevant to our modern world and the effect of the deeds of the powers that be upon it. Bear in mind, this was the period when the good ol' US of A had us in their pocket, thanks to Reagan and Thatcher's 'special relationship' ('51st State' was a NMA single written on that very subject). Seven singles in the Top Thirty, and four long-players in the album chart will tell you that 'The Army' had an intensely committed following as you would expect of an intensely committed band. It's probably narrow-minded buggers like me who have perpetuated the rather militant side of the band, when in reality there has always been a more emotive, poetic side to their music - lyrics were often inspired or even written by established poet Joolz Denby. EMI obviously believed in New Model Army's mass appeal potential, releasing four of their studio albums in their most successful period.

Compared to many if not most of the goth bands of the time, New Model Army were positively chuckle inducing. But it wasn't all West Yorkshire's pot of gloom. In the deep of night in a Barnsley crematorium, Dance Society rose from the ashes of two other bands 'Y?' and 'Lips X'. I say 'rose from the ashes' because it sounds far more dramatic, and indeed gothic than 'two effortlessly unsuccessful bands pooled their resources and formed another band'. It's all in the words, you see – for example, the name they chose for the resultant combo was Danse Crazy. Now, had I been looking for a gig to go down to and had I not known better, I'd have taken Danse Crazy to be a crazy Euro-trash disco act a la 5000 Volts. I'd have been sadly wrong, and would have looked a right pranny stood wearing my flashing Deely-Boppers at one of their gigs.

These South Yorkshire boys obviously realised that Danse Society had more of that essential menace about it. And the title of their first single left no doubt about where they were coming from – 'There is No Shame in Death'. Dance yourself dizzy.

Most goth bands were happy to have just the one label attached to them – The Society had at least two more. Positive Punk we've touched on before, but Darkwave? For such a straightforward exercise, this band of scruffy Tykes was hard to define. I suppose it was a sign of the times though – if you didn't fit in with what existed, make up your own new category and fit in there effortlessly.

Coming hot on the heels of Saxon, it seemed with Danse Society that Barnsley was on a musical roll (it was around twenty more years before the old mining town offered up its next musical act of note in folk singer/songwriter, Kate Rusby). But the *NME* didn't refer to Steve Rawlings and Company as 'Barnsley Bores' out of spite alone.

Rawlings as a frontman was far cuter in a schoolboyish way than the focal points of the other goth bands. There's footage on *YouTube* of the band making an early appearance in 1979 at the first Futurama Festival in Leeds, and young Stevie looks like he's bunked off from double chemistry and spent his pocket money on a Dracula outfit from the local fancy-dress outfitters on the way to the bus station. Bet he enjoys looking at that bit of footage.

141

The Danse Society sound – with added keyboards - was allegedly more accessible than their darker rivals. 'gothic lite' anyone? Their big crack at mainstream crossover 'Heaven Is Waiting' scraped the Top 60 of the singles chart, possibly thanks to an appearance on top TV pop show of the day, *The Tube*. Their cover of the Stones relic, '2000 Light Years from Home' however was a strange choice but perhaps illustrated the Barnsley boys' intent to break into the mainstream. It never happened. And quite frankly, thank the Lord.

These days, for anyone looking to don the black clobber and the 'Goth's Not Dead' badge, there's still the Whitby Goth Festival – home of Count Dracula and Arthur Brown, very much a gothic original back in the late 60s. But why oh why did all this goth malarkey prosper on our turf? Was it something to with all the dark satanic mill towns? Dunno, but the post-punkers lapped it up. Maybe that's it – the demise of punk (you see, it was dead after all) left a void needing to be filled and goth was the resurrection of punk, or the equivalent of as flesh-eating zombie that used to be punk? Yes, I know - time to stop ridiculing goth now just because it was never my cup of tea (or should that be 'chalice of virgin's blood'?).

It has to be said though that the hordes of Yorkshire goths were actually missing a trick, ignoring the darkest, scariest local act whose story is infinitely more rock 'n' roll than most of the goth bands put together…

From Ossett – a place we always viewed as a posh part of Wakefield – came the most frightening act of the time, and perhaps of all-time. You can keep your black hair dye, vampirish make-up, black leather, sunken cheekbones, tongue piercings, whatever, think two fun-loving blokes with highlights in their mullets and a nasty line in singalong party tunes… Black Lace. Aaaaauughh!

Black Lace had started out at the end of the seventies, attempting to ride the Eurovision train to fame and fortune and falling flat on their faces with an anonymous seventh place. If we'd have known what was to follow, we surely wouldn't have chosen these boys to represent the nation in 1979. Would we?

142

If you have to credit anyone with seeing a gap in the market for a summer holiday novelty hit, then it has to be Alan Barton and Colin Routh. Their first success with the 'sing the words and do the actions' formula was 'Superman' in 1982. But, however terrible that was, the dreadful record that everyone will remember these fun-loving boys for will be 'Agadoo' two years later. If goth seems depressing, this took the suicidal biscuit. George Michael's 'Careless Whisper' kept the blighter off the Number One slot in the UK singles chart, and for that reason alone, we should love the troubled, hirsute Greek forever. But of course it sold in truckloads all over the continent and was no doubt a fixture on the turntable of every holiday camp DJ from Torremolinos to Rhyl. The official Black Lace website – yes there is one but just one page's worth fortunately – declares that 'a DJ without a Black Lace record is not a DJ'. Judge Jules is gonna be a bit miffed with that assessment.

But, what a kick in the rocks, Black Lace saw none of the royalties. The distribution label that took 'Agadoo' all over the world, went tits-up and swallowed all the proceeds from the record sales in the process. Maybe there is a God after all. 'The Lace' followed this, their monster hit, with 'Do the Congo' and 'Hokey Cokey' – well of course they would – amongst many others, but fortunately not to the same brain-damaging effect as their masterwork.

But behind the banality lies tales of scandal and tragedy – and far be it from me not to share them on these pages. 1986 proved to be the pivotal year for the duo as they entered their own private rock'n'roll Babylon. First, in a strange piece of transfer business, Alan Barton took over as lead singer of Smokie after the Bradford quartet's long-time frontman Chris Norman decided to give it a crack as a solo artist. That was bad enough, some Smokie fans would probably have said. But he kept Black Lace going at the same time – that's very bad, most music fans would have said. But worse was to come. Colin Routh was arrested for having sex with an underage girl. The decision to sing 'Gang Bang' on the soundtrack of the film *Rita Sue and Bob Too* may not have looked such a good one in the light of this development. Routh duly left the band, and moved abroad.

But… worse news still was that another musician, Dene Michael, was happy to take his place and keep the band going. Bastard. But joking aside, the very worst was kept for last when in 1995, Smokie's tour bus veered off the road in Germany and plummeted down a ravine; Alan Barton was critically injured and died a few days later. More than enough gloom and doom even for a goth rock band, I'd say.

Is there a moral in the tale of Black Lace? No but it just goes to show that misery isn't always dressed up in black lace and leathers with 'The Death March' for a backing track.

Served up the right way, misery is a highly danceable soundtrack and what's more, it's hugely sellable. But it's probably best to have tongue-in-cheek rather than a po-face that takes itself oh-so-seriously (can you see where this is going?). How fitting, not to say convenient, then that 'International goth Day' (no, really) – 22nd May 2009 – coincided with the 50th birthday of Morrissey.

The Smiths brought misery out of the bedsit and made it a truly joyous thing in the years between 1983 and 1987. With a singer and lyricist who could put more wit into a song title than most put into a full album, and a guitarist who could weave an memorably exhilarating tune in his sleep, they proved to be the template for a whole generation of like-minded 'indie' bands. With at least two of the best pretenders to the Smiths indie crown hailing from Yorkshire, it was time to get happy again.

Chapter Nine

Yorkshire, A State Of Independents.

Most music fans toy with the idea of making music themselves during their young and stupid years. Many dabble with songwriting, the fruits of which, mercifully, usually never escape the four walls of the culprit's bedroom. Around 1983, a pair of us in Greater Manchester actually skulked outside and gave the world the gift of our songs. Via my first stab at pop immortality with The Danny Boys, I offered 'Greetings from the West', my rather clever Cold War Love Song (which actually would have been a better title – doh!). And Morrissey, with his hapless amateurs The Smiths, gave us 'Hand in Glove'.

The Danny Boys released their one and only single, 'Days of the Week', in the spring of 1987 on Manchester's Ugly Man records. You'll be surprised to hear that hundreds of dusty copies are still available even now, a fact that tells you we didn't set quite start a fire, though I swear I saw a wisp of smoke. And The

Smiths? They fared slightly better.

That Morrissey, eh? He could have almost been the nephew of Alan Bennett, couldn't he? He even dressed like The Bard of Armley in hornrims and beige cardy. Hang on! I was the Yorkshireman in this non-existent contest. Surely I was more entitled to be my generation's Alan Bennett in a pop-singing stylee?!

Well no, not really. It quickly became evident that while I'd been busy honing my drinking skills in the city's pubs and clubs for the past four years, Steven Patrick had stayed at home devouring literature on an unhealthy scale for someone not permanently bedridden.

But, finally I was having a go myself – all that bedroom strumming started to pay off (not a euphemism, missus) - and if anything the Smiths were to thank/ blame for that. By the time 'This Charming Man' had catapulted The Smiths to the front of the *NME*, *Top of the Pops* and the *Radio One* Playlist, being in an indie band was the coolest thing to do with your life.

Edwyn Collins, another of my heroes, conceded that The Smiths had taken everything that his Orange Juice and Postcard Records had been trying to do for years – lacing shiny, jingly tunes with intelligent, witty lyrics – and cracked it in sparkling fashion. No shock then that formula was borrowed seemingly on a daily basis by any number of bands eager to be the next Smiths.

Once he was accepted as the dog's whatsits, Morrissey only had to give a passing mention to another band that he liked the sound of, and all attention turned onto the grateful combo. One early recipient of the official Moz endorsement was fellow Manchester band, James, fronted by Bradford-born Tim Booth. Another, rather perversely in this context, was a band called Bradford, who, of course, hailed from Blackburn.

Booth had been demonstrating his epileptic scarecrow dance down at the disco when members of Model Team International spotted him (they were a pop group not hairdressing exhibitionists). Shortly after, Timbo was installed as the new lead singer of the renamed James. Though the band are best known for their later involvement with the Madchester scene, their early music leant more towards that distinctly less-than-sexy Folk Music, courtesy perhaps of drummer Gavan Whelan's familiarity with the genre via his folk musician father. Booth was a fantastic frontman in the early days of the band - the perfect focal point for an electrifying live music experience. But you'd have never guessed he was a Yorkshireman; I didn't, even after interviewing him more than once for various music publications. Softly spoken with a voice of no discernible origin, he was a 'herbal tea' kind of bloke, seriously focussed on music and the more serious business of finding success within it.

But whilst James were cast as Smiths protégées, supporting them on many occasions, there is one Yorkshire-based band that comes seriously close to challenging the Manc Miseries for the all-time Indie crown; in fact, once Johnny Marr's departure split The Smiths, The Wedding Present stepped effortlessly into their charity shop shoes.

Formed by David Gedge, son of Bramley, the band had come into this world as The Lost Pandas. Nothing at all to do with apples, The Gedge's birthplace, a working-class town resting within Leeds boundaries, had hitherto only put a flag on the map for giving the world of sport a perennially struggling Rugby League club. Gedge spent his first three years there before his parents upped sticks for Manchester. But even at an early age, he knew where he wanted to be career-wise.

"It sounds a bit pretentious, ridiculous even, but the urge to make music's always been there – I always knew that I'd be in a group. I dabbled with it all through school, having various bands in the sixth form and then when I got to university. It's always been my over-riding passion. But I got the education bit out of the way first."

It was further-education that took Gedge back to Leeds, studying Mathematics at the city's University in 1978. "I used to look at the gig guide and there seemed to loads of great gigs going on in Leeds. It seemed to be a happening place with a strong local scene – Gang of Four, Mekons, Delta 5. There was all the goth stuff that followed as well – it got bad press in the later years, but I think at the outset, it was really exciting. There seemed to be bands on in the city every night with loads of different venues, from the 'F Club' downstairs at Brannigans all the way up to the Refectory at the University. I remember seeing the Clash there."

Were there plenty of opportunities for a local band in the city in the early 1980s? "Yeah, loads of little venues – we played at The Royal Park Hotel in Leeds 6, right in the middle of the student area. In town there was a pub called the Adelphi and also Le Phonographique. Of course I was always badgering the Uni' for gigs as well. I think we eventually got to support someone like Suicide there, just because their actual support hadn't turned up and so the social secretary rang us up and asked us to come down quick. And we could because we were literally around the corner."

Was there a Music Community in the city at the time, offering support and camaraderie? "I think so, yeah. I might be looking back with rose-tinted glasses, but we did get along with everyone, not just bands who were musically alike. We were quite friendly with the Age of Chance who were nothing like us really. We got to know them quite well - I think we ended up doing a German tour with them. People did help each other out - when we started rehearsing somewhere in a basement, I'm sure that someone had the Gang of Four's bass amp."

Such arrangements were an extension of the 'Indie ethic', something that served Gedge and his band better than most. "There were two waves of punk, first one being the bands, the biggest of which invariably signed to majors. The second wave being when people started their own little labels all over the country and we were sucked into that. I'll be honest, we sent out loads of demos to start with and didn't get anywhere. We came to London a few times and took tapes round to 4AD, Rough Trade and people, and we were turned down by everyone. So we decided to put out our own single on our own label, like a lot of people did. It was helpful that just up the road in York was Red Rhino Records, who distributed indie records for everyone. They put out loads of stuff by bands from all over Yorkshire, I'd imagine. That was very handy."

148

That first single was 'Go Out and Get 'Em Boy', driven by what was to become trademark full-speed rhythm guitar and Gedge's quintessential Northern vocal, on their own Reception label; within two years, the band cemented their place as Indie Darlings with a full LP, 'George Best'. "We just happened to be there when The Smiths left the scene. People saw us as a replacement for them for a while. We got a lot of attention from the music press because of that."

How easy was it, as their official website puts it, to 'wilfully refuse to play the record industry game?' "It was difficult, to be honest. We started our own label by necessity and did enjoy having that control. And that's continued – I think I probably am a bit of a control freak. I do like to have my hands on every aspect of the process. But when 'George Best' came out, we got loads of attention from major record labels – I think we spoke to every major company. It was difficult because on the one hand they're offering you substantial amounts of money, which for four lads who were either on the dole or surviving as ex-students, was an attractive proposition. But on the other hand, there was this pervading attitude of 'you've done well so far lads but if you sign with us we'll take you to the next level and do this and do that for you'. We just didn't feel like we fitted in with all that.

"Eventually we sat down with RCA records - they were the first label to say just carry on with what you're doing and we'll sell the records. I think the contract we signed was almost ground-breaking in terms of the amount of artistic control that we had. It came at a really fortunate time just as Red Rhino were about to go into liquidation. And to be fair, we did enjoy the same amount of freedom there that we had on our own label. We got the best of both worlds without having to play the music business game.

"The main benefits of the RCA deal for us were financial. We'd recorded 'George Best' on a budget at a time when we didn't have any money. Suddenly it was... here's a load of money to go and record in a world-class recording studio. In retrospect. I'm not even sure it was money well spent! 'Bizarro', our first album on RCA cost sixty grand, which was an enormous amount of money,

149

and though it sounds better recorded than 'George Best', it's not sixty grand's worth better.

"The other thing was that it meant we could finally sell records around the world. The success of 'George Best' meant we were getting letters from people in America, Japan and other far-flung places, saying that they couldn't get hold of our records, which highlighted the limitations of a small British distributor. RCA as a multi-national corporation was obviously a good thing from the point of view of getting our music out to everybody."

Though they were always looked on as a Leeds band, The Wedding Present didn't have a big Leeds fan base. "We weren't a traditional local band – though I was born in Leeds, we were all Leeds students really. It wasn't like four lads from Liverpool who conquered the world! We always did well in Leeds – maybe more so now even. We had this feeling of homecoming when we played in Leeds. I've not lived there for a long time, but we're still welcomed back with some warmth now – it's a bit surreal."

The natives of Leeds – or 'Loiners' if you like - may have held the band closer to their hearts, had they named their debut LP 'Billy Bremner' or 'Eddie Gray' rather than 'George Best' (but Gedge had sadly grown up a Manchester United fan). "The main person who actually tried to talk us out of calling it 'George Best' was John Peel. When I first gave him a copy of the LP, he said there was some other band who released a record that had 'fuck' in the title, so he obviously couldn't mention or play it on *Radio One*. And he said, 'you've gone and done the same – I can't bring myself to read out this LP title. Why couldn't you call it 'Steve Heighway'?'"

If Gedge has anyone to thank for his long and continuing music career, it's Peel. The Wedding Present are up there in the Top Five in terms of the number of sessions recorded for Peel over years. A six CD box-set was released in 2007, featuring all the recordings the band made for Peel's show – "one of my proudest releases", says Gedge,

David Gedge has never stood still since that first independent single; line-up changes, quirky musical detours, another successful, if less celebrated band – Cinerama – and more personal projects feature throughout his story. "We've had a history of doing odd things – I always think the idea of just doing album/tour/album/tour is okay but can get a bit predictable. Changing band personnel brings new influences and inspirations – little upheavals have always added to the fabric of the group. It's not most commercially wise thing to do; if people buy cornflakes and go back to buy a second box, they still want cornflakes inside, not Weetabix. But it's kept it more interesting for me – maybe that's why it's lasted so long."

For the record, The Weddo's have had twenty Top 50 singles over the years, 'Come Play With Me' being their high-achiever, reaching Number 10 in 1992, the year the band released a new single every month, every single one of them charting. Not bad for a band sometimes dismissed as three-chord wonders. Eat your heart out, Quo!

Had Gedge started out with a plan beyond 'let's get a record out and try and sell enough so we can put another one out'? "No! You never do really – you put a record out, John Peel plays it and that might be it. There was always the possibility that that might happen. Fortunately it didn't. And here we here nearly 25 years later, it seems to have flown past, and I've still not got a plan!

"I was always driven to do this. I couldn't think of anything else that I'd be doing. A lot of it has been shaped by people I've met – we wouldn't have done the Ukrainian stuff without having Peter (Sowolka) in the group… and Keith (Gregory), the bass player was collecting monthly releases from the Sub-Pop label, so we got the idea for doing a year of monthly singles through that. The actual journey has been shaped by little random occurrences."

As well as Peel playing his usual big part in the more exciting musical developments of the mid-eighties, the nation's favourite music weekly, the *NME*, had clinched a starring role in 1986, by giving away a highly influential cassette 'C86', a compilation of tunes from new bands on the shiny new 'shambling' scene. The Wedding Present figured amongst the participants, but were less than enamoured by the accompanying tag.

Also present was the band about whom Peel had allegedly coined the phrase 'shambling' in the first place... Bogshed. Now, could a band called Bogshed be from anywhere else than Yorkshire? They hailed from Hebden Bridge to be precise. Great name but you do kind of wish they'd stuck with their initial handle of The Amazing Roy North Penis Band, don't you? No matter, the Bogshed sound was frantic riffage with barely discernible lyrics half-shouted on top. Though entertaining, they were never going to be pop stars of the mainstream. Not in a million years.

If not Bogshed then, just who were the other Yorkshire pop stars of the day? That'd be the self-proclaimed '4th best band in Hull'. The best three apparently were The Gargoyles, 3-Action!, and The Red Guitars. The latter of those was the only Humberside outfit to register a score on the national clap-o-meter. Their debut single, 'Good Technology', sold 60,000 copies on their own label and the band's course seemed dead set for certain success. But the pressures of continual touring (supporting The Smiths on one tour) and that of running their own independent label proved too much for the band. Their admirable anti-corporate ideology ended up being a load far too much to bear and the band folded way before they'd fulfilled their potential.

Strangely missing from that list of Humberside talents was Everything but the Girl. That might have had something to do with the fact that Ben Watt and Tracey Thorn had long gone from Hull by 1985, having met there as, you guessed it, bloody students. Of course they weren't from those parts in the first place. So the talented duo met in Hull, true, but went away and nurtured a successful career, one they're still enjoying.

Perhaps Hull is not getting the acclaim it deserves, in this book at least. Maybe that's because some of the Humberside musicians who might otherwise be celebrated were seen as mere backing to more profiled figures. Sade Adu was the singer with Sade the band – no, she's wasn't from Hull, but the rest of her band were. Shades of Bowie and the Spiders from Mars, eh? Except, I think you'd have noticed Ronson, Bolder and Woodmansey had you passed them in the street. Sorry Tom, Dick and Harry from Sade's band – you should have worn silver suits or summat.

But back to the actual '4th best band in Hull'. They were, deceptively, anything but a simple indie pop combo. The Housemartins hardly looked subversive – clean-cut lads, clean-cut sound (with harmonies for God's sake!) and oh yeah, for God's sake again, they were young Christians and proud of it. A Yorkshire pop group armed with religion?!

But that's not all, your honour; these rapscallions were also scholars of Marxism and made no secret of that either. Their early singles, whilst not blatant far-left propaganda, carried a recognisable political towards to socialism, as was fitting with the times, and their record label, Go! Discs, home to all-round good bloke and card-carrying heart-on-his-sleeve balladeer, Billy Bragg.

Though lead singer and lyricist, Paul Heaton was actually born in the Wirral on Merseyside, he was a true adopted Yorkshireman, his family having decamped to Sheffield when he was just four, and he himself taking the later decision to relocate in Hull after he completed his formal education in Surrey. Back in the Yorkshire fold, Heaton teamed up with guitarist Stan Cullimore to form the Housemartins Mk1, a busking duo at first, then on a more professional indoor footing as support act for, amongst others, them Smiths again. Adding Quentin 'Norman' Cook on bass, and Hugh Whitaker on drums, The Housemartins became a fully fledged band in 1985, with debut single 'Flag Day' receiving typical encouragement from John Peel.

Their first nationwide tour was notable for 'Adopt a Housemartin' scheme which, given that they'd had to fork out for an expensive PA for the tour (well, that was their story), was a plea for their fans to put each of them up for the night after each gig. Yeah right... The fans bought it hook line and sinker, mainly the female variety. No wonder the band had big smiles on their faces gig after gig.

This set the tone for the career of these cheeky scamps, their promotional material always endearing them to the music listening public with self-effacing slogans like 'The Housemartins Are Quite Good'. It was their third single that propelled them onto peak-time mainstream radio and TV; supported by a memorable video, replete with clay-animation figures of themselves, 'Happy Hour' went Top Ten in the charts and proved the perfect lead-in to their debut long-player, 'London 0 Hull 4'.

How could we not like them with a two-fingers-up album title like that? And even more so, when they manage to outrage *The Super Soaraway Sun* with some less-than-complementary comments about the Royal Family.

On a purely musical level, 'London 0...' was a fine representation of the Housemartins live repertoire, featuring not only the recognisable jingle-jangle pop of the previous singles, but also tracks embracing gospel and a cappella.

On the back of its success, Go! Discs released two more singles in '86, both worthy of reference. 'Think for A Minute' was Heaton at his most politically reflective without being preachy, whilst 'Caravan of Love', an a cappella cover of the Isley Brothers song, gave The 'Martins their one and only Number One.

Receiving a coveted award in any form of public life, it has been said, is usually the prelude for things going arse-shaped. And so it proved with The Housemartins. Not that they coveted any award, but the Brit for 'Best Newcomer' preceded a significant change in the Hull band's ranks. Drummer Hugh quit, claiming that the new-found celebrity was blunting the band's individual edge, mainly in the political sense. With new drummer Dave Hemmingway onboard, the recording of a second album revealed inner tensions for the first time, with musical differences actually playing a big part, honest. For one, that Norman Cook wanted the record to have a more contemporary feel, deploying loops and sampling in its production – well he did evolve into Fatboy Slim, y'know?

Nevertheless, 'The People Who Grinned Themselves to Death' came out, a more serious record than its predecessor, and was duly deemed a disappointment, not least by many Housemartins fans who hankered for the cheeky, wacky, zany, madcap antics of before.

The inevitable split became official after Heaton wrote an open letter to the *NME* stating in typical manner that "in the age of Rick Astley, Shakin' Stevens and The Pet Shop Boys, quite simply they (The Housemartins) weren't good enough." They've since revealed that their intention was always to kick in the head after three years whilst they were still 'quite good', meaning that their fans didn't have to delve too deep into their memories for the band's finest moments.

It was suggested that Heaton's controlling nature had alienated the Fatboy Norman and Stan; it came as little surprise when the singer started a new, perhaps grander venture, The Beautiful South, taking Dave Hemmingway with him, and achieving an even greater success than the Housemartins had.

More of a 'collective', featuring a female vocal alongside Heaton and Hemmingway (three different women filled that position during the band's existence), the Beautiful South was a much more ambitious musical project but still retained a manifesto recognisably evolved from the Housemartin ideology, with its subversion thinly veiled in an almost middle-of-the-road musical slant. The sarcasm of the name, and the barbed wit of the early hits 'Song for Whoever', 'You Keep It All In' and 'A Little Time' (their only Number One single) set both an agenda and a tone that served the band well for almost 20 years, though it's fair to say that the first ten years were the most fruitful, with the band at the height of their popularity.

Like The Housemartins, they courted mild controversy from the off – the sleeve of their debut album 'Welcome to the Beautiful South' featured a woman holding a revolver ready for firing in her mouth. Some of the lyrical content of their songs attacked modern British institutions, like the world of glamour models in '36D'. Heaton's lyrics were never boring or predictable, painting bittersweet vignettes of British life through singles like 'Old Red Eyes is Back', an ode to an alcoholic, and 'Perfect 10', a perfect observation of our obsession with bodily size and appearance.

For a band that managed ten Top 10 albums in their time, they were a damned fine singles band – reflected in the fact that two of those albums were Greatest Hits compilations. Of their 22 Top Forty hits, six made the Top Ten.

After selling over seven million albums worldwide, the Beautiful South called it a day in 2007, citing 'musical similarities' for the split. Perfect.

Heaton's two bands from the fair city of Hull, weren't the only Yorkshire music collectives to flirt with politics in the 1980s. The Three Johns were another politico-pop unit, very much of the times, featuring the ever-busy Jon Langford of The Mekons, who by the early 80s had added something resembling 'a proper job' to his CV, that of a graphic designer. And there really were two other Johns in there, even if one of them was really a Phillip, with John as his middle name. The Johns' repertoire was fuelled by a left-wing view on the issues of the day – South Africa, Thatcher, the nuclear threat – but whilst they were fixtures on both Peel's show and in the Independent charts, they never broached the mainstream.

But The Redskins from York just about cracked that nut. They were a band you can safely assume did have a 'manifesto' in the true sense of the word. Led by music journalist Chris Dean – he wrote under the pen-name of X Moore in the *NME* – the trio were indeed all skinheads and members of the Socialist Workers Party. Mixing their left-wing lyrics with a highly danceable soul-punk tunefulness, the Redskins stormed the bottom regions of the singles charts with catchy songs – honest - like 'Keep On Keepin On!' and 'Bring It Down' at the time of the mid-eighties Miner's strike. But their intrinsically aggressive approach always seemed destined to remain, perhaps wilfully, on the periphery of the mainstream at best. The Housemartins subsequently found the missing link and stepped inside the circle while the Redskins released their one and only album, 'Neither Washington nor Moscow' – it made it inside the Top Forty – and decided their work here was done, splitting up at the end of 1986.

There's no doubt that The Housemartins and The Wedding Present vie for the non-existent title of most successful Yorkshire independent band of the 1980s, the former because they packed so much into an entertaining, yet meaningful three-year career, and the latter because they packed so much into, erm, a much longer entertaining, yet meaningful twenty-five year career that's still going strong. It seems unfair to denigrate any other Yorkshire acts to the role of bit-players – I'm not that kind of guy. Every act is column inches in my book. Literally.

Given the hive of activity that was Sheffield earlier in the decade, the South Yorkshire city seemed strangely quiet by the mid-80s. With a cracking new venue, The Leadmill, up, running and attracting the country's top independent acts, you'd have expected the city to have continued with its production of suitably inspired locals making waves on the pond of pop. It wasn't for the want of trying.

At least one future major player from the city was making his first moves. Amazingly, Jarvis Cocker had formed Pulp back in 1978, when he was still a 15-year-old schoolboy. No matter that the band was in essence only a name at that point, and the original name was in fact Arabacus Pulp. It was 1980 before the band, with name shortened to Pulp, actually played their first gig – 'good evening Rotherham'. But, more significant was the netting of a Peel session in 1981, a golden boost for any fledgling band.

However, the decade panned out as a rather frustrating time for Jarvis and Co; despite two albums and numerous singles, Pulp didn't even start to scale the heights. A possible reason being that they were yet to find a sound of their own, their style thus far having flitted from electronica to urban-folk to dark miseribalism. It would be the dance scene of the late eighties and early nineties that would eventually inspire the definitive Pulp sound, and eventually give Jarvis Cocker that elusive success.

Another Sheffield band was a much fancied runner in the middle of the decade. Not to be confused (but they probably were many times) with Shack, the Liverpudlian combo, Chakk were very much in the tradition of modern music coming out of the Steel City. If you had to bet to bet your wage on where a top notch industrial funk band would pop up from in this indie guitar-heavy period, you'd have put your hard-earned wedge on Sheffield.

Chakk's first recorded effort, 'Out of the Flesh' was recorded by Cabaret Voltaire's Richard Kirk for his own Doublevision label. The buzz the single caused, encouraged music journo Amrik Rai to join forces and start a new label FON (as in 'Fuck Off Nazis') on which the second Chakk single, 'You', duly appeared.

That was it – the majors came a-sniffing, offering impressive advances, as they did back then. The band took up MCA's kind offer and used the cash to build FON studios, the first commercial 24-track recording studio in Sheffield. The studio's first output was their own long-player, 'Ten Days in an Elevator', which unfortunately failed to follow up their undoubted dance worthy promise. MCA dropped them like a hot brick, but at least they'd got the studio out of the exercise, so when Chakk decided to call it a day in 1987, the FON name lived on with the studio and its in-house record label.

One of the early releases on FON came from local band Treebound Story; 'My Life's Example' was a pleasant enough single with a Smith-esque feel, but it is more noteworthy for the first recorded appearance of one Richard Hawley on guitar. Hawley was not long out of school and taking the first steps on a colourful career that would gain international recognition twenty years later.

It's another FON release, more akin to the label's debut that brings another local band to our notice at this juncture... the Age of Chance, (yes, mates of The Wedding Present). Hang on, author... weren't they from Leeds? A Leeds band putting records out on a Sheffield label?! Well yes, view that either as a wonderful example of Yorkshire team work, or a rare instance of the two cities, with no love lost between them, coming together and striking gold. Because there was just one single coming out of this uncommon Tyke union, and that record was 'Kiss', a 'mutant metallic' version of the Prince classic.

Starting out as a rock/dance crossover turn in 1985, their debut, 'Motorcity' was given mucho airplay by Simon Bates. Sorry, of course I meant John Peel; a session followed, and this was when AoC first recorded a version of Kiss, at a time when Prince's original was still riding high in the charts. In the band's own words, "Prince's version is just the sound of cocktail glasses tinkling and wine bar small talk. We wanted to make a dance sound that represented iron foundries, civil unrest and motorway fatalities." Get down and boogie!

Following the thumbs-up response from Peel listeners, the band decided to give the Purple Midget's jaunty little number the full treatment in Chakk's FON studios. The resultant platter actually scraped into the Top 50 but more prestigiously took silver medal in Peel's hallowed Festive Fifty of 1986.

Age of Chance were a seriously stylish example of a set of musicians using modern technology in conjunction with more conventional instrumentation in a maverick pop manner. There was Pop Will Eat Itself doing it in a more 'grebo' style, but the Leeds band looked much better in their cycling tops, likewise their record sleeves and promos, conceived by Sheffield's Designer's Republic, giving their product the modern edge on the competition.

Maybe a case of too much too soon, Age of Chance never bettered the high point of 'Kiss', though they tried admirably before a change of lead singer signalled the beginning of the end for the self-proclaimed 'Sonic-Metal-Disco' groovers. They're worthy of an extended mention if only for their departure from the normal job descriptions of vocals/guitar/bass/drums. For the record, Steven E was 'mob-orator', Neil H was the 'power-noise generator', Geoff T was in charge of 'all nite bass frequencies', and Jan P was 'beat dominator'.

And what's more you could dance to them. A band with standard bass, drums and guitar formation that you could really dance to?! Whatever next?...

Chapter Ten

E's Bah Gum.

It was amazing, why, crazy even… one minute all the happening bands, old and new, and their avid followers were confirmed 'shoegazers', scared to get any more animated than absolutely necessary; next minute, everyone's dancing about like demented idiots. It's like they'd taken a drug or something!

As the 1980s burned down to its gutter-bound tab-end, the world was heading into a period of transition, with the end for the Cold War and the Berlin Wall just around the corner. But in the UK, even under the continuing rule of the most oppressive government in living memory , we were getting 'loved up' thanks to the small matter of a seismic shift in UK youth culture.

By 1987, Stock, Aitken and Waterman had turned the singles charts into a bland, mass-produced jingle market, but there were signs of something far more dangerous and exciting infiltrating the airwaves courtesy of the likes of the K.L.F. and M.A.R.R.s, both of them an odd combination of musical activists peddling the most in-yer-face of danceable tunes. Most significantly, the import of Chicago House music was proving to be the catalyst for a genuine clubbing revolution and the birth of a new DJ culture across the nation. I was actually still in Manchester, seen by many as the centre for this revolution. But no, despite popular media opinion, it wasn't confined to the Rainy City and the Hacienda.

Its celebrated dance nights quickly made the Warehouse in Leeds one of the places to be and at least two future 'pop stars' of the DJ/Dance age graduated via Leeds' most famous modern club. Though there were other clubs and venues active in the city - most notably The Gallery - the Warehouse was invariably in the middle of any musical happening of note in Leeds around that time.

And yes, developments there reflected the major music happening of the time, namely DJs becoming the stars of the show – at first it felt a bit like the bloke hanging the picture in the gallery getting all the credit instead of the artist. By extension, the actual clubs putting the dance nights on became bigger stars yet, with bricks and mortar for a while becoming bigger and more important than flesh and blood.

The night known as 'Downbeat' at the Warehouse was run by one George Evelyn – otherwise known as DJ Ease - and his pal Kevin Harper – otherwise know as Kev - playing hip-hop and rare groove (seventies funk to you and me). But their turntables weren't the most important bit of kit in this story.

When looking for the reasons for the new impetus in dance music, it's hard to look further than the advances in sampling technology (i.e. you'd not been able to sample sounds from other records at all until then). Evelyn and Harper played around with their bedroom-housed sampler and produced a bleep-mungous track called 'Dextrous'. The pair looked for a label to release the tune, but no one gave it a second listen until they played it to the owners of a Sheffield record store, FON – yes, most definitely related to the record label that had previously released Chakk and Age of Chance records. Store owners

Steve Beckett and Rob Mitchell decided the best way to help out the young DJs was to start a label themselves upon which they could put the dance track out. Warp Records came into the world with the help of the Tory government enterprise allowance scheme - thirty quid a week, yippee - and after selling 30,000 copies, Warp's second release, and George and Kev's first, 'Dextrous', was, and still is, credited for starting the UK dance revolution, with Leeds and Sheffield playing dual roles in its unstoppable progression.

Evelyn and Harper chose Nightmares on Wax as their 'stage name', and though Harper jumped ship some time ago, George as N.O.W. has become a relative Premiership giant in the Electronic dance world, and remains Warp Records' longest standing artist. And Warp itself has gone from strength to strength; modelled on Tony Wilson's Factory label (but thankfully with more efficient, less haphazard management) the label has developed through a twenty-year life span, even diversifying into the sphere of film production, donning the producer's hat for the recent output of maverick Midlands director, Shane Meadows.

There was something traditionally 'Sheffield' about Warp; the first record released on the label, the splendidly titled 'Track with No Name' by Forgemasters, was undoubtedly a blood relation to the likes of Cabaret Voltaire and the Human League. However, the 'bleep' sound became synonymous with Leeds, an association made all the more stronger by the success of another Warp artiste, LFO, an entity that quickly thudded to the front of the 'Yorkshire Bleeps and Bass Scene' – I haven't just made that up by the way, that's what it was referred to back in 1990.

Standing for, as we all knew or suspected, 'Low Frequency Oscillator', LFO were, and still occasionally are, exponents of bass-heavy techno. While DJ Ease and his Nightmares on Wax tunes are invariably laid-back chill-out soundscapes, LFO's creations are eardrum threatening assaults, with a bottom end sound you're unlikely to hear too often on the radio, basically because it's radio unplayable.

But even without airplay on *Radio One*, 'LFO' by LFO reached number 12 in the singles chart. The clubbers were dancing to it at night and buying it in the daytime – 130,000 of them! On record, it worked fine; but when Warp sent them out on tour, clearly it didn't. LOF suffered from in-house fighting – well on-stage fighting actually – and the duo eventually became a solo performer.

The main protagonist, again a regular down at the Warehouse, was Mark Bell, from just down the road in Lofthouse, Wakefield; he had met Gez Varley at the celebrated venue and the duo put together their first tentative efforts at electronica. One of the DJ's at the Warehouse, Martin Williams, started playing their stuff, the guys from Warp records heard it, and Robert's your uncle. Easy peasy.

Mark Bell has subsequently gone on to become a producer for Bjork and Depeche Mode; just one of many dance tunesters to be recruited by high-profile artists to direct proceedings in the control room.

Whatever else it was, the new Dance revolution was a gilt-edged Godsend for club owners and promoters, wherever they were. It was, without doubt, easier and more profitable – you didn't need to pay for a couple of bands, put up with their egos and demands, you just had to pay the DJ to play dance tunes all night. Sorted.

House music and its variations inspired the kind of mass gatherings not seen across the nation since the days of ye olde Hippy. The result, as far as the tabloid-reading public were concerned, were House Parties of a different, highly undesirable kind – illegal raves. It was one of these events that put a rather unremarkable suburb of Leeds on the map in July 1990, in what became known as the Big Gildersome Bust (it didn't, but it should've). 'Love Decade', a bunch of rave-loving Yorkshire blokes, set up one of said raves in an empty warehouse on an industrial estate in Gildersome, but such was the furore about Ecstasy and acid house, that seemingly the whole of Yorkshire's constabulary were mobilised, stormed the site and going ever so slightly over the top, arresting 863 people in total, though only eight people were actually charged. It remains one of the biggest mass arrests in British history. Rave on! Or rather, Rave off.

Of course, while these exciting underground dance events were taking place in the clubs and warehouses, or whatever enclosed space could house a rave (a disused abattoir was one such improvised venue), back in the less-than-hip mainstream discos, there was actually an alternative sound of Yorkshire whipping 'em up into a frenzy.

Apart from the bass player from Muse, the only 'pop star' ever to have come out of Rotherham was a man-sized rabbit with a musical content and style that made Black Lace seem as seminal a music act as the Velvet Underground. Jive Bunny – yes, I'd erased him from my musical psyche too – was a South Yorkshire DJ, Andy Pickles, who had the smartarse idea of using his sampler to lace together a bag of old hits in a 'Stars On 45' type medley. What was more overwhelmingly irritating than the actual aural result was the fact that enough people bought enough Jive Bunny records to make him/it only the third artiste - and I use the term as loosely as is possible - to score three number ones with his first three singles. Oh Rotherham, so much to answer for – the Chuckle Brothers and Jive Bunny.

But stepping back from the banality… what if you were playing in a band and wanted to adopt the Rave ideology? No problem. Musically, the incessant House breakbeats were borrowed by every drummer under the age of 25, heralding the great indie rock/dance music hybrid, with 'Madchester' leading the way. Madchester, in reality, can be summed up as the Stone Roses, the Happy Mondays, perhaps The Inspiral Carpets and every other band trying to sound like them. Even the originally folk-influenced James adopted the baggy vibe, to great and successful effect.

Manchester was a great place to be in the late 80s as a music fan looking to go out for a good time. But let me tell you from experience, perhaps not the best place to be if your band sounded like Aztec Camera with the occasional pretension of modernity. Right place wrong time?

My latest stab at pop super stardom was as singer/songwriter with Raintree County, and as local musical developments sped past us in 1989, we realised we had to at least sound a little bit in keeping with the times. Luckily, our manager at the time was going out with Graham Massey, head honcho of Manchester ambient dance beepers, 808 State. I'd met Graham before, interviewing him in his long-time Factory Records band, Biting Tongues. He agreed to produce a track for us, which became our debut single, 'Take' and first track on a mini-album released by Native Records of Doncaster. We made the pages of the *NME*, getting our piccy taken by a Manchester-based snapper who gave us a sparkling piece of advice if we wanted to advance our career – 'get on one'. We never did get on one. It was still a good time to be Manchester band – even if your profile didn't really fit into the Madchester groove. But was it such a good time to be a Yorkshire band, specifically a Leeds band?

The nearest that Leeds got to the Madchester baggy sound was The Bridewell Taxis. There was hardly a shortage of music-loving scallies in Leeds, and the Taxis certainly looked the part, sounded the part, but in a departure from the norm, they deployed a brass section of sorts – well a trombonist anyway. To these ears they were at their best when they sounded like a distant relation of the Teardrop Explodes rather than when they resembled, sonically at least, a watered-down Inspiral Carpets.

At least they came close to breaking the Manchester stronghold on indie grooviness. Apart from the garage band feel, they had the prerequisite laddish feel to them, with regular spates of football chanting breaking out at their gigs. However, releasing a cover of 'Don't Fear the Reaper' was perhaps not their wisest career move. Fair play to them though, they did do a Peel session, and built up a considerable following across the county, not just their home city. Their standing in Leeds can be plotted by the fact they packed out each of the venues they played in their heyday, from The Duchess of York pub to

The Warehouse to The Town and Country Club to the Town Hall. Even if they didn't conquer the globe, they conquered Leeds, becoming the city's Mondays or Roses. They supported all the baggy Mancs at various times, of course and played all the expected venues including the Hacienda, La Locomotive in that Paris, and er, somewhere in Blackpool.

Their name came from a local police station and has since become local slang for a police car. But after five singles and just the one album, the Bridewell Taxis called it quits in 1991 before the 38-inch flares started to look ridiculous. Probably a good move since they're still talked about in hallowed terms these days. They even enjoyed a successful reunion in 2005, but it seems they've parked up for good now.

There were still more orthodox indie bands from Leeds doing it – apart from the ever-popular Wedding Present, there was Cud. Cud were... exhales slightly wearily ... ex-students at the Leeds University, who got their first break when Peel gave them a session in 1987, then a second break when the Wedding Present's label Reception released their debut single, 'Mind the Gap'. Cud played unmistakably, and unsurprisingly, student-orientated indie rock, and though they did inject a modicum of danceability into subsequent recordings – tracks on the 'Leggy Mambo' LP in particular - they never came near to the cool, almost effortless grooviness of the Madchester rabble. Maybe that was partly down to natural 'attitude' as the personnel of the Stone Roses and the Happy Mondays were 100% 'local lad', with nowt added and nowt taken out.

To be fair, these Cud boys were slightly at odds with what was going on elsewhere in 1990, specifically on the other side of the Pennines, and stayed that way, possibly wilfully so. Retaining a sense of humour in your records was admirable at this seriously cool time – singles 'Hey! Wire' and 'Only (A Prawn in Whitby)' being the best examples of Cud's enduring light-heartedness. It's said that Cud may have found themselves high in the mainstream charts as well as the indie charts had they left the Imaginary label earlier. Sadly, the pressures of an eventual move to major label, A&M, finally did for Cud. They have since taken a walk down the regulation reunion route, an exercise that proved that their appeal was less than completely transient but they were always much more Wonder Stuff than wonderful stuff, and that wasn't just down to the 'Grebo' haircuts.

Less orthodox on the indie front, and filed under 'Very Close to Making It Big' were Leeds duo, the Rhythm Sisters, and not just because they were females in predominantly male territory. Mandi and Debi Laek were indeed sisters, aided and abetted by Normanton boy Bill Byford – no relation to Biff, but since he came from my own town, he feels like family to me, kind of. Their debut LP, 'Road to Roundhay Pier', was rightly lauded by the NME and The Guardian alike, with its songwriting qualities leading to comparisons to no less than The Kinks. The acoustic pop of the Rhythm Sisters should have propelled them to the same heights as The Proclaimers, but the follow-up LP, 'Willerby', didn't appear for another four years by which time… well, times change, don't they?

There was an interesting compilation LP released around this time on Stolen Sounds, 'Knowing Where It All Leeds' which included tracks from Wedding Present, Cud, and the Bridewell Taxis as well as the evergreen Mekons, and another band-most-likely, the Pale Saints. With their usual home on 4AD Records – the hippest of indie labels at the time – the Pale Saints was an interesting yet slightly frustrating proposition that had started out as a jingle-jangle combo a la early Primal Scream but then developed into an entity capable of both beautiful ethereal sounds and more bombastic guitar-driven indie-rock. Their heyday was probably in the early 1990s though they'd first seen light of day in 1987; one of their early gigs is cited as the occasion of the term 'shoegazing' being coined by a smart-penned reviewer. The addition of original Lush vocalist Meriel Barham coincided with a near brush with bona fide pop stardom, most teasingly in 1991 when their version of Nancy Sinatra's 'Kinky Love' reached the much sought-after Number 71 slot in the singles chart. It was progressively more downhill, but not in a free-wheeling way, from that point on and the band split for good in 1996.

But back in 1991, as the Dance Revolution looked under threat of petering out, there were new Saints in town. The Utah Saints were definitely no relation, being probably as far removed from the Pale Saints as one could get at the time. Numerically a duo, the Utah Saints comprised Jez Willis, originally from Carlisle, and Tim Garbutt from Lincolnshire, but both were proud for theirs to be counted as a 'Leeds band'.

The Utah Saints may have become one of the most respected Dance acts springing from the House scene of the late 1980s/early 1990s but Jez Willis certainly paid his dues before tasting success. Back in Carlisle, he played in a covers band and had his own mobile disco, playing weddings, birthdays and retirements, like you do. He migrated to Leeds, ostensibly to study, but with a more telling plan to get the job as Entertainment Secretary at Leeds University. "I thought it'd be a good way to learn about the music industry.... but I hadn't anticipated the politics involved." After a shorter stay in the post than anticipated, Jez's musical education continued when he ran a musicians collective in Leeds called 'Music for the Masses', a project originally run by Simon 'Jazzwank' Denbeigh, he of the March Violets.

"This was about 1983/84, and we had over 400 members. We were the first external promotions company to put gigs on at Leeds Polytechnic (now Leeds Metropolitan University). We put on bands like the Three Johns and The Redskins – it was a highly politicised time because of the Miners Strike. We raised a bit of money – but the way things worked at the time, you had to spend whatever money you'd made in order to get a grant the following year. So we bought a drum machine and a little PA system – our claim to fame with that is that the Wedding Present used that PA a few times."

But that drum machine purchase could well have been a watershed moment as Jez's studies duly went by the wayside completely after he got involved with not one but two bands. "Cassandra Complex was an electronic band who had a couple of Number One indie singles in Germany. After that, I formed MDMA – we chose the name prior to the whole rave thing kicking off (*MDMA was the abbreviated scientific term for Ecstasy*). At the time I was more into industrial electronic, so was already making electronic music before House arrived – it was the same instruments but just stripped back a bit, so it wasn't too aggressive. You sat back and listened, and realised that the two scenes were very similar apart from the fashion aspect – they were completely different. If you broke down the components on the music side, they were pretty similar.

"All the way through all this I was DJ-ing, running a night called the 'Mile High Club' in what became the Gallery in Leeds around 1987. The Gallery became a forum venue – an epicentre for rave, with loads of name DJs like Sacha and Pete Tong playing there. 1989 was probably the year when it really started to gain a lot of momentum – 'Acid House' was such a wide-reaching term, it grabbed music from everywhere to start with, everything than was electronic and had some energy to it was working. It was just a really exciting time."

Inevitably it was the DJ-ing side of activities that brought Jez into contact with his eventual partner in Utah Saints. "Tim was doing Friday nights in Harrogate club The Mix and I was DJ-ing there on Saturday night – we were playing the same kind of music but we were off each other's radar. When I met Tim, MDMA had just about finished, and he was recording stuff for a label called Ozone in Sheffield. The first track we started working on together was 'What Can You Do For Me?', sampling Annie Lennox and Gwen Guthrie.

"Tim went to oversee the pressing of 'What Can You Do For Me?' and decided to put it on coloured vinyl so it'd stick out a bit more than other 12-inchers. He came back and said 'it's gonna be this nice orange'. I only found out five years later that he's red/green colour-blind, so when the vinyl came through, the record was basically sick coloured. Kind of punk rock-y! We sent one copy off to Pete Tong, and Tim, ever the optimist, said 'he'll play that on Friday'. Sure enough he did. The week after we got a phone call from 3 Beat Records in Manchester asking for 300 copies – I said how many shops you got, the guy

169

said one! It was that mad – we sold the first pressing out in a week. We had no idea that was going to happen and it took off straight away. We signed to Pete Tong's FFRR label, two months later we were on *Top of the Pops*, and we ended up selling 135,000 copies."

That immediately set the Saints on a roll… "once we sampled Annie Lennox and got that cleared, the next one had to be Kate Bush. Around that time, when there were awards for best female vocalist it was always Annie Lennox or Kate Bush. It felt like such an obvious step to sample Kate next – we were amazed that no one else did it. Our record was the only time she has ever cleared a sample from one of her records. We had to go crazily high in 'the biz', up to the powers that be, to clear it, but it happened. We asked nicely…"

The result was 'Something Good' complete with samples from 'Cloudbusting'; KB obviously respected their intentions, because she also allowed Jez and Tim to use footage from her 'Cloudbusting' video for their own video. "Yeah. It was a massive compliment to us that she let us do that."

Utah Saints completed their initial 'trilogy' of singles with 'Believe in Me' featuring samples lifted from Human League's 'Love Action'; the three records are now cited as examples of the pioneering use of the sampler. So how important was the sampler in the scheme of things? "Massively. It just short-cutted production. The process had been painfully laborious before that. The moral argument over sampling will go on forever but the arrival of the sampler was incredibly exciting. You could get sounds that already sounded powerful and put them into your track. It was so expensive to get those sounds in a studio before the sampler came along – all of a sudden you could get the sound you wanted from a record you liked and your record sounded all the better for it."

So they obviously encountered more than their fair share of Luddite attitudes? "Oh yeah – there'll always be someone who takes exception to something new like that. For some reason sampling instruments was more acceptable than sampling voices, so we went and sampled the voice. We were quite proud of that, being on *Top of the Pops* with a vocal but no singer. To their credit *TOTP* went with it but I know it was a major headache for the show's director because there were just four blokes stood there and no singer to focus on."

But after 'Believe in Me', it was 'step forward to the mic, Jez' – "we wanted to make a big departure after the third single. For the fourth one, we sampled Slayer and I ended up singing on it. I realised that if you want to be in control of your band and its future you don't want to be relying on an external singer."

Sounds like they had a plan? "No, a lot of people think we had some kind of plan but we've always been much more organic and chaotic than that. We were in too much of a hurry up to that point – we should have been looking to reinvent ourselves album after album, not single after single.

"Suddenly we were asked to go and do PAs – we'd both been toiling away for years and not really earning any money out of it. We saw that as an opportunity to move onto the live circuit; we started to get a lot of love from the festival crowds for what we did. We were completely taken aback. Things got big quick... we got offered the support on the U2 *Zooropa* tour. It was Adam Clayton's preference to have us, while Bono wanted the Stereo MC's - we got the gig. We weren't prepared for how big we got and how quickly it happened, and we were certainly unprepared for the amount of media we got."

It was hard not to know the name 'Utah Saints', not least because the duo had deployed the most blatant promotional device on their early singles. "We'd put the 'Utah Saints-U-U-Utah Saints' bit in the first two records because the KLF did it in their records, getting the 'KLF' bit in. We thought, you're on the radio for two and a half minutes it's best to get the name of the band in, and get the name established... and it worked almost too well. It almost made the idea of the band bigger than the band itself in a way."

Speaking of the KLF, there's the famous Bill Drummond quote when he cited the Utah Saints 'the first true stadium house band'. Jez still finds that more than flattering: "for Bill to even know that we existed was amazing for us at the time. It was a massive compliment to just be on his radar. We looked up to the KLF such a lot, because they were completely ground-breaking and they kind of publicly handed us the baton when they called it a day. It's very humbling when something like that happens."

You know you're doing something right when U2 invite you on tour, REM's Michael Stipe name-checks you in interviews, and Pendulum come up to you backstage to tell you they used to listen to your records when they were kids! But you sense that Utah Saints are still less than secure with their standing. "I think it's something that's always held us back – lack of confidence. I've seen Tim DJ and I've seen top DJ's next to him – Sacha, Oakenfold – and they all know how good he is, and it's a genuine talent he's got. But we always kind of assume that we just got there before everyone else not that we're better than everyone else."

But surely that's what being pioneers are all about? "Yeah. But we've had a bit of self-doubt in everything we've done to be honest. It's only now that we are thinking that we are quite good at what we do."

I'd got it in my daft old-school head that these dance-y DJ types were as all as cocky as East 17 after a very strong coffee but Jez Utah seems uncommonly grounded – "perhaps that has something to do with being based in Leeds… it's sometimes hard being a Yorkshire band, writing from there because it's sometimes hard to explore your more sensitive side. It's good when you find out U2 as a band really are down to earth. You don't have to put on a diva act, you can just be yourself. If your music's good it'll stand up on its own."

And just to make sure that they both stay completely grounded, Jez and Tim have continued to DJ around the country, sometimes under their SugarBeat banner and sometimes under more anonymous names – "some of the requests you get on a Saturday night are for the kind of music you'll never play. You have to placate people who've had a few pints and want to enjoy their night. You quickly learn distraction techniques if you haven't got what they want."

Though they had one of the year's big dance hits in 2008 with a remix of 'Something Good', Utah Saints these days are all about 'multi-tasking'… "but we see ourselves primarily as musicians – that's what it says on our passports.

I'd like to see ourselves as composing musicians. But not in a Mozart way, obviously. We're not particularly adept musicians but we can put things together to make a new piece of music, transposing different pieces of music into a different context and make them work in a different way. It's terrible at Xmas when someone says, you're a musician, come and play this piano..."

It's no surprise that they're in constant demand as red-hot re-mixers for artists as diverse as Girls Aloud, Simple Minds, and even the Osmonds! But it's the thrill of making their own records that really does it for Jez – "when people say I used to just be into indie music or dance music before I heard your band and it changed the way I look at music. That's the best thing because that's exactly what we're trying to do. A lot of the time people say, no you can't surf different musical genres and that's the reason we took so long to bring a second album out. I think that's held us back though. Maybe we've been unfocussed in the past – instead of flitting around as we have done, it would have been much better to re-invent ourselves from album to album. It'd have given us a steadier inflow of income for one thing!"

The odd regret aside, the last eighteen years have been good to the Utah Saints. And yes – it all started back in Leeds, and Harrogate...

"London and Manchester, as usual were very good at stealing everyone else's thunder and taking the credit for something that was happening all over the country. Leeds in the late 80s and early 90s... the whole rave thing was brilliant, and Leeds and the surrounding area did have a big scene. The Mix in Harrogate used to be rammed with 300 or 400 people. And it never got any national coverage at all but it didn't need it. The Gallery in Leeds – the feeling there was we didn't need to become a national name, we were always full having brilliant nights. We didn't need the added hassle of having too much attention. It was incredibly exciting because people really were there just for the music, it was nothing to do with fashion. You were part of something that potentially could shake everything up... and it did.

"It's an easy comparison to make between Punk and Acid House because of the DIY element. You didn't have to be great musicians but you could make something happen. It was a very exciting time and Leeds definitely had a huge part to play as a city in it all, and it had nothing to do with being marketed."

The dance scene in Leeds has continued to flourish since the early 90s. Utah Saints' old road manager Dave Beer started 'Back to Basics' in 1991, and it's since become a legendary night out in the city. Leeds itself has become something of a dance mecca in a, to use the much bandied phrase/trade name, Dance Nation. Though DJs have enjoyed continued respect, it was inevitable that focus would eventually switch back to the traditional group format. At least the dance revolution was by and large a British movement, albeit inspired by a music genre born in the States. But the next definable British scene would have to see off another Yank import first.

Chapter Eleven

Who You Calling 'Common', Speccy?

Some of us can recall when Ibiza was actually a nice quiet place to go on holiday, read a few books, get a few early nights in, and listen to a bit of Ned's Atomic Dustbin on your Walkman whilst sunning your spotty carcass on the beach. If you were a music fan of the 'indie' variety in 1991, there's every chance that you'd tolerated rather than actively enjoyed the dance scene of the previous three years or so, because you'd really had little choice. The 'Madchester' phase had pulled almost every young person with a pulse in the direction of dance beats but blowing on whistles and waving your arms in the air in tribute to a faceless DJ was understandably a step too far for many.

Rap and Hip Hop had been coming over from the U.S. of Yankyland since the beginning of the 1980s and though we'd embraced all manner of cutting-edge acts from Grandmaster Flash through to Public Enemy, I'm not sure we'd gone so over-the-top so quickly for a Trans-Atlantic import – Chicago House included - as we did for the new American guitar-driven genre that started dominating the UK's alternative airwaves at the beginning of the 1990s. The stupid thing is, Grunge was at odds with the general up-ish mood of the day; in 1990, Thatcher had moved out of Number 10 with a full set of knives in her back, the Berlin Wall had been pulled down signalling a decidedly warmer era in East-West relations, and Saint Cliff nabbed his 700th Number One single.

Grunge was very much the counter culture of its day – unless I'm much mistaken, no-one felt 'luvved-up' listening to Grunge. As Nirvana, Pearl Jam, Soundgarden, Mudhoney and all that Sub-Pop Seattle stuff started getting a grip of the UK's indie scene, any home grown Grunge of a comparable standard was thin on the ground. Of the British pack of bands touching on the style, Teenage Fanclub were the only protagonists really worthy of mention, and even then there was always something more substantial hiding in the Fannies' overdriven guitar bashes. The Wedding Present employed grunge alumni Steve Albini for a brace of EPs and their 'Seamonsters' album, but they were all still recognisable Weddo's records. Gedge's dalliance with the Seattle sound was the extent of Yorkshire Grunge in those days (strange how the two words actually sound like they were made for each other though).

Nevertheless, the influence of grunge was in evidence on every city street, in every bar and at every live venue, dressed in checked shirt, loose ripped jeans and baseball boots. And if possible, with long, lank, greasy hair. Mmmm sexy. Like many looks associated with over-hyped movements, the grunge style was perversely, given the attitude it was supposedly representing, a uniform with next-to-no individual identity inherent. The same could be said of much of the actual music. Any deviation from the norm, or – wait for it – 'subtlety' marked out the band responsible as world beaters. Surely we could count on this nation's musical youth to do something in response?

It's quite obvious then that our county's opening shot in the new decade should have sod-all to do with this, coming from a predictably unpredictable source. The first Yorkshire Number One of the Nineties came from a prodigal son. Born in Leeds, but leaving for Darlington aged five, Jim Moir wasn't content being Britain's brightest new comedy figure, oh no. Better known as Vic Reeves, this 'Tyke in the closet' teamed up with The Wonder Stuff to send a new version of Tommy Roe's 'Dizzy' to Number One in 1991. Obviously, that record and his other two hits had a taste of novelty about them, Vic delivering in trademark 'Mr Songwriter' style, but for a short time, Reeves was, in his own lingo, 'tip of the top, cream of the crop, *Top of the Pops*'.

Non-comic chart-topping songstress, Tasmin Archer, appeared to come from nowhere. She came out of Bradford, in actual fact. Not quite a One-Hit-Wonder, Tasmin had been a sewing machine operator, singing backing vocals for a local band until she started helping out at a Bradford recording studio, where she started making her own demos. Snapped up by EMI in 1990, her first single saw the light of day two years later and struck instant gold as, ahem, Archer hit the Bullseye... no? Please yourselves. Though a fine record, 'Sleeping Satellites' really was against the grain of everything else going on in the music scene at the time, sounding more like a Judie Tzuke track from the 1970s. There were four more Top 40 hits for Tasmin, though I'd be hard pressed to name them, or even recognise any but the last of those, which was a cover of 'Shipbuilding', the sublime classic co-written by Elvis Costello. Good taste as well as talent.

There were actually two Yorkshire bands making their mark on the lower end of the charts but neither of them were what you'd call hip and happening. Little Angels were far from hip, being – you won't hear this often - Scarborough's answer to Bon Jovi. Very successful they were too in the rock world, not totally surprising since they'd read the 'Do it like Def Leppard' manual, and geared up accordingly in every department, even down to the Poodle Perms. Fair play to them, they scored 11 Top Forty hit singles between 1990 and 1994, and their last album 'Jam', even went to the top of the album charts. Amazingly, they never made a significant dent on the American Rock Market, something they were surely equipped to achieve. But lead singer Toby Jepson was allegedly

177

approached to take up the vacant vocalist position in Van Halen, an opportunity he surprisingly turned down.

The other square peg combo was Kingmaker, a very Indie band from Hull, even though they were signed to major label, Chrysalis. I say very Indie, because they were in the tradition of the aforementioned Wonder Stuff and Cud, a style increasingly old-hat in the period between Madchester and 'the next big thing'. Still, they too had hits, six of 'em in the Fab Forty, and two charting albums too; 'Eat Yourself Whole' was their defining moment, both the album and its title-track single. So what was the problem with them? Paul Heaton put his finger on it when he called them 'middle-class pretenders' – there was just something too contrived about them at a time when bullshit was instantly detectable. I think I can safely say that, as my own band, Raintree County called it a day, having been something of an odd-band-out in danger of trying too hard (good little combo though – should have been moderately big).

So where was the anticipated real-deal response from the Bright Young Things of Blighty to those Grunging Yanky fellas? Lads and Ladettes, I give you 'Britpop' – a term conjured up by latter-day broadcaster Stuart Maconie, still a humble *NME* scribe at the time. And yes it really did feel like an antidote to what became the manufactured misery machine seemingly feeding off the cult of Kurt Cobain. Finally, indie music fans were reminded that 'fed up' didn't really mean 'fucked up'. Though it wasn't without its own shade and shadows, Britpop at its best at least had an identity indigenous to this complicated island, with an onus on having a good time.

Maybe the 'laddish' attitude of the Gallagher brothers said more about the State of the Nation than their actual music did; Blur's songs did actually attempt to emulate the likes of The Kinks and The Jam, in representing vignettes of British life, and often succeeded. The third group that came to represent the Britpop echelon was perhaps the most British of the lot in essence, with kitchen–sink-dramas for songs, the mail-order catalogue look for an image, and a spectacularly ordinary manner for attitude.

Pulp were no ordinary band though, and their leading light Jarvis Cocker certainly neither dork nor dullard. Already introduced within these pages, Pulp had played their first gig in 1980 but had spent the subsequent seven years trying to get a foothold in the crazy world of rock 'n' roll before public indifference prevailed and Jarvis decided enough was enough – for the time being at least – as he took up a place on the film course at St Martins College of Art and Design in London.

If the White Rose County can claim to have a modern day equivalent to Morrissey, then it's surely Jarvis. A deep thinking chap with a pleasing turn of phrase, not immune from the odd spot of controversy, and of course with a long career that has touched on art, film and literature as well as, obviously, music. He may not have been as trigger-happy with the quotes as old Mozzer, but he's certainly a fellow aesthete of the first class variety. Can you imagine a meeting between the two over a plate of scones in a Lake District tearoom – now there's a film-script for you.

After Jarvis finished his film course, Pulp was brought out of cold storage and the classic line-up of Cocker/Senior/Doyle/Banks/Mackey recorded the third album of the band's topsy-turvy career at the end of the 1980s; the fact that it didn't see the light of day till 1992 was all to do with the pitfalls of being on a DIY indie label like Fire Records. But, the release of 'My Legendary Girlfriend' and 'Countdown' as singles in the preceding year brought enough press acclaim to make the eventual album release worthy of renewed attention; it displayed the first influences of dance music on the Pulp sound. But by that time the band had grown impatient and looked to their hometown's Warp Records for a boost – Warp's imprint label Gift released three watershed singles for the Cocker Crew, starting with 'Do You Remember the First Time?' It all started going right from that point, as Island Records picked up the band and released their breakthrough album 'His 'n' Hers' in 1994. Reaching the Top 10 of the album charts and being nominated for the Mercury Music Prize confirmed that Pulp had finally arrived, a mere 14 years after their first gig.

But it was the following year that catapulted Cocker to the pop star status that he'd always craved. On the back of a true classic single, 'Common People', Pulp stepped in for The Stone Roses at Glastonbury, played the set of their lives and stole the show. A double A-side single, 'Mis-Shapes'/'Sorted for E's and Whizz' copied 'Common People' with another number two placing, and predictably caused tabloid controversy for obvious reasons. No matter - at the height of Britpop, 'Different Class' topped the album chart and bagged the 1995 Mercury Prize. Just for good measure, Pulp finished their stellar year with another spanking Top 10 single, 'Disco 2000'. Could they ever top 1995?

Of course they couldn't. The 1996 BRIT awards did transform Jarvis Cocker from pop star to national hero/villain depending on your point of view. During Michael Jackson's ludicrous Messiah-like performance, a sozzled Cocker chose to mount the stage and ridicule the spectacle with a couple of well-directed bottom wiggles. The fallout from the incident was even more ludicrous with the tabloids going to town, some supporting Wacko in his condemnation of Cocker's antics, but one or two others actually in support of our Jarvis. The rational, un-hysterical response was one of understanding as to why the Pulp frontman felt moved to do what he did, with most other musicians present wishing they'd thought to do it themselves. Cocker himself has spent years playing down the incident – he is best known in some quarters for that tongue-in-cheek protest than for his music (and even the cracking impression of Rolf Harris he did on *Celebrity Stars in Their Eyes*).

It's well known that Jarvis struggled to cope with his new-found mega-fame even without his new-found notoriety. 'This is Hardcore', a much darker album in 1997, reflected the problems in his private life, and not surprisingly failed to achieve the success of its predecessor. Pulp recorded one more album – the Scott Walker produced 'We Love Life' in 2001 – before the band once again took a sabbatical. This one however looks to be of a permanent nature. Cocker has remained active however, releasing two well-received solo albums – the second in the summer of 2009 - as well as indulging in several other multi-media projects. He actually featured on the soundtrack of *Harry Potter and the Goblet of Fire*, and also in the film itself as the lead singer of the fictitious band 'The Weird Sisters'. Just as likely to be invited to talk on *Question Time* as perform on Later, Cocker is unlikely to disappear from public view for the foreseeable. There's far more to the man than a controversial arse, y'know?

Surprisingly perhaps, York has only figured fleetingly in our ongoing story since the days of John Barry but, though it's hardly rock 'n' roll capital of the world, the old historic Yorkshire capital (for that it is, if you hadn't guessed) features rather strongly during the 'Britpop' years. Following his well-chronicled exit from the Stone Roses in 1996, John Squire didn't waste much time kicking off his next musical project. Within months, Squire had recruited the other three-quarters of The Seahorses in York, firstly snapping up bassist Stuart Fletcher who he saw playing in a pub band in the old town, then singer Chris Helmes who he'd witnessed busking outside Woolworths in York. A tic-tac man at York races was apparently under consideration for the Bez-esque stage-dancing role, before Squire thought again and stopped recruiting after Andy Watts had been drafted in as drummer.

A debut album, 'Do It Yourself' received mixed reviews, though the four singles released from the collection did make the Top Twenty, including 'Love Me and Leave Me', a track co-written with the decidedly non-songwriting brother from Oasis, Liam Gallagher. It was a promising start by any standards; so it inevitably fell apart before a second album even had the chance of seeing light of day. It seems the musical differences all rested with Chris Helmes, less than complimentary was he of Squire's musical input, and it is said, rather fond was he of developing a solo career. Hmmm... John Squire has of course gone on to build on the artistic talent first demonstrated on Stone Roses record covers; Chris Helmes hasn't gone back to busking outside Woolworths in York though... Woolies has closed down, he's busking outside Poundstretcher now.

Only joking, Chris – call off the heavies.

But despair ye not – there was a York band that lasted the course during that mid-90s period, and indeed, are still wowing them in a familiar 'we-broke-up-years-ago-but-nothing-else-has-worked-quite-as-well-so-we're-back-together' fashion. Famously named after singer Rick Witter's train pulled into York Station (of course it wasn't Rick's personal train in a mega-huge rock star's plaything style), Shed Seven came into being back in 1990. But it wasn't until 1994 that they made their breakthrough with their second single for Polydor, 'Dolphin' making the Top Thirty and giving the band their first *Top of the Pops* appearance when that still meant something.

The Sheds' personnel had been playing together in bands from school days and Rick Witter had always known he wanted to be a singer in a band. "It started coming together seriously around 1989, when we got into the Stone Roses and that Madchester scene. We realised we were good at what we were doing and thought we could make a go of it. There was only really us in York playing that kind of stuff. We'd gone through school listening to the Smiths and that really good indie music. And we always knew that it would kind of come back round again – not that we were waiting for a scene. What we weren't aware of was that there were a lot of other like-minded bands – Oasis, Sleeper, Bluetones – all in little pockets of the country, all doing the same thing as us and biding their time."

And along came Britpop, well kind of. "A lot of bands say that they didn't feel part of it though they were included in it. We were British and we played an element of pop music, so if we had to be pigeonholed as Britpop then that's what we were. We were doing similar stuff before the phrase was coined and recognised as a movement – but then we were classed as 'New Wave of New Wave', with bands like S*M*A*S*H and These Animal Men. A lot of it was the journalists trying to create a scene, which worked to an extent because it made the public aware of it but then it becomes overkill. We never really wanted to be part of any scene."

Shed Seven's relationship with the music press was always a bit iffy to say the least… "It was good at the beginning because we were a bit of an enigma. It slowly started to go downhill because we wouldn't play ball. We didn't want to move to London and start stroking Peter Stringfellow's hair, we were happy where we were, which I think pissed the *NME* off. Without the strong fan base that we had, we'd have probably gone under. Every article seemed to start with 'Shed Seven, the band from the unfashionable back of beyond, York' – always a patronising comment on where we were from. It got to the point where a review wasn't talking about our new single, it'd be about how I stink of piss. I don't – just to set the record straight."

Wasn't that indicative of Britpop being more about style and attitude than content? "Yeah, I think Oasis have a lot to answer for there. As much as I liked their music and still do, it pissed me of the way they insisted on giving it the 'we're the best and if anyone says we aren't, we'll fuckin' have you' attitude. Just grow up, y'know!"

So, not much Britpop camaraderie? "Everyone was nice to your face obviously. We had loads of bands support us, happy to be playing a good size crowd with us, who went on to be bigger than us, selling more records. That's when they slag you off, saying you weren't cool. You just think 'fuck you.'"

That two-faced attitude is just one of many wonderful things you can't control in the pop music industry; the week that Shed Seven were due to be on the front cover of the *NME*, Kurt Cobain blew his one face off and took their front page along with every other front page going.

Britpop was a double-edged sword for bands like Shed Seven, finding themselves in the shadow of Big Britpop Three but also spared the continuous scrutiny and allowed to get on with the music process. Which was no bad thing, as Rick concurs until "the pressure to sell records became ridiculous". The band made a rod for their own backs in 1996, scoring no less than five Top Twenty singles, amazingly making them the most successful chart act of the year; "the timing of the 'Maximum High' album was perfect, the scene was there and there were plenty of celebratory songs to be taken from that album and put out as singles. We had a lot of hits but could still walk down the street and people wouldn't know us".

Surely inspired by the crap yet strangely compulsive lunchtime BBC TV quiz show, *Going for Gold* gave the York band their only Top Ten hit. But 15 hit singles in total, four chart albums and a large solid fan base is success by any standards, and certainly by Yorkshire's. However, Rick and the boys still regret their decision to sign for Polydor back in 1993. "We signed to them because of their tradition with The Jam and The Who. In hindsight I wish we'd signed with a good indie label. We got our way for quite a while before people started seeing pound signs instead of quality."

Polydor's insistence at the decidedly premature release of a Greatest Hits album in 1999 signalled the beginning of the end of Shed Seven's relationship with their label, and after similar fallouts with subsequent smaller labels, Shed Seven called it a day (the first time) at the end of 2003. But 13 years wasn't a bad innings for these, or should I say, those modern transient times.

Hats off to Rick Witter and The Sheds; honest enough to admit they never set the recording world alight – "we were never a great studio band" – and thankful enough for what they did achieve. "We had our time then and we're fortunate enough that we still organise tours and sell loads of tickets. We put the work in live and that created our fan base. We were always renowned as a good live band. That's what got us back together and keeps us going now."

The mid-1990s are quite rightly seen as the high point of activity for the UK's pre-digital media circus. *Loaded* magazine officially heralded the age of 'the Lad', ably assisted by Chris Evans with his *TFI Friday* TV show, and more bizarrely, the Labour Party. 'New Labour' spun its way to power in 1997, but not before inspiring the instantly annoying term 'Cool Britannia' and all the fake 'let's celebrate being British like we did in the 1960s' stuff that rang the death knoll for anything meaningful that threatened to surface from the hype.

The 'Blur versus Oasis' rubbish inevitably meant that most new bands strived to emulate one or the other, and happily the majority fell at an early stage before we had to endure them. Yorkshire be credited here – we at least offered a handful of acts that were, if nothing else, different, odd or interesting.

Chumbawamba could conceivably be labelled all three.

Okay, strictly speaking they weren't a Yorkshire band as such, their origins being in Burnley, in the old enemy territory of Lancashire. But because they decamped to Leeds, setting up home in an Armley squat, Yorkshire has come to be seen as their spiritual home. And quite right too; their first recording in 1985 was in support of the striking Yorkshire miners of Fitzwilliam, a town that was being torn apart by the proposed pit closures. Chumba's music was very much in the folk tradition back then, but they proudly announced themselves as Anarchists. 'Agit-pop' was a badge quickly pinned to their lapels, and they even called their record label 'Agit-Prop'.

Twelve years on, and with a more electric, even dance-influenced sound, Chumbawamba unexpectedly made the move from the deep underground to the spot-lit mainstream with 'Tubthumping', a celebration of the 'common man' and specifically his ability to carry on in the face of adversity, not to mention his ability to survive the drinking of a full off-license's worth of booze. The rabble-rousing single went to Number Two in the UK, and even more bizarrely, Number Six in America! The song still turns up regularly on film and TV as well as radio – for years it was the tune the DJ at Elland Road played as the subsequently hapless Leeds United and their opponents ran out onto the pitch. In the context of Britpop and its aftermath, it fitted in nicely with its football-chant chorus, and lyrics of determined British defiance. It probably wasn't what they intended, but Chumbawamba gave the Britpop generation an anthem to rank alongside anything that Oasis, Blur or Pulp had supplied.

But their new-found fame didn't distract them from their political agenda as they sought to heighten public awareness of pertinent political issues and the hypocrisy of the nation's so-called leaders. The emptying of an ice bucket over

185

the head of Deputy Prime Minister, John Prescott, at the 1998 Brit Awards by the band's Danbert Nobacon was a gesture of disgust aimed at the New Labour Government's lack of support for the striking Liverpool dockers. The front page incident was a welcome comment on the tiresomely fake 'Cool Britannia' circus actively encouraged by the Labour marketing machine.

Though they have continued to release albums on a regular basis, 1997-1998 was undoubtedly Chumbawamba's prime-time period in the spotlight (the 'Tubthumper' album went triple-platinum and the band had two more chart singles), perhaps helped by the fact they were on nasty old EMI records at the time. Though the line-up has changed – my cousin, Neil, last chronicled here as guitarist/vocalist with The Donkeys, has been in the Chumba fold for a goodly while – the aim remains the same… singing songs of rebellion to highlight the issues that are otherwise deemed best left unsaid. In recent years, they've returned to their acoustic folk roots in a stripped down line-up, but their following remains strong and committed. More power to 'em.

Hull had another of their 'pop moments' in the mid-90s when female duo, Scarlet, scored a Top 20 hit, seemingly out of nowhere, with 'Independent Love Song'. Though they did have a minor success with their follow-up, the pair disappeared from view almost as quickly as they appeared on the scene, though they did a little better than most flash-in-the-pan popsters after the song was used for a terrible, but inevitably popular American 'rom-com' movie, 'Bed of Roses', in 1996.

Another act sometimes viewed (mistakenly) as a One Hit Wonder is Babybird. To all intents and purposes, Babybird is, and always was Sheffield's Stephen Jones, deft exponent of 'Lo-Fi' music, a term covering a multitude of sins – at its most double-edged, it describes the beautifully simple, recorded organically and unfussily, or, it's an amateurish effort recorded on a cheap Portastudio, in desperate need of spit, polish and real production. To be fair, Jones's musical career developed out of an experimental theatre project that required songs to be written and recorded. The result as far as Jonesy – or Babybird as he chose to call his project – was concerned, fell somewhere between the two alternatives just offered as a definition of Lo-Fi.

After a minor hit with his debut single on Chrysalis's Echo label, the follow-up catapulted Babybird towards a preposterously elevated pop profile. 'You're Gorgeous' was played with such frequency on the radio, and TV for that matter, that you swore you'd kill an innocent bystander if you heard it once more. It got to Number Three in the charts, and Number One on the Hate List. Not yer man's fault of course (unless you hate him for writing and recording the thing in the first place). He did have minor hits with follow-ups and has continued to record in his own sweet way, in a less commercial, more off-the-wall style but there always appeared to be something of the maverick about Mr Babybird. The commercial success of 'You're Gorgeous', it has been suggested, has meant it's been difficult for Jones to be viewed as a serious independent artist. It's hard to fathom whether he actually cares one jot; suffice it to say that he's continued to happily make music, commercially successful or not (which by and large is the case). You could say he's probably best known now for supplying the theme music for Gordon Ramsey's *'F-Word'* TV show. Except, erm, not that many people know that it's him.

Also from Sheffield, but in more traditional band shape and size, came The Longpigs. Not the sexiest band-name going, I grant you (second only to Bogshed in the blunt Yorkshire band-name chart) but in the scheme of things, i.e. the Britpop period - I'm getting sick of using the term now, Stuart – they appeared to be the band that seemingly snatched disappointing failure from the jaws of joyous success. 'Failure' is a harsh assessment actually, because the Longpigs did in fact register five Top Forty hits in the UK, together with two Top Forty albums. But it feels like failure when you discover that but for, let's say, the more erratic, less desirable aspects of the music industry, things could, and perhaps should have been so much better for the band.

187

Revolving around quirky voiced singer/songwriter Crispin Hunt, The Longpigs was the latest gig for Richard Hawley, then 'merely' a renowned guitarist of not a little talent. Hawley had been last heard of with his long-time band Treebound Story, treading gingerly through the Indie minefield. "I was playing with a band called the Lovebirds, post-Treebound Story, when the Longpigs asked me to join them. They were just about to sign to Elektra Records, and record an album produced by Gil Norton who'd done all the Pixies stuff."

So far so promising. What could possibly go wrong? Well, apart from Crispin Hunt being involved in a car accident that put him in a coma for days, and knocked their schedule back, Elektra UK folded, leaving the band in limbo. Luckily, U2's label, Mother, stepped in and bought up their contract. The next couple of years saw a period of solid gigging, supporting the likes of Radiohead and Supergrass to promote their early singles, none of which made a noticeable impact chart wise. But it was their fourth single. 'On and On' – a ballad no less – that finally cracked the Top Twenty, and whetted the appetite for the debut album 'The Sun is Often Out', a record that Hawley still rates very highly: "people look back, press whatever, and write the Longpigs off as Britpop also-rans. But they sold a lot of records that band. The first album just fell short of going platinum in Britain."

Both *Q* magazine and *Melody Maker* also rated the album, placing it in their Top 50s of 1996. A re-issue of their debut single, 'She Said' went Top Twenty too, putting The Longpigs on the verge of the Britpop Premiership. And that's when a rather inadvisable career move took the band down the long dark road to a premature end. As well as doing the business in Blighty, 'On and On' had made waves over in the States enjoying a full year of regular airplay on College Radio and taking its place in what they call their 'Modern Rock' countdown. When the opportunities to capitalise on this unexpected success came up, the Longpigs naturally packed their bags and dug out their passports. Well you would, wouldn't you? "We started off supporting U2, then toured with Echo and the Bunnymen... then toured with the Dandy Warhols ... *and then* went on a tour of our own. We just went round and round America. That could test the patience of any musician."

The price for Hawley personally was almost too much – "the night my new baby daughter was born, our tour manager came to get me from the hospital and I didn't see her again for nine months. Having a young family and touring is virtually impossible – you've got to have a very strong and tolerant woman."

The Longpigs were, shall we say, well known for indulging in the more excessive side of that there rock'n'roll, and it was nigh on impossible for Hawley not to join in. "I went bonkers even though I was the only one who had a missus and kid. When I say I was fucked, I was beyond that - I didn't know Shit from Shino. Our lass has been amazing in terms of what she's had to put up with. But she was really shocked when I came back from this tour – I was no more than eight and half stone, wet through. I was in real trouble."

If the state of the individual personnel was bad enough, the relationship between band and recording company was critical. "Our second album has some truly great moments on but Universal bought out Mother Records, and they wanted to close the label down. The fact is, all the other acts on Mother sold nothing apart from us. So they just shipped 10,000 albums even though we had pre-sale orders of 90,000 and that gave them a reason to close the label down. It's stuff like that that tests your faith in it all."

To say the writing was on the wall for The 'Pigs is an understatement, and to his credit, Hawley stayed in the fold, though by now he was well in-demand as a guitarist. "I would have stuck with Crispin to the bitter end – I'm a loyal person, and I don't believe in leaving sinking ships. But it was just time to call it a day because the pressure was crazy and I was a mess with everything. It was either we split up or someone was going to die, really. It was a shame because The Longpigs started off as a really great band."

It won't have gone unnoticed that most, if not all of the music so far featured thus far, has been of the confirmed White and Western variety. Good to report then that from the West of Yorkshire in the 1990s, came forth Black Star Liner as part of the emerging Asian underground - though that was a tag they were less than fond of. Formed in Leeds, personnel drafted in from various local combos including the baggy-ish Hollow Men, Black Star were a far more interesting proposition than most traditional bands surfacing in the mid-decade soup, but they were perhaps more than a little hidden in the shadows of Cornershop who made the breakthrough to the mainstream with 'Brimful of Asha' in 1997. Like Tjinder Singh's band, Black Star mixed Asian music, born of traditional instruments such as sitar and tabla, with more Western dance music. But where Cornershop had more than a smattering of mainstream pop tunefulness, the Leeds combo brought in even more underground sounds into their mix, such as dub reggae.

First gaining notice via a pair of self-released 12-inchers, Black Star Liner earned a deal with EXP Records after co-owner Feargal Sharkey (yes, he of the Undertones) heard their session recorded for the John Peel show. An acclaimed debut album, 'Yemen Cutter Connection', led to them signing a major deal with Warner Brothers. Their second album 'Bengali Bantam Youth Experience' took up with the plaudits where their debut had left off, earning a Mercury Music Prize nomination. But the album turned out to be their swansong as relations in the bizarre union between underground band and major label turned sour and the band fell apart as prolonged legal wrangling ensued.

Back in the mainstream, it wasn't just about bands with mod haircuts, sixties riffage and laddish behaviour. Terrorvision hailed from Keighley, another West Yorkshire outpost hitherto nearly famous for having a rugby league team. Definitely more rock than pop, but no worse for that, success was a while in coming for Terrorvision, the band having started out as Spoilt Bratz in 1987. Though they'd flirted with single chart success in 1993, their breakthrough came with the following year's 'How to Make Friends and Influence People' album, the five singles plundered there from all breaching the Top Thirty. By 1996, the Bradford based quartet were at the height of their profile, with their first Top

Five single, 'Perseverance', and lead singer Tony Wright becoming something of a celeb in his own right, thanks to his endearing TV appearances.

Strangely, this is where the roller coaster started its decline for 'The Terrors'; their fourth album saw them detour away from the old accessible rock formula toward a more subtle(-ish) melodic tone. The result was that radio-friendly 'Tequilla' was a big hit with casual listeners but a no-no with their hardcore fans. So regardless of the single peaking at Number Two in the Hit Parade, the end was nigh for Terrorvision – they were dropped by EMI after the follow-up to 'Tequilla' struggled to Number 42. Just how fickle is this business, eh?

The band have inevitably done the reunion thing since their original break-up in 2001, and will doubtlessly continue to do so at regular intervals; the nice thing about Terrorvision was you didn't need to be a fan to at least warm to them, if that makes any sense. Proof that with a modicum of self-effacing wit, you could be a bit 'rock', quite 'lad', but still endearingly 'likable'.

If any band went out of their way to replicate the Oasis model, it was Embrace, Brighouse's favourite/only pop prodigals. Just a few miles outside Halifax, Brighouse seemed an unlikely source for these latecomers to the Britpop party but nonetheless, Embrace quickly picked up a suitably laddish fan base. Why, they even had a pair of brothers at their heart but the antics of Danny and Richard McNamara come a poor second to those of the mad-for-it Gallaghers (though Danny did hit the tabloid headlines fleetingly courtesy of a fling with Gina 'Ooh Just a Little Bit' G). Noel's only comment of note on the McNamaras was that he thought Richie needed guitar lessons.

It was around this time that the gloss of Britpop faded – I'm not blaming Embrace, you understand – and the term was wisely locked away; and it has remained so until numpties like me see fit to resuscitate it. As for Embrace, their early recordings seemed to be forever striving to be 'anthemic'. Once they stopped trying so hard, they actually made some rather decent music, especially the singles from their second album, 'Drawn from Memory'.

But… they never looked like reaching Oasis-like heights, maybe the reason

191

that their record company Hut eventually dropped them. Independiente Records picked them up and reaped the benefit; Coldplay's Chris Martin gave the band a song to record, 'Gravity' went Top Ten and Embrace were back on track. Their 'Nature's Law' single took them to Number Two in 2006, and 'Out of Nothing' went one place better in the album charts. Then they were invited to write and record England's official World Cup song for that year... oh dear. It's got to be said that 'World at Your Feet' was probably one of the worst football songs ever committed to record or CD. But at least Embrace were back in some health even if it wasn't quite rude.

Now if you're thinking that's the total sum of Yorkshire's involvement in this period's pop evolution, you'd be wrong – in fact you could hardly be wrong-er. Of course, there were other developments in the music mainstream while all this Brit-bloody-pop nonsense was going on. Manufactured pop acts became the biggest of business in the music industry, thanks to the American boy bands like New Kids on the Block, and their UK counter-parts, Take That. What next? Well obviously, girl bands... introducing the most successful Yorkshire Pop Star of the 1990s, Melanie Brown. Mel B to me and you... no? 'Scary Spice' then! Yes, she of the all-conquering Spice Girls.

If success is measured in terms of sales, the Spice Girls were the UK act of the decade, selling an inconceivable number of units globally. And if it's measured by the criteria of personal wealth accrued... well, ditto. In any normal group, young Melanie from Leeds would have just been one of the girls, but such was the in-yer-face marketing of the Spice Girls, that every member was almost a solo act before they made that status official years later. At least 'Scary' wasn't the least talented of the bunch, and didn't marry an annoying, overrated footballer.

In a funny sort of way, the Spice Girls were the most 'Britpop' of any acts, selling their Britishness to maximum effect and profit. Hurtling towards the end of the century, British pop music was in a healthy state, at least as far as the accountants were concerned. The Spice Girls were one Britain's major exports, Oasis were being touted as the biggest band in the world (by Noel and Liam that is), whilst, from the less laddish leftfield, Radiohead were being exhaulted as the new Pink Floyd (how I wish they'd been from Rotherham).

The question was... how do you follow something as super-hyped as Britpop?

Chapter Twelve

The Calm Before The Storming Of The Stage.

So there we were... 'Britpop', despite being fifty-percent marketing toss, had given the UK pop scene a timely boost; 'New Labour', despite being fifty-percent toss, had given UK politics a timely boost; and a new millennium was fast approaching. Surely there were good times ahead. Of course, fifty-percent toss would have been a good result there; none of us knew the world, and the way we look at it, would change forever within two years of those millennium celebrations.

But even as 2000 sped forth from the horizon, Yorkshire chucked new quality ingredients into the mainstream music mix. Dance music hadn't gone away while Noel, Liam, Damon and Jarvis were taking centre-stage. If anything, it had actually got stronger than ever with club brands like the Ministry of Sound and Cream carving out a multi-platform niche that cut across the whole division of youth culture.

Gatecrasher was Sheffield's club giant – it had started out as a club night in Birmingham, doing the rounds of that city's venues, but once it had relocated to the Leadmill in Sheffield, it was on the path to being officially 'massive', eventually taking over The Republic nightclub in the city, and renaming it 'Gatecrasher One'. A full Gatecrasher empire has subsequently been built, including another pack-'em-in venue in Leeds.

The point of that bit of information? To illustrate that dance music was a thriving entity, independent of the mainstream. Yes, serious dance was on the High Streets of every major UK city, meaning you didn't have to go to the Balearic Islands for that authentic dance experience, and dance DJs were now National radio DJs with their own specialist shows. But there was still something exclusive and underground about the dance scene. Though every now and again, a dance record infiltrated the daytime airwaves, the charts and *Top of the Pops*.

It had escaped my attention – no surprises there then – that Sheffield electronica collective, All Seeing I, had registered three times in the singles chart; not just with the Tony Christie/Jarvis Cocker collaboration 'Walk Like a Panther' in 1999, but with 'The Beat Goes On' the previous year (they also produced a version of the song by Britney Spears on her debut album), and '1st Man in Space', also in 1999, a strange Space Oddity-esque dance-pop track featuring the ubiquitous Phil Oakey. Dance but not as we know it, Jim.

For a more recognisable dance hit, step forward Moloko. Comprising one of the Sheffield's long time music activists, Mark Brydon, first seen as bassist in Chakk and subsequent key player in the building of FON studios, and Irish vocalist, Roisin Murphy, the pair broke through to mainstream success with 'Sing It Back', a funky Latino-tinged track that had been a massive club hit in 1998. Given the remix treatment by German house producer, Boris Dlugosch the year after, 'Sing It Back' rose as high as Number Four in the Mighty UK Hit Parade. Good enough, you might think but hold the bus, stop the front page

195

- the follow-up, 'The Time is Now', scored even higher, hitting Number Two and subsequently being used, seemingly forever, as background music for Sky's Football coverage. Quids in!

Though Brydon and Murphy enjoyed three more Top Forty hits, they never quite hit those heady late 1990s heights again, and while Roisin inevitably went solo with no little success, 'Brydo' continued enjoying a career as a respected studio-dudio, taking up re-mixing duties with a whole host of dance acts. But… the fact that were actually a romantic item during their chart heyday surely makes them the biggest Yorkshire based hubby/wife pop act of all time – the Peters and Lee of the Dance Scene? (We won't let the fact that they weren't married and neither of them actually originally comes from Yorkshire get in the way, will we?) And of course while other young fellas were dreaming of drinking Bacardi with Linda Lusardi, some of us were fantasising about having a cocoa with that bird from Moloko.

As Roisin said, the time was indeed now, or rather then. Five… four… three… two… one… whayhay, it's the year 2000! (Or it was). Aaahhh, very good, how we drank. Then… nothing. Well, not much really. I suppose we shouldn't have been too surprised that all this new Millennium hoo-hah led to something of an anti-climax as we finally left the Twentieth Century behind.

But there was something happening… Kate Rusby was earning the first of her four BBC *Radio Two Folk Awards*.

Underwhelmed by that musical landmark? There is a kind of significance in there, trust me. Singer-songwriter Kate Rusby had been making her name as the bright young thing of English folk music since the mid-1990s. Born in Sheffield, but growing up in the Barnsley area, Kate played with other like-minded folkies, making her recorded debut with fellow Barnsley folkie, Kathryn Roberts in 1995, before releasing her first solo album 'Hourglass' two years later. The debut received positive reviews but it was her next album in 1999, that brought Rusby to real national notice as 'Sleepless' was nominated for the Mercury Music Prize.

196

Not a chart act though, I hear the cynics cry. Au contraire. In 2006, the singer-songwriter tasted her first chart success, rather unexpectedly in a duet with winsome Boyzone warbler Ronan Keating, 'All Over Again' hitting Number Six in the singles countdown of June 2006.

But Kate's original success came at a time when the singer-songwriter was starting to come back into mode. When I say 'come back in', it had hardly been out, it's just a proposition that's never been seen as sexy or exciting a spectacle as a band. A young woman or bloke with just a guitar or piano for company never seems like the most mouth-watering prospect until you actually hear the songs presented in their most organic form (the way that most songs are brought into this wacky world anyway).

Another South Yorkshire musician was surprisingly heading down the path of the singer-songwriter as the 20th Century flicked over into the 21st. Surprisingly, not least in that though he'd been playing guitar in Sheffield bands for over ten years, no one had any idea that he had the stuff of singer-songwriters in him. Not even Richard Hawley himself.

Though the Longpigs were still clinging onto dear life by their fingertips, Hawley's main gigs in the late 90s were as additional guitarist for Pulp on the road – he's a long-time friend of Jarvis Cocker and Steve Mackey - and as session musician on numerous recordings for other artists. "From 1996, I'd started doing session work for various people and did thousands in the next few years. Looking back, I don't know how the fuck I did that given I was still in the Longpigs and playing in Pulp. I used to get offers all the time – I even did the *Romeo and Juliet* movie soundtrack with Nellie Hooper, as well as stuff for All Saints and Robbie Williams.

"At that time songwriting was something that had taken a back seat for six or seven years, though I still wrote stuff when I was with the Longpigs. But in my mind it was always something of a sideline – I was primarily a guitar player and certainly never thought of myself as a singer. In early 1999, Crispin

197

(Hunt) started writing songs for the next Longpigs album. I asked politely if I could have some studio-time with my songs as well and they said 'no'. I'd been writing songs pretty much since I was 14 but I never tried to foist my stuff on the Longpigs. I didn't mind 'cause Crispin was a good songwriter."

But the opportunity to record some of his own stuff did eventually arise for Hawley. "There was a bit of studio-time left over at Yellow Arch in Sheffield – can't remember what from – so I recorded nine tracks in six days. I went out with an old friend, Graham Wrench, who was working at the Leadmill at the time. We got pissed, came back to my place and I played him what I considered to be demo songs from this session. He listened six or seven times, then said he wanted to be my manager. I just laughed. The only reason that I'd sang on the tracks was because I couldn't find a singer who had a deep enough voice – there are not that many baritone singers really.

"I'd played this stuff to Jarvis and Steve Mackey from Pulp as well and they loved it – I'd known Steve since we were five and he said 'it's like hearing for the first time the person I've known all my life'.

"We chose seven tracks from the session, and Graham took them to London, touted them around and eventually got round to a guy called Keith Cullen who ran Setanta Records, that put out Divine Comedy and Edwyn Collins's stuff. Keith put my first mini-album out and it went down really well, to my utter shock and horror!"

From the word Go, it was clear that Richard Hawley 'solo' was a different fish kettle from the music produced by the bands he'd previously been part of. "A lot of what I do is very gentle. I might be a gobshite in reality but I have got a very soft thoughtful side to me that's reflected in the music."

For the uninitiated, Richard Hawley's music takes in a whole raft of classic music influences – Johnny Cash, Scott Walker, and even Jim Reeves being just three of the named influences often bandied in reviews. And this is where Hawley's musical heritage, steeped in the blues and country of the American

South but most definitely made in Sheffield, marks him out as a true musical scholar, as well as accomplished singer-songwriter and all-round good egg.

There was never any danger than young Rich wasn't going to be a pro' musician. "It was all mapped out for me with me Dad, Granddad and Uncle all being musicians. It was around us all the time as kids - me Dad worked with Charlie Rich and backed Sonny Boy Williamson, and me Uncle, Frank White, played backing for Little Walter at the Esquire Club in Sheffield."

Both Dave Hawley and Frank White are 'names' to drop in Sheffield's musical circles, both having played with the legendary Hillbilly Cats, the Steel City's long-running Rockabilly combo, and having been instrumental in the city's burgeoning R 'n' B scene of the 60s - Frank even played guitar for our good friend Dave Berry in his Cruisers.

Hawley Junior didn't stand a chance, and not much else got a look in – music's gain was perhaps his beloved Sheffield Wednesday's loss. "I absorbed music like a sponge as a young man - me Dad had 3000 vinyl albums and me Uncle 2000. Me Mum was a singer – I learned to sing while she was ironing, she always put the Everly Brothers on. But that's the kind of music I listened to when I was a kid – plus loads of blues."

It didn't take long before he was learning to play it too, picking his first guitar up at six. "Finding my Dad's 1963 Fender Stratocaster under the sofa was like a Hallelujah moment for me."

Not only did Hawley Senior pass guitar lessons onto his son, he gave him his love of rockabilly; Richard still takes his rockabilly side group 'The Feral Cats' out on the road from time to time. His early musical heroes obviously included Elvis in a "list that could go on forever. But my real heroes were and still are my granddad, father and uncle. I didn't think about it at the time, but now I think back and there were musicians popping in and out of the house all the time."

But it was another Uncle – 'Uncle Chuck', a friend of the family, who gave young Hawley his first experience of life on the road. "I went on tour with him in Holland and Germany when I was only about 14 or 15. He told me mother

199

we'd be playing theatres and dance halls; we were actually playing strip clubs. Me Mum didn't want me to go but me Dad's attitude was that 'the only way he can get experienced is by having experiences like this'. They basically couldn't get an adult guitar player and so they phoned me Dad up. But he was in semi-retirement by then, not playing live anymore. He'd had a nervous breakdown during the seventies, brought about by working in the steelworks in the day and going out playing gigs at night, every night for years. He just pushed himself too far because he loved playing music so much. Eventually, it gets to the point where you can't do both, you have to do one or the other.

"But anyway, we were literally playing behind a curtain in these strip clubs, while a girl in front of it would get her clothes off. Then we'd play a 15 minute set in front of these dirty old blokes who just picked their papers up and ignore us. I'd played with Uncle Frank at the Pheasant but that was the first tour I ever did."

It's clear that Richard Hawley's always had the wherewithal to be a professional musician but at what stage did he think he could or should try making a good living at it? "I'd done a lot of Working Men's Clubs when I was playing in me Uncle's band – it was fun when I was 17. But I remember playing Healey Bottom Social Club when I was about 19; it was a Sunday evening, we were on this little stage playing Chuck Berry stuff and there were this couple at the front. She had a scarf on with curlers in her hair, 'nighty' on underneath her overcoat and furry slippers, and the bloke had pyjamas and dressing gown on underneath his coat. When they announced the 'pie and peas have come', everybody rushed to the back of the hall apart from this little old bloke. His missus went for the pie and peas, came back and took a hanky out other handbag… he spat his false teeth into this hanky. Then, as we carried on playing, she started spooning his chopped up pie and peas into his mouth. The gravy was dribbling down the side of his mouth… and it was at that point that it dawned on me, I should start giving music a proper go, writing my own songs. I knew I wanted to make music but I didn't want to play it in front of an audience like that – I could see it would be soul-destroying. But if everything went tits up now and I had to go back to it, I'd still be proud to be making a living out of making music. I admire people who go out and do working men's club's night after night."

It is highly conceivable Hawley could have been playing guitar for Morrissey instead of pursuing his own solo career – "I was in me early twenties, and still doing Treebound Story. I remember being with me mate Anthony who'd done me star chart – he said it'll be a long struggle but eventually with the last throw of the dice, it'd come right for me. That same day, the phone went and it was Morrissey on the other end! He wanted me to audition for his band – so I went and played along with Boz Boorer and all these other rockabilly guys. Me and Morrissey went off for a chat, and we were talking about Helen Shapiro, the Stooges, and the MC5, and I started singing 'One Night' by Elvis. He asked me why I was singing. I said he might need backing vocals and I think that was it. He said 'I'll be in touch'… and I never got a call. I don't think it was anything malicious – just don't think I was good enough."

Just one of many disappointments in Hawley's musical career but it's obvious that he's been well equipped to cope with them. "One thing that kept me going when things went tits-up was something my Granddad said to me when I was a little lad – 'If you're going to be a musician, you have to accept before you even start, that you might fail.' Best advice anyone's ever given me. I was never in it for a Ferrari and a villa with swimming pool in Miami – I was in it for the music. When everything went tits-up and I was left with our lass and me guitar, it all boiled down to love – that's what kept me going. Love and the music was all I needed – everything else can go fuck itself. There have been so many points in my career when it's been the last throw of the dice time – I can't think of any other musicians who've had more bites of the cherry."

After the trials and tribulations of Treebound Story and The Longpigs, not to mention joining Pulp at a tricky stage of their story, you'd think that Richard's solo career has been comparative 'plain sailing', especially after the praise dished out to his first two albums. Wrong…

"I did one more record for Setanta – 'Lowedges' – that was critically acclaimed but went down like a lead balloon in terms of sales. Setanta went bust after overstretching with their releases, and though we reached an agreement over royalties and distribution of the first three albums, we were left in limbo. Graham said we needed to get the money to pay for me to record a full album's worth of material, so he could take it round and get me another deal. It became a case of writing and recording under major fucking pressure."

But out of this adversity came 'Coles Corner', eventually released by the EMI supported Mute Records. The album was Hawley's breakthrough, and it deservedly gained nomination for the Mercury Music Prize, losing out to the Arctic Monkeys, whose frontman Alex Turner received the award with the words 'someone phone 999… Richard Hawley's been robbed'. (Hawley was to play a part in a Mercury triumph however when Elbow picked up the 2008 prize for 'The Seldom Seen Kid' – he co-wrote and contributed vocals to 'The Fix' on the album).

'Coles Corner' was the second album, after 'Lowedges', to reference a Sheffield landmark; and its successor 'Lady's Bridge' followed suit. They're indicative of the Hawley style of songwriting, very much a personal exercise. "I got it in my mind the way I wanted my music to sound from the age of 14. I wrote 'Just like the Rain' on my 16th birthday. There are songs that have just hovered around until I got round to recording them much later. I kept this hidden really. The stuff that I really loved was influenced by my Dad, my Uncle, and Granddad. It was stuff that was deeper down inside me. In the '80s I was a big Bunnymen fan, and I loved music like that but it doesn't go down as deep as the rockabilly and country stuff, and folk music as well. These are the sounds deep down in the mountain where Gollum lives. If you write music deliberately to appeal to other people – that's commercial basically – I don't see that people can believe fully in that. It's a smokescreen and there's no heart in it. I write about things that are real – me Mum and Dad used to tell me about meeting on Coles Corner in Sheffield so it means something to me."

'Lady's Bridge' took Hawley into the Top Ten of the album chart for the first time; the first single from the lovingly crafted collection, 'Tonight the Streets are Ours', scraped into the Top 40. Though he himself might say these things mean nothing, fans and observers see them as vindication for a musician who's stubbornly stuck to his guns.

But even now, Hawley's not sure about his ability as a singer. "I was always embarrassed about my voice. All the singers I knew were indie screechers, y'know, and a deep baritone voice seemed so monumentally unfashionable. I was always happy to be at the back in bands, I wasn't interested in being the frontman and to this day I wish someone else would fill that fucking job! Being a singer and guitarist on stage might only seem six, ten or twenty feet apart but they're really a thousand miles apart in terms of the role. I never fancied being the frontman, because to be honest, with the exception of Jarvis, Nancy Sinatra and a few select others, most singers I've ever worked with are complete arseholes. To fill that role you do have to have an ego the size of Saturn and all its rings. The way I was brought up was to be one of the lads, and don't be a pain in the arse."

Hawley's been making music professionally for nearly 25 years but remains determinedly independent of the music biz – "there are some great people in there, but otherwise, to coin a phrase, it's full of cunts. Their whole reason for being is something I don't want to be part of. I find it astounding that I get invites to the Brits and this, that and the other but I don't belong there, I don't feel comfy in that environment at all. It's not something I aspire to. I can see it for what it really is… which is a bag of shit."

If any modern-day musician can be said to have carved out a niche with a music that's hard to define, it's our mate Richard Hawley – is that the way he likes it? "Yeah I do. Just being on me own little boating lake or whatever. For me I just wanted my solo stuff to be something that had some meaning rather than be another attempt to cash in on the charts. I never thought I was going to

203

sell any records, and now to be in this position where I've just finished me sixth album, just played on Jarvis's new record, and I'm meeting Lisa Marie Presley to write some songs with her, is just fucking bonkers. I never expected this to come out of that encouragement from Jarvis, Steve, me wife, me Mum, Dad, Graham and people – that encouragement to open me mouth… without them I would never have done it. It was me Dad turning round to me and saying 'son, you've gone thirty now, you've got a good voice, you've got good songs – you've avoided the issue for all these years, it's about time you give it a try'. I did and here we are… me talking bollocks to you for two hours."

With another album, 'Truelove's Gutter', out in Autumn 2009, Hawley will undoubtedly be hitting the road again with the regular live band that's helped earn him a gigging reputation second to none. People have been known to go to a Hawley show just to enjoy your man's entertaining between-song banter. In my mind at least, he's everything a Yorkshire Pop Star should be – a grounded, unpretentious talent, supremely aware and proud of his roots, yet with the enduring potential to be a star anywhere in the world. Only a matter of time I'd say.

Oh yes, we've been turning potential global stars out on a regular basis for a while, don't you know? Young Corrine Bailey Rae was making the first meaningful moves in her musical career in the early 'Noughties'. Her childhood and formative years in Leeds make for interesting reading – enjoying a happy middle-class upbringing, singing in church every week, being obsessed by Led Zeppelin, that ordinary sort of thing. Oh yes, and at 15, Corrine, wielding an electric guitar, fronted an all-female indie band called 'Helen' in the style of celebrated American combo's L7 and Veruca Salt. Amazingly, Corrine's band became the first indie act to sign to confirmed heavy metal label, Roadrunner Records, one-time home to Slipknot, no less! The union was short-lived however as Helen's bass-player fell pregnant and the band split.

Not one to dwell on disappointment, Corrine discovered soul and jazz when she started working in the cloakroom of a Leeds jazz club, a part-time job that helped to support her English Literature studies at the city's University. Developing a more soulful approach, she started writing her own songs whilst collaborated with local dance acts on various obscure recordings, before getting noticed and signed up by Global Talent Publishing. Working with Craig David's old collaborator Mark Hill, got Corrine more serious attention, culminating in EMI snapping her up at the beginning of 2005. Her debut single 'Like a Star' was a prelude for a best-selling debut album and a Top Ten single 'Put Your Records On', quickly became her signature tune. The best indicator of her star status on both sides of the Atlantic was the number of music awards she was nominated for – just the 18 in 2006. She ended up winning four; two of them coveted MOBO awards, for best UK female singer and best newcomer.

However, tragedy struck in 2008 when her husband, Jesse Rae, a highly respected session saxophonist, was found dead, his death blamed on a suspected drugs overdose. Corrine is poised to bounce back from this personal low with a new album later in 2009 – you'd guess her already heavily-celebrated career will prevail for years, hopefully in happier times.

But stepping back to view the bigger picture, was it just solo acts making headway at the beginning of the much heralded decade, century and indeed Millennium? Of course not… but frankly there wasn't much going on in the line of bandology from our part of the island. What was going on, quietly at first but later with some gusto, was a teenage Leeds band called, rather precociously, The Music.

A debut indie single 'Take the Long Road and Walk It' had garnered rave reviews in all quarters from the *NME* to *Radio One*'s Steve Lamacq, and the bigger labels started sniffing round the indie rock quartet from the Kippax area. Hut Recordings it was who snaffled up the band, releasing their self-named debut that took The Music into the Top Ten of the album chart. All good then… with a charismatic frontman like Robert Harvey and potential guitar hero in Adam Nutter, a powerful sound sometimes touching on psychedelia, even earning comparison to the Stone Roses, a record deal with Capitol in the States, and a legion of fans eager to worship them as the biggest band since Oasis. What could possibly go…

Well, no sooner had The Music released their second long-player 'Welcome to The North' than they stepped out of the limelight, while, it transpires, singer Harvey sought professional help for his alcohol and drug problems. To say it was bad timing for a Yorkshire band, as we will witness, is something of an understatement. It was the summer of 2008 before The Music resurfaced with 'Strength in Numbers', their third album. A few things had happened while they were away.

That's not to say that The Music have missed the boat – they've had six Top 40 singles in total, with the re-issue of their debut single claiming their highest placing at 15. And, they're not without success on foreign shores either, being a popular act in Australia, of all places. And of course, they're still going, relative young men that they are. But it has to be said that for a band that were flavour of the month for a fair few months, and the band most likely for more than one 'musical authority', The Music have yet to become the headline band they threatened to become in their infancy. Perhaps that's still to come?

It's mighty difficult to write a book chronicling the modern developments in music without mentioning the media circus that shanghaied the evolution process in the infancy of this new decade. What is it they say... reality bites? Reality TV came to the fore in the 1990s but back then there was something of artistic value in producing a documentary series about ordinary people's lives in an unusual setting like an airport or on a cruise liner. The voyeuristic nature of the exercise was at least controllable, in that the public participants had the ultimate say about what made it onto the viewer's screen. The series about the cruise liner – 'The Cruise' – made a star out of a Wakefield singer called Jane McDonald. An average club singer never got so lucky; on the back of the TV

206

series success, the lass from Wakey's debut album stayed at Number One for three weeks, and the snappily titled seasonal single 'Cruise into Christmas Medley' (can you see what they did there?) took her into the Top Ten. Though she's continued to sing, with her albums invariably charting, she's now whittled out a career for herself as a 'TV personality'.

Tip of the iceberg? You betcha! Some bright spark producer realised Reality TV was a great platform for showcasing the most basic of human traits – competition. It was only a matter of time before what is basically 'the talent show' was resurrected for the Reality TV generation.

Pop Idol first aired on our screens in 2001, brainchild of pop impresario Simon Fuller; though yes, record company executive Simon Cowell was present from the start as a judge, he only became Lord and Master when he introduced his vastly different *X Factor* format a few years later. The winner of the first UK *Pop Idol* was Will Young but who – hands up – can name the inaugural runner-up? Have a cigar… yes, Gareth Gates!

No disrespect to the Bradford lad, but Gaz was pure gold, in a vulgar bling-stylee, for the show's producers. A normal looking young fella who could sing a bit but… had a 'human story' to tell. Unlike many of the heart-rending secrets that only get revealed in a short film before the contestant actually sings, Gareth's little back-story was there for all to hear before he'd sang a note – he suffered from the cruelest of stutters, taking a good five seconds or more to announce his name at the first audition. Yet when it came to singing, there was no problem (some less kind critics would say there was a big problem with his singing voice – it was crap. But not me).

Hats off to him though as he seized his chance, courtesy of Cowell's BMG record label of course, scoring four Number One singles and eight Top Twenty singles in total. And he has used his unexpected celebrity to do good works for several high profile charities, and qualified as a speech coach, the youngest person ever to do so in the UK.

He seems a very nice young fella, so any attack on the process that gave him success, and hopefully happiness, is certainly not a personal attack on him. But, it's hard not to line up the banal entity that is the modern popstar-spotting show against the old organic process of finding your way in music a la Richard Hawley, and think that there is something that is ludicrously wrong about it.

Hawley himself sees such shows as "just cruel", watching people with genuine dreams of stardom being destroyed by a dozen unkind words in front of several million sniggering viewers. And such a crass presentation of 'talent' says much of our 21st century world – instant celebrity, instant gratification, instant disposability. But is that the point – view it as a Pot Noodle and not a five-course feast? That's another book…

Sticking with *Pop Idol* shows and indeed, sticking with Bradford, there's another 'Pop Star' from our neck of the woods, who unlike our Gareth, is still at the height of her stardom. *Popstars: the Rivals* took place in 2002, with five girls being sought to make up a new girl band to compete against a new boy band, built by the same process. Kimberley Walsh from Allerton, Bradford was one of those lucky five girls, but only just. When the last ten hopefuls were announced, Kim hadn't made the cut. It was only when one of the original ten, refused to sign a contract claiming the pay the band would stand to receive was substandard (ouch - wonder if anyone ever dares mention that to her these days?), that the Bradford gal stepped in as a happy substitute.

Seven years, four Number Ones, 20 Top Ten singles, dozens of awards, and several million pounds later, Girls Aloud are arguably the most successful British Girl band ever – although The Spice Girls would probably have something to say about that (and there are grown men who'd pay good money to see the fight that settles the argument). Kimberley herself, it has to be said, has had her rock 'n' roll moments, not least causing controversy when pictured enjoying a crafty toke on a spliff.

By 2005, Kim and Girls Aloud were firmly established at the top of the pop tree. And but for a few of our less mainstream acts beavering away in the background, the music landscape was as you were, with our ever-growing fascination with celebrity meaning that 'Style over Content' was very much the predictable order of the day.

Halfway through a new decade, weren't we due a band from Yorkshire making the odd wave or two? The Music had been prime candidates for the job but circumstances kind-of beyond their control governed otherwise. It'd be good to have a local combo on the front of the mags and papers again, getting regular daytime airplay, getting talked about excitedly at school after making a TV appearance, being everybody's 'favourite new band'. Be careful what you wish for. In a bus-like scenario, you don't have a successful Yorkshire pop band for ages, then two come along at once…

Chapter Thirteen

It's Up To You, New Yorkshire New Yorkshire…

Overnight Success… it used to be the stuff of Hollywood movies. These days it's the stuff of Reality TV talent shows. Where else can a middle-aged spinster from an anonymous Scottish outpost be sneered at one minute, then be hailed as a global singing sensation within hours, courtesy, of course, of the Internet? One thing for sure, it isn't the stuff of Yorkshire Pop History. Even Gareth Gates and Kimberley Walsh had to go through weeks of absolute agony before they got the TV viewers vote and became 'stars'. So did we. Luckily, I discovered there is an 'off' button.

Ask any working musician, and they'll tell you that 'overnight' in Yorkshire entertainment circles, as probably everywhere else beyond the casting couches of California, invariably means years. If it's as few as two or three years, then you're very lucky as well as talented. And the remarkable rise of Yorkshire pop bands in 2005 may have seemed to smack of 'overnight success', it was far from it.

Runston Parva started their long road to pop success back at the tab end of Britpop, forming in Leeds back in the medieval times of 1997. Adopting a deliberate misspelling of Ruston Parva – a small village in East Yorkshire – as their name, Nick Hodgson and Andrew White found their lead singer Ricky Wilson prancing around as a would-be Mick Jagger in a local Rolling Stones tribute band. But it wasn't until they recruited old pals Simon Rix and Nick 'Peanut' Baines, and shortened their name to Parva in 1999, that anyone took a blind bit of notice. Luckily for them, that 'anyone' was Mantra, a subsidiary label of Beggars Banquet. The Leeds quintet delivered three singles and one album – '22' – but to a less-than-rapturous reception. And listening to those Parva recordings now, you can see why. They're very much a potpourri of every indie band of the nineties, from Nirvana to Radiohead, Primal Scream to Blur, often resulting, not altogether surprisingly, in a less than inspiring aimless thrash. As it was, Parva came to their crossroads in 2003 when Beggars Banquet decided to dispense with the Mantra label and all the bands recording on it. A serious re-think was on the cards.

Meanwhile...over in Sheffield...a set of spotty youths barely out of school were playing their first gig at the city-centre pub, The Grapes. After a few more performances, The Arctic Monkeys made the decision to record a set of demo tracks, burn them onto CDs and give them out to the audience at their gigs. Though that might, in retrospect, appear to be have been a masterstroke of marketing, it was actually really just a reaction to the regular practice undertaken by other unsigned bands who actually sold their recordings, however ropey, after their gigs, an enterprise that particularly pissed off the Monkey's singer and chief songwriter, Alex Turner.

The demos were ripped, burned and passed around via computers and before long fans were turning up at Monkeys' gigs and singing along to the

211

songs en masse. Next thing you know, these same fans had created a *MySpace* page for their new faves – though the band still claim they knew knob-all about that development and had no direct part in it, it was undoubtedly what first attracted the attention of the record companies eager to snap up the proverbial next big thing. Alongside Lily Allen, the band are cited as the first artists to take full advantage of the age of social networking on the Net.

So what was all the fuss all about? Well, only a young band playing guitar music as exciting as the best angular punk but also as tight as hell, with a singer with the nasal delivery of John Cooper Clarke singing the undiscovered prose of a young Alan Bennett. There was no doubt this band were from the North of England, and a second listen told you they were specifically from Yorkshire. While the A&R execs were falling over each other in an effort to get to the shiny new prize, the Arctic Monkeys released their first recording proper, an EP 'Five Minutes with Arctic Monkeys' which featured the stand-out track of their early days, 'Fake Tales of San Francisco'. Its success only fed the hype surrounding the band, so by the time they played the unsigned stage at the Reading and Leeds festivals, half the bodies in the audience were singing along while the other half were waving cheque books.

Back up the M1…Faced with the need for a radical rethink after losing their independent label, Parva had become Kaiser Chiefs in 2003. Named after the South African club side from whence Leeds United's hugely popular Lucas Radebe had arrived, the band's most important development came in the music department, with the blatant influence-dipping sound of yore being stripped away to reveal a catchy-chorus-encrusted set of songs more akin to post-punk Power Pop. As keyboardist Peanut said, "when we became the Kaiser Chiefs, we were so settled we knew the style we were performing, and the band was a genuine band. We're not trying to be like anybody else, and that was our aim."

Respected 'webzine' offshoot label, Drowned in Sound gave the Kaiser Chiefs the opportunity to put a single out in 2004, and 'Oh My God' duly and pleasingly paid a brief visit to the lower reaches of the charts, peaking at number 66. That original version of the song, recorded in Nick Hodgson's bedroom, was given immediate endorsement when it was made 'Record of the Week' in the *NME*. Suitably impressed, B-Unique picked up the band, offering them a five album deal, and they were truly underway. The first Kaiser release on their new label was the song that was to become their signature tune, 'I Predict a Riot'. The song was inspired by an evening down at the Hi-Fi Club in Leeds city centre, where another promising local band, Black Wire, were playing at one of the 'PIG' nights that Hodgson and Wilson ran on a monthly basis; as things started getting slightly out of hand, it was the Kaisers' drummer who sensed trouble with the immortal words, 'I predict a riot'. I personally had hoped that inspiration had surfaced on an occasion when the boys were down at Elland Road watching the Mighty Whites – as they often do – and the crowd had been perturbed by some dubious refereeing decision – as they often are – and had launched into the old terrace chant of 'there's going to be a riot'. Bang goes that theory.

Whatever. Apart from being as catchy as hell, the song was notable for its sheer 'Yorkshireness', telling the story of a hazardous night out in Leeds with references to 18th Century 'Leodensian' dignitary John Smeaton, after whom Wilson's comprehensive school had been named. The use of the word 'thee' – 'you' in Yorkshire-ese – was a rare use of local parlance in a modern record, the kind of thing you might expect and hear from a Jamaican reggae band but not from a guitar-driven pop group from the suburbs of Leeds. Its release in November 2004 took the band into the Top Thirty of the singles chart and paved the way for the debut album 'Employment' in March 2005.

And it was 'Employment' that really established the Kaisers in 2005, though the re-issue of the first two singles and a further pair including 'Modern Way', the first song they wrote as the Kaiser Chiefs, obviously did them no harm either. While the album was given a near unanimous thumbs-up, not least for its 'quintessential British' flavour, there were inevitably detractors too. The first shot fired in what's become a long-running slanging match between the Kaiser Chiefs and Oasis, came courtesy of Liam Gallagher as he dismissed the Chiefs as a 'bad Blur'. Whilst Damon and Co may have taken that comment as a backhanded compliment, the remark was nothing if not obvious. The Leeds band had gladly cited Blur as an influence, and 'Employment' was actually produced by none other than the highly sought-after Stephen Street, who had earned his studio spurs with the Smiths in the first place, then of course, Blur.

No matter. 'Employment' was a celebrated debut, eventually going platinum six-times over and being nominated for the 2005 Mercury Music Prize, not to mention peaking at number 2 in the album charts. If that wasn't enough, The Kaisers were one of only two British bands invited to play at the Philadelphia concert of Live 8 Day in July 2005. The other Brits? Our old rockin' mates, Def Lep of course.

Back in old Def Leppard territory, the Arctic Monkeys were still making a buzz as loud as a chainsaw, with all the ears of the music industry now listening in. But with a healthy disrespect for most of the record companies courting them – many of which were making rather less welcoming noises about the Monkeys making 'slight' changes to their act – the Sheffield band eventually plumped for a deal with Domino Records, home to Franz Ferdinand, and well-respected for their old school, minimum bullshit, 'DIY' approach. Domino reaped an immediate dividend for their investment as The Arctics' debut single for the label, 'I Bet You Look Good on The Dancefloor', went straight into the charts as a big badass Number One in October 2005. And that's about as 'overnight' as it gets in the real world of pop success. But in the Arctic Monkeys story, it gets better. The following January saw another top-slot single with 'The Sun Goes Down' and a Number One album with 'Whatever People Say I am, That's What I'm Not' officially becoming the fastest selling debut album in British pop history. The band had achieved this despite having to deal with a potentially disruptive personnel change when original bassist Andy Nicholson left, citing

214

an inability to cope with the increasing attention and resultant fame that the band had thrust upon them – Nick O'Malley stepped into his shoes without too much fuss.

The Brit Awards for 2006, presented in the February of that year, confirmed that Yorkshire was most definitely back on the Pop Map with a vengeance. The Arctic Monkeys won the award for the Best Breakthrough Act whilst The Kaiser Chiefs went and won three of the blighters, for Best Group, Best Rock Act and Best Live Act. But while those two combos were collecting their prizes, giving drunken speeches and very possibly pinching themselves, there was another local act, often forgotten but nonetheless closing in on the blind side to take their place at the vanguard of what became known as – courtesy of the *NME* – the 'New Yorkshire' music movement…

The Cribs are unique. No really. Starting out in 2002 with twins, Ryan and Gary Jarman on guitar and bass respectively – both taking up vocal duties - and younger brother Ross on the drums, The Cribs is no cuddly family affair; anyone expecting the Wakefield version of Hanson would be sadly disappointed. The Cribs are a punk band.

From the off, The Cribs have been an uncompromising unit with a distinctly barbed lyrical content and an unswervingly purist attitude towards their craft as recording artists. Hitting the scene as The Strokes and The Libertines were setting the indie agenda, the Jarmans' early output can be classified as 'Lo-Fi', with the emphasis on achieving the rawness of their live performance. Little surprise then that their eponymous first album in 2004 was recorded in just seven days in an old eight-track studio, Toe Rag - the result was distinctly 'garage rock', as intended.

Don't be thinking that The Cribs are a set of musical amateurs though. As Gary Jarman reveals, music's been a big part of their lives for a long time: "I had always been involved in music to some degree in the Yorkshire area, be it in bands, the symphony orchestra, promoting shows or running a studio with my brothers. We started to play together purely because we had the same musical interests, which was hard to come upon at that time... it seemed pretty obvious. There was never any masterplan or even a shred of expectation we would be signed, as that just didn't happen back then, especially not to people from the North."

A self-confessed fan of The Beatles and Queen when he was very young, Gary's tastes changed as a teenager when he became "a huge Sex Pistols fan, with The Ramones a close second. Nirvana, Sonic Youth and a lot of the US 'alternative' bands were very important to me throughout my teenage years, as well as being pivotal in turning me on to a lot of the more obscure acts that I would later cherish. Locally, The Real Losers were an incredible garage rock band from Leeds, the most uncompromising band I have ever come across. Boy racer were an influence to some degree in the formative years of the The Cribs, and Pop Threat were an awesome noise/shoegazer band. Karren Ablaze who ran the 'Ablaze!' Fanzine is someone who I have enormous respect for too."

So was there a 'Yorkshire scene' as such when The Cribs started out? "Not one that I was aware of. That seemed to come from the press later on. But Wakefield was slowly getting better at that time; there were a handful of like-minded bands that would play shows together, while not necessarily sounding anything alike. We would play late night shows with art rock bands, or squats with hardcore bands - stuff like that. Running a studio gave me an interesting insight. There were a bunch of bands with everything in common except the way they sounded! We would put on big warehouse shows in the studio from time to time, people would party all night and travel from miles around - we had hope if nothing else."

Did The Cribs set out with a 'manifesto' of sorts? "Yeah. I had just got out of music college, which I fucking hated, so my original 'manifesto' was just to maintain a very back-to-basics DIY approach, and throw off all the useless nonsense/rules that I was forced to adhere to at university. My views have mellowed a little since then; I absolutely value musicianship, just not necessarily in a traditional sense. I feel proud that we have really stuck to our DIY approach throughout it all though."

That was the music side of things; what about early encounters with the industry? "I was a kid from a nowhere town, down in London for the first time, so I could absolutely smell a phony, and a lot of the major label reps that would come and schmooze with us in the very early days didn't get very far for that reason. Wichita (Records) were, and still are, awesome guys - we talked about weird American underground bands, or cutie bands and post-punk obscurities for hours in the pub. We immediately knew we wanted to be on this label."

It won't surprise anyone to hear that Gary and his bro's have a healthy disrespect for the industry – "I don't want to sound cynical, or like the whining 'rock star', but all the fucking clichés are true. I get disillusioned with so many facets of it - the bigger you get the more you are exposed to, the more disillusioned you become. We are lucky enough to work with a label and management that we love - I can't imagine how some bands deal with it."

It was The Cribs' second long-player in 2005 that put them in the bigger picture, and inevitably in the freshly minted bracket of 'New Yorkshire'. Produced by the rather splendid Edwyn Collins in his own West Heath Yard studio, 'The New Fellas' was championed by the usual commentators as the work of a highly individual act, sounding like no other band at the time. Opening track and single, 'Hey Scenesters!', quickly became something of an indie anthem. Though they'd registered in the lower chart with earlier singles, 'Scenesters' finally put them in the Top Thirty. The intention of recreating some of the endearing ragged energy of Orange Juice, by putting the Jarmans and Collins together, definitely paid off.

2005 was a good year for Gary and his brothers, apart from being roped in as part of this 'New Yorkshire' thing: "I thought it was ridiculous. I hated it. It was strange for a band like us, who had always been totally independent, not to mention the fact that at the time we were already 2 albums into our 'career', to all of a sudden be regarded as part of a 'movement'."

Was there actually 'a scene' as such? "People did drink together, and socialise I suppose. I think the key to the scene as I knew it was a night run by Nick Scott - the guy that does all our artwork - called The Village Green Preservation Society. It was at a tiny bar in Leeds called Milo's and only played British music. It was ace. Bands would play impromptu shows, crushed in the corner. Every band that was good in Leeds came out of that club. As soon as it started to be recognised for that, Nick, all respect to him, shut it down. There were also people like Johnny Strangeways promoting really great shows and festival weekends, as well as a really great club-night. He had been doing that for years, but it was just more underground so it slipped under some people's radar. It's a shame that the press focussed so heavily on the county after a few bands had got big, rather than scratching the surface to find some of the more important stuff that had been going on for a long time."

But there was support and camaraderie amongst West Yorkshire bands at least? "I suppose there was, yeah. For example, at the height of their initial fame Kaiser Chiefs would take us on tour with them, and in turn we would do the same for other local bands, such as Black Wire or The Research. I don't think it is because we are all Yorkshire folk, so much as the fact that these people were friends, and you were frequently exposed to what they were doing, so if you liked it, you supported it.

"There were some good sides to all the attention. The best thing that came out of it was the fact that people were all of a sudden mobilised and very pro-active, at least in Leeds. A lot of new club nights and independent promoters sprung up, so the old guard all of a sudden lost it's stranglehold over the city. It also took the focus away from London. That was gratifying, as some people still believe that culturally nothing exists outside of the capital. I think the down-to-earth nature of a lot of the Northern bands helped kill off some of that hipster culture that everyone was so fascinated with in the early part of this decade."

Apart from 'The Big Three' – Kaiser Chiefs, Arctic Monkeys and Cribs - there was many more pop acts coming out of the county besides, with Sheffield and Leeds turning out smart new bands on a monthly basis. From the former came The Long Blondes, Milburn, The Harrisons, Little Man Tate, Bromhead's Jacket, Pink Grease, and Reverend and the Makers; from the latter, the Pigeon Detectives, Forward Russia!, Sunshine Underground, Your Vegas, Black Wire, Lodger, and Dead Disco. Strangely though, most of these have come and gone, some rather at an inexplicable point in their timeline, some rather tragically just as they were on the verge of good if not quite great things.

The Long Blondes were only yards, even feet away from unqualified success, when cruel circumstance nipped their rapidly opening bloom prematurely in the bud. Centred on the charisma and vocals of Kate Jackson, the band comprising three women and two blokes, and sounding like a cross between Pulp and Blondie, were forever being touted as the best unsigned band in the UK before Rough Trade put that right and signed them at the beginning of 2006. Originally from Bury St Edmunds, Jackson, it is said, had moved to Sheffield to be closer to her hero Jarvis Cocker.

All was proceeding swimmingly – debut album 'Someone to Drive You Home' and its follow-up, 'Couples', peaked at numbers one and two respectively in the indie charts, and both infiltrated the Top Fifty of the album charts proper. Purveying pure pop songs with added quirk, and a voice with Chrissie Hynde potential, The Long Blondes were set to take the step up. Then guitarist Dorian Cox fell ill, with what turned out to be a stroke - terrible enough to happen to anyone, but to a young guitarist with a band on the cusp on mainstream breakthrough, just cruel. The band split as it was unknown when or if Cox was going to be able to play guitar again. It's a credit to their solidarity that the idea of recruiting another guitarist doesn't appear to have been a serious option. It's hardly surprising that Kate Jackson is now being groomed by Rough Trade as a solo artist, with Bernard Butler writing and producing as he did for Jackson's wildly successful label-mate, Duffy.

Of the other new Sheffield bands, Milburn seemed most likely to follow in the Arctic Monkeys' footsteps. Though eventually charting with singles and album in 2006, they did seem to be a little too like their more industrious city-mates, but not as good. After a second album saw them going backwards, Milburn split in 2008. Ironically, they'd been selling out gigs in Sheffield as The Monkeys were playing their first gigs. Such was the rapid rise of Turner and Co, that Milburn were supporting the Arctic Monkeys when they broke big. The same could be said of many Sheffield bands, some who are still cracking on – they've been left in the dust cloud of the Arctic Monkeys.

There is an exception. Enjoying Top Ten success with their debut single in 2007 were the splendidly named Reverend and The Makers. Of course singer Jon McClure's not really a man of the cloth - he got the nickname because he was looked on by some of his Sheffield contemporaries as something of a 'preacher'. He has subsequently proved himself to be a very capable spokesman for young people, appearing on TV and radio, most impressively when offering a considered opinion on the success of the BNP in the European elections of May 2009. It's clear that McClure's is very much a politicised voice; well known in the Sheffield's cultural and political community, he's been integrally involved with the ongoing 'Instigate Debate' project. As well as being an ex-flatmate of little Alex Turner, he was responsible for much of the written material on the Arctic Monkeys website when it first took to the internet screen. And it's his brother who appears on the front of the Monkeys debut album 'Whatever People Say I am…', smoking a fag with relish.

Back with the music, Reverend and the Makers scored a hat-trick of Indie Number Ones with their first three singles, the first two of which made your actual Top Twenty singles chart. As of summer 2009, it's still their debut 'Heavyweight Champion of the World' that they're best known for; not surprising since it reached the heady heights of Number Eight in the charts. Possibly even less surprising, is the fact that Jon the Rev tends to sing in a recognisably Yorkshire accent. With a spanking new album about to be unleashed in the late summer of 2009, Sheffield 'legend' McClure is poised to become a recognisable figure on the national stage.

It's been a similar scenario with the Leeds collective, outside of the Kaiser Chiefs, where one band in particular seemed to be in pole position to progress to relative stardom, only to miss out when they decided to split, while another has built steadily on initial success whilst maintaining its independent status.

The notoriously rabble-rousing Black Wire – it was thanks to them that the Kaiser Chiefs originally predicted a riot, remember - were surely destined for relative greatness, perhaps not in a mainstream chart sense but definitely in the realms of the cool and the influential. 'Attack Attack Attack' was a startlingly good debut single, not surprisingly a *NME* Record of the Week. With an intense New York punk vibe running through their debut album, Black Wire sounded like the real deal. Anti-climactic then would best describe their fate, as they decided to go their separate ways in 2007 for not apparent good reason. They are possibly the great lost Leeds band of the 21st Century.

Tenuous link alert… Speaking of New York, not many local bands have taken the decision to decamp to the City of Big Apples, have they? That'll just be Your Vegas then. Originally from Otley, the five-piece took the indisputably brave decision to set up base in New York after main man Coyle Girelli visited friends there and played some of his band's music to, ahem, 'influential' people. With a look of Razorlight and a whiff of Stadium Rock about them, I'd fully expect these sons of West Yorkshire to be modelling designer gear, talking with Trans-Atlantic accents, and opening for Bon Jovi anytime soon.

And though they hardly troubled the chart compilers, it would be remiss not to mention Dead Disco. Victoria Hesketh from Blackpool, was the singing third of the electronic popsters, the trio having met up at Leeds University in 2005. The all-girl band released four singles to moderate response before Hesketh left the Leeds fold and planned a solo career as Little Boots (any link to success is precious in this book, however tenuous).

But currently residing as runners-up in the 'Successful Modern Leeds Band League' behind The Kaisers, is the Pigeon Detectives. It's not altogether a shock then that they're often viewed as a poor man's Kaiser Chiefs. They do play a similar kind of indie rock but the Pigeons are infinitely more 'shouty' with a direct approach that make Ricky and Co sound as subtle as Radiohead. Not that the Pigeons care; since their debut single 'I Found Out' sold out in a morning, the band have enjoyed a highly successful indie existence, invariably hitting the Indie Number One spot with every release, breaching the Top 40 singles chart on five occasions and going Top Five with both their albums.

Sharing that success with the Rothwell band is their label, *the* Leeds independent label, Dance to the Radio. Named after the recurring line in Joy Division's 'Transmission', DTTR was founded by Whiskas, guitarist with Forward Russia!, themselves serious pop contenders. Fronted by Tom Woodhead who once reached the final of the British Air Guitar Championship – respect is due – their funk-tinged punk sound has infiltrated the singles Top 40 twice, with 'Twelve' and 'Nine' (very fond were they of titling their songs as numbers). The slight irony though is that their label has enjoyed more profile and success than they themselves. They're currently taking an indefinite sabbatical, with Whiskas joining another much fancied Leeds band, Duels. Watch this space.

So Yorkshire had a few bands doing quite well... what was all the fuss about again? If you don't know then you haven't really read the rest of this book. Until now, two bands or acts emanating from the county at the same time had been good enough to announce the birth of a 'movement' or a 'scene', no matter how big, respected or cool those acts were gleaned to be. Around 2005 through to 2007/2008, the number of pop acts from the cities and towns of Yorkshire making a dent in the charts, or making waves in the industry were – admittedly at a stretch - into double figures. Okay - approaching double figures. At least.

The Big Three of this last wave were/are vastly different animals when you look closer. The Kaiser Chiefs embraced the mainstream with songs often overloaded with hooks and sing-along bits beyond the chorus; they remain very much a traditional chart act – a disappointing chart placing does hurt. The Arctic Monkeys still have the whiff of 'underground' about them even though every release gets high profile attention and is expected to register high in the mainstream countdowns. You suspect that it really wouldn't kill them if they had 'Miss' rubber-stamped across one of their singles. As for The Cribs, you get the feeling that there's a point at which unqualified mainstream success would be both viewed with curiosity and handled with caution; they value the 'cult' appeal that allows them to avoid playing the music biz 'game'.

After their 2006 awards-fest, The Kaiser Chiefs' sophomore long-player picked up where 'Employment' left off. 'Ruby', the first single taken from 'Yours Truly, Angry Mob', quickly became the band's first Number One. The album itself followed suit in the album charts, and even broke into the *Billboard* Top 50 in the States. Surely a backlash was on the way? Course it was! It'd already started with the reviews of the album, viewed in some quarters as 'predictable'. And of course, there was always the brothers Gallagher waiting to stick the knife in. Noel compared the KC's to The Monkees (the manufactured variety from the sixties, not the Arctic variety from the Noughties) saying he didn't like the band despite the fact that he 'did drugs for 18 years'. Nick Hodgson told the *NME* – "when I was 17 and Noel was going on about Blur I was watching it, and now I'm 30 and he's 50 and he's talking about us, it's brilliant". They weren't about to stop enjoying their purple patch. As Ricky Wilson said, "it took ten years of playing in this band to get lucky".

And there was inevitably talk of rivalry between the Kaiser Chiefs and the Arctic Monkeys. The media even invented a story about the two bands having a go at each other at some *NME* awards event or other. Naturally it was, to put it in suitable Yorkshire parlance, complete and utter bollocks.

The Arctic Monkeys themselves could do no wrong, winning friends, fans and awards aplenty. Not that they really gave a flying one about awards. Rather than pick up the two Brits they won in 2007, the band sent 'acceptance' videos through, one featuring them dressed as characters from *The Wizard of Oz* and the second with them dressed as Village People. They won the 2006 Mercury Music prize for their debut album, and were nominated again the following year for 'Favourite Worst Nightmare', but lost out to The Klaxons. Quickly hitting top slot, 'Nightmare' was a louder, often heavier affair than the Monkeys' debut, spawning two Top Ten singles. A mark of how big the band had got, was the fact that the album charted highly in 20 different countries, including the States – which begs the question, they think they speak the same language but how can they understand what Alex Turner's singing?

The Yorkshire revolution wasn't confined to the cities either. The market town of Helmsley in North Yorkshire was the highly unlikely source of Top Ten band, One Night Only. On the back of surprise hit 'Just for Tonight', the young quintet scored a Top Ten album, 'Started a Fire'. Their radio-friendly soft indie-rock has undoubtedly been propelled forward and upward by wise utilisation of the Internet – it's hard now to imagine a young band not having a *MySpace* page that showcases their music. Promising Wakefield trio, The Research, are similar beneficiaries of the social network revolution.

But you can't put the Yorkshire surge down to that alone. The live circuit in the county's major cities has grown and prospered more than steadily throughout the 2000s. Sheffield had, and still has The Leadmill, The Board walk, The Plug and The Grapes amongst other buzzing venues, whilst Leeds has been able to boast perhaps even more clubs attracting live music – the Cockpit, The Faversham, The Brudenell, Joseph's Well, The Irish Centre and the Hi-Fi Club. Even Wakefield has a truly buzzing venue in Escobar. Of course, the two big city's have bigger venues, ranging from University Unions (the University Refectory is still a big draw for Leeds), to the Carling Academies. And then there are the big venues in the Sheffield area – the Sheffield Arena and the Don Valley Stadium. Since the

Queens Hall was demolished in 1989, Leeds has been without a large indoor venue. In terms of open air events, The Leeds Festival is now an annual fixture in Bramham Park, running in tandem with the Reading Festival. Roundhay Park has been used in the past, staging many high-profile gigs including Michael Jackson and Robbie Williams. But the only other big gig option in the Leeds area has been Elland Road, home of Leeds United. Queen, U2 and the Happy Mondays had all appeared at the stadium but no local band. That is until May 2008…

The occasion of the Kaiser Chiefs playing Elland Road was a cherry on the cake of their career thus far. The homecoming gig in front of 35,000 fans came at a time when the Kaisers' star was at its highest, after spending a full four years in spectacular ascent. The third album was eagerly anticipated, even more so after the single 'Never Miss a Beat' announced its imminent release in the autumn of 2008. The Top Five single was a worthy Kaiser Chiefs sing-along effort, another 'weird pop song', as they put it, their trademark. The album 'Off with Their Heads' was a departure; for one, production duties had been passed to Mark Ronson, hot and fresh from his 'Version' album, which had featured his take on 'Oh My God' with vocals by Lily Allen. The intention had been to record a few tracks for an EP release – almost inevitably, enough new material survived Quality Control, and a whole new album was the result. Though the press reviews were hardly gushing, there was enough of a positive response to suggest the exercise had been successful. Stateside, *Rolling Stone* loved the album, comparing it to The Jam, The Kinks and XTC, and ranking it Number 21 in its albums of the year.

But…it seems that other people, apart from the Brothers Gallagher, were ready for a rest from the KCs, and that included the band themselves. After the second single from the album, 'Good Days Bad Days', failed miserably, there was a round of Chinese whispers; the band had decided to take a well-earned break after five years of solid recording and touring, but before long

225

the story going round was that B-Unique were dropping the Kaisers after the relative disappointment of 'Off With Their Heads'... so obviously they were about to break up. This observer tried in vain for months to arrange a chat with one or more of the band for this well-meaning tome but was eventually left disappointed. I ripped their posters from my walls and melted their CD's down into ashtrays. But, I have no doubt that this is far from the end of the Kaiser Chiefs story – they've worked far too hard to achieve mainstream success to just give up on it now.

Mainstream success is rarely straightforward, even in these push-a-button-and-download days. The third Cribs album – possibly their breakthrough recording – was 'Men's Needs, Woman's Needs, Whatever', a collection that had a relatively polished feel, thanks to producer Alex Kapranos, he of Franz Ferdinand. The single, 'Men's Needs', became the Cribs' biggest hit thus far, reaching number 17 in the chart. There's every chance that it'd have peaked higher had the accompanying video been shown more extensively. The problem wasn't that the video featured a naked woman mooching amongst the band as they played (black boxes had been strategically placed across her bits and bobs anyway). No, the problem was that she was seen to decapitate one Jarman, and then chop the arm off another, resulting in hilariously bad blood spurt shots that would shame an ancient Hammer Horror film. The fact that the song was addressing the subject of sexual politics in a refreshingly 'anti-lad' fashion was lost on the censors. The Cribs may sound like stroppy punks but it pays to listen closer.

When in 2008 *Q* magazine described The Cribs as the biggest cult band in Britain, it felt like a backhanded compliment to this punter. Do bands really want to be seen as a cult, wilfully exclusive and not quite popular enough to be a household name? The Jarmans apparently do. An *NME* review of a Cribs gig carried the telling overview of the band's set - 'songs that have meant so much to so few fans'.

Does Gary Jarman think the band's cult status allows them to address the 'issues' they do? "I think that, regardless of status, if you weren't comfortable addressing something that you had strong feelings about through your art, then you might as well be in a covers band playing weddings or cruise liners. That is the greatest thing about being in a punk rock band - artistic freedom. In the early days we just wanted to be a beat group, the lyrics were pretty innocent and straight forward. I think that you instinctively write what you know about, sub-consciously sometimes, so it manifests itself that way."

Would a big mainstream hit compromise what The Cribs are about? "I don't think so. It just allows you to do more. There is no point in having something that you think is valid and care about and then hiding it away. When you get in the mainstream you can do way more damage – if the coverage through magazines, TV, radio or whatever is so much broader you have this incredible platform to try and turn people onto other things, or subvert it. It's a privileged position realistically. We would probably end up resenting the song, though."

While we're on the subject, what are the Cribs 'about'? "Reality, romance, sincerity, no pretence."

After the unqualified success of their second album in 2007, the following year was something of a detour for the Arctic Monkeys. Alex Turner had the sheer audacity to embark on a sideline project. Cheeky (and talented) monkey. The Last Shadow Puppets featured Turner, his pal Miles Kane of The Rascals and producer/drummer James Ford who had overseen the Mercury Prize-winning 'Myths of the Near Future' for the Klaxons. The result was an interesting departure from Arctic Monkeys fayre, replete with full orchestral arrangements and taking in influences as wide as Bowie, Ennio Morricone and Scott Walker; single 'The Age of Understatement' went Top Ten, and the album, titled the same, went top-of-the-heap, Numero Uno.

Not to be outdone, Monkeys drummer Matt Helder was involved in his own side project, resurrecting the band's old rhythm section with bass player Andy

Nicholson and joining up with 'Reverend' Jon McClure and rapper Lowkey to record under the name Mongrel. Best described as political hip-hop, lyrically challenging government policies, their album, 'Better than Heavy', was appropriately given away with The Independent newspaper in March 2009.

However, back with the day-job, Turner and Helder have spent most of 2009, writing and recording the third Arctic Monkeys album, 'Humbug'. The preceding single 'Crying Lightning' suggested that that traditionally difficult third outing is a definite departure from the norm. Darker and slower than previously, the song bears the undoubted influence of producer Joss Homme from Queens of the Stone Age. But there's still a recognisable Alex Turner song in there – not many songwriters reference 'Pick 'n' Mix' sweets, do they?

A new Arctic Monkeys album is big, big news, eagerly anticipated by fans and press with equal fervour. Perhaps the new Cribs long-player, 'Ignore the Ignorant', won't inspire quite as much opinion, hype or discussion but the fact that it's their first with legendary Smiths guitarist, Johnny Marr onboard, means there'll be more than a passing interest for most fans of ye olde indie rock, regardless of what they thought of The Cribs before, and Gary Jarman knows it – "we all expected it, Johnny included. I can see why it's a big deal to people, so I am not pissed off about it; it's just natural human curiosity. It feels weird to us as a four-piece now though, because we are all so close and don't consider it a big deal at all."

How did this rather unlikely union come about? "Me and Johnny bonded as Englishmen in Portland, Oregon. I was living there and Johnny was playing with Modest Mouse, and our paths crossed one day. We became firm friends pretty quick. It turned out he was a big fan of the band, the first conversation we ever had was him telling me what a big fan of 'Hey Scenesters!' he was. Very flattering, and also a great ice-breaker, as I was always a huge Smiths fan, and of Johnny in particular. Made my life much easier! I introduced him to my brothers at Glastonbury about a year later, and then at the Q awards a couple of months after, he and Ryan hatched a plan to collaborate on some songs - which just grew and grew to the point it's at today with Johnny a full-time member of the band. It's pretty bizarre, but cool."

The Cribs hit the front cover of the NME (for the third time) at the end of July 2009. The music paper might not be the weekly hip bible of the music scene that it once was, but even with bona fide guitar legend in their ranks, the Wakefield band are still the uncompromising punk combo they've always been (the single 'Cheat On Me' even sounds like a punk title from 1977).

Gary Jarman agrees that with The Cribs, the onus is on steady progress; "as a punk band you never expect mainstream success from the off, so it has been fun knocking the dominoes over, kicking in doors, competing on whatever level you want."

Has Wakefield, and Yorkshire for that matter, had an important role in The Cribs story so far? "I believe that it's instilled me with the realist outlook that I, and we as a band, have, as well as the 'no pretence' element. Where I grew up you weren't supposed to step outside of your social position, and if you did, people gave you a hard time for it, like 'who does he think he is, thinking he's better than everyone else?!?', so you are naturally inclined to catch yourself before you get pretentious, or self-indulgent as you are used to the consequences of ego and vanity. You have to remember when we were kids, we would get attacked for having long hair and carrying guitars around town, that damages you really. But I am proud of my core values."

By the time the Cribs and Arctic Monkeys albums have been judged and ranked for the various awards events that'll roll round again at the beginning of 2010, Kaiser Chief fans will perhaps have an idea of what lies ahead for their boys. By then it'll be five years on from that Golden Year of 2005 when Yorkshire was viewed as the epicentre of all that was good, shiny and new in the Q Magazine-reading, MTV-watching, MySpace-hitting music world. It would be interesting to know if anyone at the time thought to ask any of the hip and happening young Tykes involved where they thought they would be in five years time. More interesting still would have been the answers…

Chapter 14

Now Then... Think On.

August 1st 2009... not only is it my Dad's birthday, God bless him, but – put it in your diaries – it's officially 'Yorkshire Day', first celebrated in 1975 as a protest against the Local Government Act of 1972, the bureaucratic folly that came into force two years later, re-jigging county boundaries across the country, and most seriously, re-naming the Yorkshire Ridings for no apparent reason. It's a day when Tykes everywhere rejoice in their 'Yorkshireness' and all that entails. There'll no doubt be some scallywags imagining that, on this, our rather special day, every able Yorkshireman dusts off his flat-cap, and takes his whippet to the Brass Band concert down at t'mill, indulging in a spot of plain speaking, a la Geoffrey Boycott, with anyone he encounters on the way. Sounds smashing. But it's the first I knew about it too.

I've not lived in the county of my birth for thirty years now. But at the risk of stating the bleedin' obvious, researching and writing this book has felt like a journey back in time, not just because of the music involved and the people who made it, but also because I've had to revisit aspects of Yorkshire that I'd forgotten about, maybe some of which I'd happily chosen to forget. 21st Century Yorkshire is, at once, different from the place I grew up in, and yet, exactly the same. The county now boasts many modern cosmopolitan cities – Leeds, Sheffield, York – where the ethnic and cultural diversity is both embraced and celebrated regularly. But I'm neither stupid nor naïve; I know that much of the narrow-minded prejudice I encountered in my youth still exists. The selection of a BNP candidate in the region's 2009 European elections confirmed as much. But these days, the more positive aspects of Yorkshire tradition manifest themselves more regularly in the county's younger generation. Where else can you find such a heady cocktail of effervescence and belligerence?

It (nearly) goes without saying now that the world is a much smaller place, thanks to the advanced technologies of travel and communication, and Yorkshire doesn't feel like it's in its own little bubble anymore, and it's certainly no cultural backwater. It probably never was – it was just viewed as such.

I've found out a bloody lot about Yorkshire music in retrospect, thanks largely to the new set of friends I've met through my exhausted laptop computer, including perhaps my new best friends, *Wikipedia* and *YouTube*. I really have listened to hours and hours of Yorkshire music, even watching the artists who made it wherever possible. I'd go further and say I've physically made myself read about, and listen to the music made by people who I would never have even dreamt of giving the time of day to in the past. And do y'know what? I won't be doing that again.

But I have at least learnt to appreciate the less conspicuous qualities of some of these people – for example, I never thought I'd have such respect for David Coverdale, a man who obviously has pride in his roots (we've done the hair gag – leave it). And while I won't be rushing out to buy their back catalogues, I will think of these musicians in a different, more favourable light in the future. I feel like a better man for this experience, as you can readily tell.

In writing this book, the big temptation was to veer into the territory of the Pop Encyclopaedia. Though it has probably skated perilously close in a few chapters, a big, heavy fact-fest was never the idea; the real aim has always been to sketch a landscape illustrating the contribution made by the county to the development of popular music in the UK. In doing so, it is very possible, and highly probable that some Yorkshire musicians have been overlooked, and apologies, of course, are due to them all.

Bob Hardy, the bass player from Franz Ferdinand, comes from Dewsbury apparently. They're a band whose music I have liked in the past, especially their debut album, yet Bob could actually come from Swaziland and I wouldn't care too much. I view Franz Ferdinand as a Glaswegian group – they all met in that fair and vibrant city and shaped the course of their pop career there. It's rather like Gang of Four plotting their musical path from Leeds despite none of their number being of Yorkshire blood. But different.

Similarly, the bassist from Muse, Chris Wolstenholme, was actually born in Rotherham but that hardly seems important in their story since 'Wolsto' left South Yorkshire when he was barely out of nappies, moving down to Devon where he eventually hooked up with the other two Muse 'musos'. They'll just have to share their own 'Devon Pop' book with Joss Stone and Chris Martin (wouldn't want to share a lift with them though, eh?).

Pete Thomas is perhaps my favourite drummer of all-time – that makes me sound like a muso but I've been called many worse things - and I would recognise his snare sound anywhere (but don't test me on that). Most of the Elvis Costello recordings I like the best feature the drumming of Pete Thomas. Yet, I didn't know that the great sticksman hails from Sheffield. But within the realms of punk and new wave, the period from which Elvis and the Attractions first sprang forth, the justified attention to the importance of the Gang of Four-led scene in Leeds, and the Human League's first beeps in Sheffield, meant that skin-slammer Pete is only a bit player in our story at best. Now if it had turned out that Elvis C was actually from the market town of Elland, that'd have been a completely different matter.

You want 'obscure'? I can do 'really obscure'. Guy Manning, apparently, is a highly respected multi-instrumentalist, singer and song-writer from Leeds. He has a considerable fan base and has released albums under the names Manning, The Tangent, Parallel or 90 Degrees. The reason he's dealt with here in just the one short paragraph, is that he writes and plays progressive rock – I know! - and these days, progressive rock really is under the radar, less likely to make an impact on the mainstream pop consciousness than I am. But like me, I'm sure Guy still lives in hope.

Yorkshire folk, for all their faults, are a proud people. And music is a matter of local pride too. Some may even call it tribalism. Yeah, whatever. In the same way I enjoyed a private moment of Yorkshire pride when, at eleven-years-old, my daughter Ruby announced that the Kaiser Chiefs and Arctic Monkeys were her favourite bands, and she had their respective debut albums to prove it, I was truly proud to know that another band from Wakefield – The Cribs - were following the footsteps of Be Bop Deluxe, and making people take note on a national, even international level.

I've enjoyed some unexpected prangs of pride whilst rummaging through the archives in the name of research. And, like a true Yorkshireman with his fingers fumbling around for anything resembling a pulse, I've discovered some good stuff (and frankly, some dreadful stuff) long after the rest of the country has encountered it - years after, in some cases referred to in these pages. And I'm still doing it.

A big, almost-up-to-date 'for instance'? It appears that a lot of 'the kids' are listening to Hadouken! (That's their own self-contained exclamation mark by the way). Who? Well yes, precisely. Prime exponents of Grindie music, captain, that's who. Er, Grindie? A cross between Indie and Grime. Grime? A kind of

Garage, Hip Hop, Dance hall hybrid. Come on, Granddad, get with the beat!

I prefer the alternative description 'Dance Punk', a combination I can imagine, even one I've probably already encountered without realising. Listening to Hadouken! confirms that the sonic picture in my head wasn't far off the mark. They started getting talked about and danced to back in 2007; course it's no surprise that it's taken two years for yours truly to even hear of them. Just two years though - impressive.

But there's more. It's good to report that there is a diverse range of new music still coming out of Yorkshire and getting noticed. For 'diverse', feel free to read 'extreme'. Bring Me the Horizon are far-removed from most of the genres outlined in these pages thus far. We're talking... Metalcore! Metalcore? Is it a bit like Grindie? Well no, we're talking a fusion of heavy metal and hardcore punk, aren't we? Obviously. They're not likely to get they're own *An Audience with...* show anytime soon on ITV, but this Sheffield band are big news in their particular arena. And getting bigger; their second album 'Suicide Season' breached the Top 50 chart in the UK in 2008, made inroads into the various countdowns in the States, and made them rock stars in Australia, where they've already toured twice.

Not a zillion miles away, geographically or musically, comes Evile – as in 'eeee, vile' – a (or maybe the) thrash-metal band from Huddersfield; it was only a matter of time. Their rise, apparently, has been stellar, with their debut album 'Enter the Grave' winning them the kind of attention that any new metal band can only dream about. Apart from all the usual plaudits, that meant the band even got to support metal gods 'Megadeth' on tour. Their new 2009 album, 'Infected Nations', is said to be influenced, content-wise, by the swine flu pandemic that's put the fear of God into the world and his wife. The album cover is very metal, and yup, rather vile.

Not to be confused with Yorkshire Pudding, or Yorkshire Tea (endorsed these days by South Yorkshire's finest all-round entertainer, John Shuttleworth), watch out for 'Yorkshire Grunge'- like I said, it takes us a while to catch up with trends going on elsewhere. Not that the protagonists call themselves that but this is a real movement, honest. With glorious band names such as Dinosaur Pile-Up, The Old Romantic Killer Band and, best yet, Pulled Apart by Horses, the new, new guitar sound of Yorkshire has distanced itself from the likes of Kaiser Chiefs and Pigeon Detectives whilst declaring a loving respect for The Cribs with their punk credentials. Mmmm, grunge... the cynic in me says it's both too late and too soon; but the Tyke in me says, go for it, boys!

As a county, we know that Yorkshire has a tradition for producing rock bands, be they metal or punk. But there are genres – some of them modern genres – that don't appear to have been embraced in any meaningful way at any point in Yorkshire's music development. So while some general questions have been addressed in these pages, there are other, more specific ones to be raised.

Where are the black acts from Yorkshire? And what about Asian acts? For all the white boy rock and pop we've produced in abundance over the years, we've come up with very few Soul, Jazz, Blues, Funk, Rap, Reggae, Bhangra or Hip Hop acts of any mainstream note. Corrine Bailey Rae announced herself in fine style winning all manner of awards in 2006 with her best-selling debut album of self-penned songs in a soul/jazz vein. But before and since? We've struggled, to say the least. But...

There has been a hot Hip Hop underground in and around Huddersfield for years now. Who knew? Spearheaded by the World Hip Hop Freestyle Champion (no, it's true), Jack Flash, the old town is the unlikely Beats capital of the county, boasting highly respected acts like the esteemed emcee and producer Asaviour, an eminent figure on the wider UK Hip Hop scene, and Practical Headz, a full posse responsible for the acclaimed 'Who Iz It?' album of a couple of years ago – not many artists have been able to bring the Yorkshire accent into Hip Hop with the same success.

And it's not just Huddersfield. Sheffield has its Hoodz Underground (or had

– they seem to have gone a bit quiet, apparently), Constant Creation and Bare Knuckle Soul. And Leeds, not surprisingly, probably has more Hip Hop acts of relative note than any other White Rose city. But I'll be honest here to prove a point. Skinnyman, Alphabetix, Yorkshire Terrierz and D-Cypher are all acts from the Leeds area, highly rated by fans of Beats, as they say. But how do I know? I've trawled the Internet and come up with their names, that's how. It's no surprise that they're off my own personal radar – I'm sure everyone's realised by now that I'm not quite the music mag-reading, club-going, dance-crazy dude that I perhaps used to be (you'd be shocked) but I'd wager these Hip Hop acts are also off the radar of most music fans outside their county of origin. They're names on the underground scene, mostly confined to the Yorkshire region – fact.

Like any other musician playing within a genre appealing to the music-buying mass public, you can hardly claim to be residing in the realms of pop success until your name and your music is known across the country. And, call me an old stickler, but that's not going to happen until your music is given a national platform via the radio, TV, press... and we're back to where we started.

'Underground Respect' and 'Commercial Success', are like oil and water – they don't mix. Once an act gets that mainstream thumbs-up, and starts shifting significant units, much, if not all of the original respect that fuelled its early development invariably gets left behind and forgotten. I'm surely not the only person who has considered himself a fan of a band in their early formative period, then dropped them when everyone else started to like them too. They no longer 'belonged' to me - they'd gone out into the big soulless world of mass consumption, just another product. Give me a minute, I'll be fine.

The nature of Hip Hop, as is the case with much if not most dance music, is that it thrives on 'underground respect' – the club-based underground is its natural habitat. Discuss...

Perhaps the only current Yorkshire-based Hip Hop act with a real chance of making the big breakthrough is the Matt Helders/Jon McClure side project,

237

Mongrel, perhaps because of the personnel's association to existing mainstream success. But even then, purists might argue that Mongrel is a predominantly white collective and their featured rapper, Lowkey, is London-born of Iraqi descent.

Stepping sideways but still with a similar subject, most observers would probably offer the opinion that Bhangra music is never likely to feature on a regular basis in the Nation's mainstream chart, making 'stars' of its musicians. But then again, why not? Musicians of all races have been mixing the influences of Asian music with House and Hip Hop for years now. Black Star Liner didn't quite manage to bring their hybrid styling through to a level of mass acclaim in the 1990s but taking a more wilfully mainstream pop route, Cornershop showed that it could be achieved.

The bottom-line for all these music-makers, however talented they are and how vibrant their music may be, is they're yet to register on a significant record-selling scale. Until they do, their potential remains just that. And the fact remains that many are happy to remain 'underground'. Who needs or even wants the mainstream?

Another big question that has arisen from this crazy journey into the world of the Yorkshire Pop Star is, what about the women? 'They'll have half a lager and lime each and be glad of it' would have been the typical local answer back in the 1980s (who am I fooling – political correctness hasn't yet reached half of Yorkshire), but it's outrageous to think that barely more than half-a-dozen women have played a part in our story.

The fact that Kiki Dee is still probably the most high profile female solo performer to figure in our overview tells a story in itself. But for the life of me, I can't put into words what it is. Or perhaps I'm scared to try since it could perpetuate Ye Olde Yorkshire stereotype, of the man of the house going out to earn a crust and 'our lass' staying home to look after t'house and t'nippers. We have come on since those days, haven't we?

Of course there are female figures prominent in more recent years but, erm, these success stories are not without reservations. Joanne and Susan in the second incarnation of the Human League were always the subject of ridicule from some observers – were they really integral to the music or were they to a large extent just window-dressing?

Two other local lasses have done extremely well for themselves in chart-topping girl-bands since manufactured pop acts became de rigueur in the 1990s. But therein lies the reservations about Mel B of the Spice Girls and Kimberly of Girls Aloud – they're both part of a product essentially put together by some male Svengali, and to be absolutely and brutally frank, if it hadn't been Mel and Kim getting the gig in their respective bands, it'd have been two other highly marketable, good-looking girls, and the end result would probably have been exactly the same. That sounds harsh, sexist even, but you know that it's true.

That's possibly why the emergence of the likes of Corrine Bailey Rae and Kate Rusby in the last decade has been refreshingly organic in comparison. Here's to more women coming through the county ranks; perhaps 'Blue Roses' will be the first of many.

Blue Roses is, in essence, singer/songwriter Laura Groves, from Shipley, near Bradford. In the tradition of her obvious influences, Joni Mitchell and Kate Bush, Laura has a captivating emotion-raw voice and songs of a refreshingly old-fashioned beauty. And what's more, her steady rise to prominence owes nothing to the more banal, manipulative developments in the entertainment industry of recent years. That in itself has got to be a triumph.

Five years is a long time in music; some might say five minutes is a torturously long time in Yorkshire. What were new pop propositions in 2005 are in danger of becoming 'old-hat', unless that is, they evolve and stay oven-fresh, surprising and interesting. Easier said than done. The Arctic Monkeys could have carried on doing what they were doing so well on their debut album, but their 'Favourite Worst Nightmare' album suggested they weren't prepared to stay still, and their 'difficult' third album has confirmed it. Citing old influences like Cream and Hendrix will please old hippies everywhere, while Alex Turner recommending the work of Jake Thackray delights those of us old enough to remember the cheeky minstrel poet from Leeds.

The 'New Yorkshire' bands of 2005 are now the establishment, so there's room for the next wave of local acts to step forward. It's a fair bet that the best is still to come from the likes of Sunshine Underground, Pink Grease and The Lodger, all bands who have been beavering away for years, earning not much more than favourable mentions in despatches. As we know, many bands, such as these, got left behind in that whole New Yorkshire thing.

These days there seems to be three distinct routes to 'making it' in the Pop industry. There's the method employed by the likes of The Cribs or Richard Hawley, with little or no compromise, doing things their way or not at all, working their way up in the traditional learn-your-craft-honestly-and-pay-your-dues-on-the-road manner. Then, at the other extreme, there are the desperate Reality TV talent show hopefuls who might as well all be wearing a T-shirt that says 'Whatever it Takes'.

But what do I know? The next winner of the *X Factor* could be the chanteuse from Sharlston who finally picks up the Yorkshire solo-female baton from Kiki Dee. And the next star 'created' on Britain's Got Talent could be that long-struggling black rapper from Ripon. Good luck to them.

Somewhere in-between, owing much to Trend and Technology (wasn't that an early Human League album?), are the hoards of *MySpace* hopefuls. Thanks to the digital age we find ourselves in, anyone and everyone has a fighting chance of making a go of it in the music industry at the push of a button. It's something of an exaggeration I know but you really do only need a moderate knowledge of computer technology to post your own recorded music online and let the world witness your musical genius. Then - moving swiftly along in the process to artists who are established enough to be on a recognised download site - you only need a moderate number of downloads to register in some chart or other. There used to be just one chart to my knowledge back in the day. And no one gave you its rundown better than Alan Freeman. Not 'alf.

But it's a matter of opinion whether this technological revolution has made for a better pop music world or not. It's an argument that applies to everywhere not just Yorkshire. This isn't the place to list all the pro's and cons. But suffice it to say - and very relevant this is - at the top of the pro's list is the fact that no one really needs a record label anymore, making the industry much less London-centric. One thing that has to be said in terms of cons though is the lack of quality control; there used to be a perfectly good quality control system in place before, especially in Yorkshire, the home of Plain Speaking. The first audience a Yorkshire band would have to face was a Yorkshire audience. If enough people said you were crap, you got the message and gave it up as a bad job. Now bands can cut out the middle man and get their music straight out to the listening masses, however dreadful it might be.

But that's a bone of contention outside our specific concern. What has all my retrospective probing told me about the local folk who made the music that made the grade? Many of Yorkshire's pop stars are individuals who became professional pop musicians in the first place either by accident or default. Many of them have admitted to having an in-built reluctance to stand in the spotlight, especially in periods when there was an onus on theatrics and showmanship; and there are certainly instances when songwriters have had to become the singer of their song if they wanted to have their music heard at all.

Some of them didn't think it was something they could ever do, let alone think it was something they could ever make a living from. Some never thought anyone would ever give them the chance to do so. But that's not to say it wasn't something they always wanted to do. Since it's not been possible to speak to every Yorkshire Pop Star who's ever been, it's impossible to judge whether such determinedly driven musos as the Def Lep boys, Jarvis or The Gedge are rare creatures on the local pop landscape. A steely resolve obviously has a place in every success story outlined within these pages but it often takes second place to circumstances/events beyond the control/influence of the Tyke involved (there's another great/terrible album title in there somewhere).

What of the influence of the nasty old music industry on Yorkshire over the years, and, vice versa, the influence of Yorkshire on the music industry? It doesn't take a genius to work out that the latter has been greater than the former. We're not talking London or San Francisco in the 1960s here. An alien invasion probably wouldn't change Yorkshire.

Come on now, would we really ever want Yorkshire to change? Moves on quickly... The Beatles changed Liverpool for its natives, and changed the city in the eyes of the rest of the world. But that really was the exception rather than the rule – I don't think The Smiths changed Manchester though millions of Smiths fans viewed the city in a much different way than they did before the Smiths (that's if they even considered Manchester at all in pre-Smiths days).

I don't think that Yorkshire's in danger of being radically altered by the success of one or more acts from within its boundaries. The Arctic Monkeys changed Sheffield in the same simple way that the Human League did before them – lots more young people there took up the idea of making music themselves.

The recent spate of pop success stories has made our county look brighter and more exciting in the eyes of young outsiders looking in. 'Fashionable' is probably pushing it – I personally have always liked to think that Yorkshire transcends fashion. That's definitely pushing it. However, the wit, talent and drive of the current crop of Yorkshire popsters have blown away many of the dusty old misconceptions of the place that have been handed down generation to generation. Any talk of the county in a positive light has to be a good thing – these mere musicians have done the job of a dozen or more tourist boards.

Which brings us to the two big questions this book has sought to answer... the first being, why, compared to other celebrated cities and regions, has the nation's largest county produced so few successful pop acts? Taking into account that we just don't blow our own trumpets as much as other provinces, and you do have to delve a little deeper for yourself, there are, in fact, many more success stories than I'd estimated. Going further, I'd suggest that we haven't produced significantly fewer, per se – we've produced relatively fewer substandard, yet successful pop acts. It sounds rich when you consider Black Lace and Jive Bunny, but bear with me.

Cue final controversy. Some places have had individual success stories where the artists involved really didn't merit that success. These have usually come about as the result of a scene becoming a bandwagon to be jumped on - Liverpool in the Merseybeat era springs to mind, as does Manchester when it morphed into Madchester. Being a bit more backward in coming forward, Yorkshire acts are less given to jumping on the back of someone else's endeavours, being less than fond of being attached to a press-inspired scene or movement. Yes, it might help to catch the attention, but there was not one band in the supposed 'New Yorkshire' scene that didn't want to be talked about as being individual or unique, rather than a mere component of something deemed bigger and possibly better. Yorkshire artists are nothing if not proud of their individuality.

And the second question was, what took us so long to start turning out pop stars in numbers? Well, perhaps because this first decade of the new century has proved to be the prime-time for it to actually happen. It would take a more learned scholar than me to make any big meaningful link between world events and the perspective of the ordinary man. But, without doubt, we're in a less innocent, more knowing age where there's neither room nor need for the promotional nonsense of old. In the ultra-accessible world of modern pop music, you just don't need marketing flannel or gimmickry to get yourself noticed. It makes for a much more even playing field with perfect conditions for Yorkshire I'd say. And so, of course, with talent, drive and determination in abundance, we're well and truly in the game.

The last question I asked Gary from the Cribs was what he thought it was that set Yorkshire bands aside from bands from other parts of the country. 'I don't know,' he said, 'humility?'

Success in pop music, as in everything, is a relative concept. Where I come from, getting up and doing it in the first place is a result in itself. Being asked to get up and do it again is tantamount to being a Pop Star.

The Author's Top 20 Yorkshire Singles

1. *Maid in Heaven:* Be Bop Deluxe
2. *Common People:* Pulp
3. *Theme from 'Midnight Cowboy':* John Barry
4. *Poison Arrow:* ABC
5. *Tonight the Streets Are Ours:* Richard Hawley
6. *Temptation:* Heaven 17
7. *I Predict a Riot:* Kaiser Chiefs
8. *At Home He Feels Like a Tourist:* Gang of Four
9. *Bet You Look Good on the Dancefloor:* Arctic Monkeys.
10. *Sound of the Crowd:* Human League
11. *Crying Game:* Dave Berry
12. *Tainted Love:* Soft Cell
13. *Fatman:* Southern Death Cult
14. *Happy Hour:* Housemartins
15. *How Long:* Ace
16. *Avenues and Alleyways:* Tony Christie
17. *Where Were You?:* The Mekons
18. *Hey Scenesters!* : The Cribs
19. *Eloise:* Paul Ryan
20. *Kiss:* Age of Chance

Top 20 Yorkshire Number One Singles

1. *Wannabe* Spice Girls (featuring Melanie Brown) (7weeks)
1= *(Is This the Way To) Amarillo* Tony Christie (with Peter Kay) (7 weeks)
3. *No Other Love* Ronnie Hilton (6 weeks)
3= *Don't Go Breaking My Heart* Kiki Dee and Elton John (6 weeks)
5. *Don't You Want Me* Human League (5 weeks)
5= *Swing the Mood* Jive Bunny and the Mastermixers (5 weeks)
7. *Unchained Melody* Gareth Gates (4 weeks)
7= *The Long and Winding Road* Gareth Gates & Will Young (4 weeks)
7= *Sound Of the Underground* Girls Aloud (featuring Kimberley Walsh) (4 weeks)
10. *That's What I Like* Jive Bunny and the Mastermixers (3 weeks)
10= *2 Become 1* Spice Girls (3 weeks)
10= *Mama* Spice Girls (3 weeks)
10= *Anyone of Us (Stupid Mistake)* Gareth Gates (3 weeks)

14. *Tainted Love* **Soft Cell** (2 weeks)

14= *Dizzy* **Vic Reeves (with the Wonder Stuff)** (2 weeks)

14= *Sleeping Satellite* **Tasmin Archer** (2 weeks)

14= *Say You'll Be There* **Spice Girls** (2 weeks)

14= *Too Much* **Spice Girls** (2 weeks)

14= *Viva Forever* **Spice Girls** (2 weeks)

14= *Spirit in the Sky* **Gareth Gates (with The Kumars)** (2 weeks)

14= *I'll Stand by You* **Girls Aloud** (2 weeks)